Squatters and the
Roots of Mau Mau

EASTERN AFRICAN STUDIES

Squatters and the Roots of Mau Mau 1905–63

Tabitha Kanogo

Lecturer in History
Kenyatta University

James Currey
LONDON

Heinemann Kenya
NAIROBI

Ohio University Press
ATHENS

James Currey Ltd
54b Thornhill Square, Islington
London N1 1BE

Heinemann Kenya
Kijabe Street, P.O. Box 45314
Nairobi, Kenya

Ohio University Press
Scott Quadrangle
Athens, Ohio 45701

BRITISH LIBRARY CATALOGUING IN PUBLICATION DATA
Kanogo, Tabitha
Squatters and the roots of Mau Mau –
(East African Studies)
1. Kenya–Race Relations   I. Title II. Series
305.8'9676'2 DT433.542
ISBN 0-85255-018-9 ISBN 0-85255-019-7 Pbk

LIBRARY OF CONGRESS CATALOGING-IN-PUBLICATION DATA
Kanogo, Tabitha M.
Squatters and the roots of Mau Mau, 1905-63
Includes bibliographies and index
1. Migrant agricultural laborers–Kenya–History–20th century
2. Squatters–Kenya–History–20th century   3. Mau Mau–History
4. Kikuyu (African people)–History
I. Title
HD1538.K4K36 1987 307.3'36 87-11202
ISBN 0-8214-0873-9 ISBN 0-8214-0874-7 (pbk.)

Typeset in 10/11 pt Baskerville by
Oxford Publishing Services, The Old Toffee Factory,
120a Marlborough Road, Oxford OX1 4LS
in association with Selina Cohen

This edition printed in the United States of America
Ohio University Press books are printed on acid-free paper ∞

*For my mother
and in memory of my father*

Contents

Three
Social Organisation among Squatters

Four
The Crisis: Decline in Squatter Welfare 1938–48

Five
Politics of Protest: Mau Mau

Acknowledgements

I am greatly indebted to the many people and institutions that have been helpful in the course of preparing this work. The study began as a Ph.D. dissertation for the University of Nairobi. I would like to thank my two supervisors, Prof. Godfrey Muriuki and Dr Atieno-Odhiambo for their constructive and stimulating criticism of the drafts. Prof. Ahmed I. Salim kindly joined hands with Prof. Muriuki during Dr Atieno-Odhiambo's absence on sabbatical leave and offered valuable help.

The United States Agency for International Development funded the initial two-year grant while the University of Nairobi awarded me a one-year grant between December 1977 and November 1978. Both grants went a long way towards financing the research.

The members of the Department of History, Kenyatta University College, deserve special thanks for sharing my teaching load while I completed the dissertation. I am especially grateful to them for shouldering my departmental duties while I took a Rhodes Fellowship at Somerville College, Oxford, between 1982 and 1985, during which time I completed the research necessary for the revision and restructuring of the thesis and its conversion into this book. I would also like to thank the Rhodes trustees for funding the fellowship that has enabled me to write this book. Somerville College was my home away from home and I am grateful for the support and welcome that its staff and Principal, Miss Daphne Park, extended to me.

The staff of several libraries were very supportive during the various stages of this work. Librarians at the Kenya National Archives, the McMillan library and the University of Nairobi libraries in Kenya deserve many thanks. I spent long periods at Rhodes House library and at the Institute for Commonwealth Studies library. In both places the staff were most helpful. The Public Records Office library rendered good service.

Dr John Lonsdale deserves special thanks. He read all the draft chapters of this book and offered invaluable advice and support. David

Throup and David Anderson made useful suggestions on earlier drafts. Mrs Selina Cohen sub-edited and typed the whole manuscript. I am very grateful for her patience and good work.

I wish to thank my various informants who willingly took time off for the interviews. The data thus gathered has been vital in the writing of this book. I am grateful to Lady Pamela Scott, Penina Nyawira and the late Selina Lyndall, who provided me with accommodation at different times of my fieldwork research. I would also like to thank Jane Nandwa, Gill Short, Tom Forrest, Niamh Hardiman and Tajudeen Abdul-Raheem for their encouragement. My family has patiently supported me, always. To them I say 'thank you'. However, the responsibility for any errors or distortions is entirely mine.

List of Abbreviations

AAD	African Affairs Department
AIM	African Inland Mission
AR	Annual Report
CMS	Church Missionary Society
CN	Central Nyanza – including the Kisumu Londiani area
CNC	Chief Native Commissioner
CO	Colonial Office documents held at Public Records Office, Kew Gardens, London
CSM	Church of Scotland Mission
DAR	*District Annual Report*
DC	District Commissioner
DO	District Officer
EAISR	East Africa Institute of Social Research
EALB	East Africa Labour Bureau
EAPH	East African Publishing House
EAS	*East African Standard* (newspaper)
EBU	Embu
FH	Fort Hall
HAK	Historical Association of Kenya
KADU	Kenya African Democratic Union
KANU	Kenya African National Union
KASU	Kenya African Students Union
KAU	Kenya African Union
KBU	Kiambu
KCA	Kikuyu Central Association
KER	Kericho
KISA	Kikuyu Independent Schools Association
KLFA	Kenya Land Freedom Army
KNA	Kenya National Archives
KPSA	Kikuyu Private Schools Association
Lab.	Labour

Leg. Co.	Legislative Council
M.A.	Master of Arts
MAA	Maasai
MLC	Member of the Legislative Council
NAD	Native Affairs Department
NDI	Nandi
NKU	Nakuru
NSA	Njoro Settlers Association
NVA	Naivasha
NYI	Nyeri
NZA	Nyanza
PC	Provincial Commissioner
PRO	Public Records Office, London
RH	Rhodes House Library, Oxford
RNLO	Resident Native Labourers Ordinance
RV	Rift Valley
RVP	Rift Valley Province
SP	Southern Province

Glossary of Kikuyu and Swahili Terms used in Text

ahoi	landless people among the Kikuyu
aruithia	surgeons who performed circumcision ritual
baraza	public meeting
bibi	wife/woman
boma	cattle pen
ciama	elders' councils
ciondo	Kikuyu baskets
debe	tin container
Gigikuyu	the Kikuyu language
Gikuyu na Mumbi	mythical founders of the Kikuyu tribe
githaka	system under which land was acquired/Land acquired under such a system
gituiku	handleless blade often given to surgeon as a circumcision fee
guciarwo	adoption
gukaywo nyori	to pierce the upper ear lobes
gunias	gunny-bags
harambee	self-help
iganda	temporary huts
igweta	high social standing, fame
irua	circumcision
ithaka	plural of *githaka* (land)
jembe	hoe
kamuirigo	killer
kanyanga	trespass
karani	clerk
kiama	singular of ciama
kifagio	broom – signifying period when the squatters lost their livestock, i.e. it was swept away, or officials involved in de-stocking

kihiu-mwiri	the age-group circumcised between approximately 1914 and 1918
Kikuyu karinga	pure Kikuyu
kipande	identification pass
kirore	fingerprint in lieu of signature – used on contracts
kuna	breaking up virgin land
Lumbwa	Kipsigis (in slang)
madaraka	affluence
maisha	lifetime
mashuka	piece of cloth worn wrapped around the body
maskini	poverty stricken, poor
mathace	skimmed milk
mbari	clan
migoma	she-goats
mubara	toy-wheel
muingi	community self-help group
muruithia	singular of aruithia (surgeons)
muramati	trustee of the land
mzungu	white man
ndarwa	skins
ndigithu	gourd
Ndundu Ya Hitho	Inner Secret Council of Mau Mau
nduriri	non-Kikuyu, especially from Western Kenya
ngoima	ram
njahi	black peas
nyakiburi	form of sweet potato
nyapara	foreman/farm overseer
posho	ground maize flour
purko	Maasai
rutere	frontier
saidia	helpers
shamba	plot of land
siasa	politics
siri	secret
thenge	he-goats
thigari cia bururi	soldiers or guards of the land
thu	enemy
totos	children
uhuru	independence
ungumania	hypocrisy
utuuro	dwelling place/permanent residence
Wamera	Kikuyu slang for Luo
wazungu	white men, plural of mzungu
weru	pasture-land

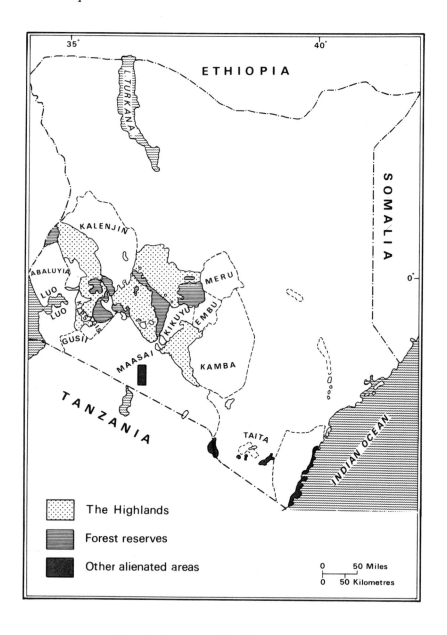

The Highlands

Forest reserves

Other alienated areas

Map 1   Location of the White Highlands

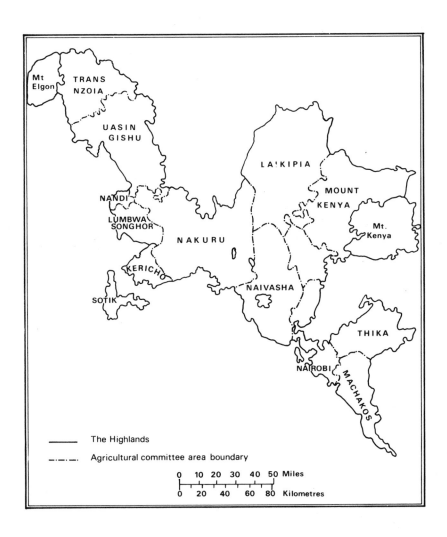

The Highlands

Agricultural committee area boundary

0   10   20   30   40   50 Miles

0   20   40   60   80 Kilometres

Map 2   Agricultural Districts of the White Highlands

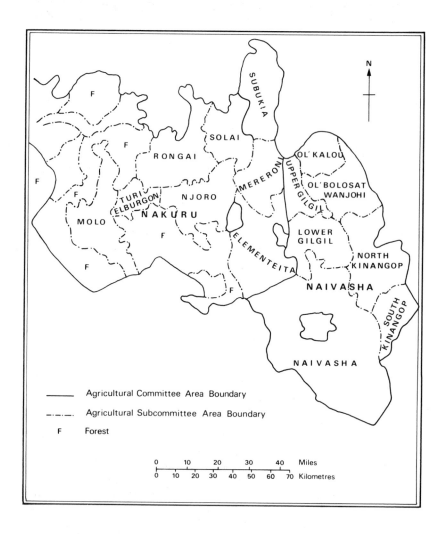

Map 3   *Nakuru/Naivasha Districts of the White Highlands*

Introduction

> The nature of the squatter problem is too familiar to require
> recapitulation. The way in which it should be solved has been a
> matter of controversy for many years, but in general it is true to say
> that the policy of evolution towards the cottage labourer has been
> accepted by both the farmer and the government.[1]

Establishing colonial rule in Kenya and attempting to turn the country
into a white settlement area had a profound affect on the local African
population. Not only did the alienation of African lands (for European
settler occupation)[2] disinherit and dislocate many Africans,[3] but the
subsequent development of settler plantations and mixed farms created
a demand for a large number of wage labourers.[4] But, since no African
labour force was readily forthcoming, the colonial government adopted
a combination of financial and political measures to create the required
labour supply. Attempts to coerce Africans into seeking wage
employment included imposing taxes, creating reserves, disrupting
local economies and denying Africans the right to grow major
commercial crops.

This is a study of the genesis, evolution, adaptation and subordination of the Kikuyu squatter labourers, who comprised the majority of
resident labourers on settler plantations and estates in the Rift Valley
Province of the White Highlands. The story of the squatter presence in
the White Highlands is essentially the story of the conflicts and
contradictions that existed between two agrarian systems, the settler
plantation economy and the squatter peasant option. Initially, the
latter developed into a viable but much resented sub-system which
operated within and, to some extent, in competition with settler
agriculture. This study is largely concerned with the dynamics of the
squatter presence in the White Highlands and with the initiative,
self-assertion and resilience with which they faced their subordinate
position as labourers. In their response to the machinations of the
colonial system, the squatters were neither passive nor malleable but,
on the contrary actively resisted coercion and subordination as they

struggled to carve out a living for themselves and their families

In collaboration with the European settlers, the colonial government set out to create a cheap, malleable and readily accessible African labour force.[5] Most of the settlers were themselves rather poor and could only afford to hire labour if it was cheap and could be paid for mainly in kind, in the form of land for cultivation and grazing. The pioneer Kikuyu squatters, on their part, looked upon the opening up of the White Highlands as an opportunity for expansion. Both the Kikuyu who had lost access to land in their Central Province homeland (the *ahoi*) and wealthy Kikuyu herders visualised the White Highlands with its vast expanses of unutilised virgin territory as a land of opportunity where the enterprising could make their fortunes and establish permanent residence (*utuuro*).[6] There was unlimited land for both cultivation and grazing.[7] On a more mundane level, the White Highlands offered the squatters an escape from the extortionate authority of the village chief and the opportunity to earn enough to meet tax demands, and their accumulation of wealth, in the form of livestock, was quick. This study looks at how the Kikuyu squatters reacted to the various socio-economic and political pressures that were imposed on them and how their opportunities were frustrated and thwarted by the settlers and colonial government alike.

To a large extent the aspirations of pioneer Kikuyu squatters were similar to those of the early colonial settlers. Both wanted a fresh start in life and both anticipated that their productive ventures would bring them quick returns. But this was where the similarities ended, for the settlers and squatters were locked in an unequal political and economic relationship. As the exclusive owners of the land, the settlers expected, with political backing from the government, to be able to limit the squatters' role solely to that of providing the necessary labour. The squatters, however, were determined to maintain independent and extensive cultivation and grazing, which put tremendous strains on their relations with the settlers.

Because it was important for the colony to become financially self-sufficient, the colonial government threw all its weight behind settler agriculture providing it with vital services and financial subsidies. More significantly, the government enacted a series of legislative measures intended to create and maintain a constant supply of labour. These included the Hut and Poll Taxes, the Masters and Servants Ordinance and the *kipande* system, to mention but a few. However, in Kenya, and particularly in the White Highlands, the shortage of labour and the dissatisfaction with what labour was available, became endemic. The labourers and the employers did not always see eye to eye.

While the settlers were wrestling with the novelty of farming in the tropics and trying to cope with unfamiliar crops, animal diseases, insufficient capital and unstable market conditions,[8] squatter production thrived. The first chapter examines the various factors that pushed Kikuyu squatters from Central Province, as well as those that pulled them to the White Highlands. Perhaps the most important, however, was that during the pioneering stage of settler agriculture, demands imposed on squatter labourers were minimal and, until 1918, squatters were allowed to engage in extensive and unregulated cultivation and grazing which, together with a lucrative trade in livestock and farm produce, enabled them to amass 'wealth' through accumulating large herds of goats, sheep and cattle.

By 1918 the golden age had arrived in which squatters were realising their economic aspirations. Unlike the settler economy, theirs was well capitalised, had plenty of labour and land and required no financial outlay. During this period of *laissez-faire*, the squatters evolved a rewarding socio-economic system, which they sought to protect after 1918. But their independence was short-lived, for the settlers were beginning to emphasise the need to regularise the squatter presence in the White Highlands. After all, they were labourers, not co-owners of the land.

Like that of the squatters, the presence of settlers in the White Highlands was both precipitated and motivated by financial aspirations, the realisation of which largely depended on exploiting the available land and labour. With the wartime boom and profitable commodity prices in the mid 1920s, the settlers sought to diversify from their monocultural maize production into the stock and dairy industries, but were fearful that squatter livestock would spread disease among their expensive grade stock. Hence the call for reducing and/or eliminating squatter stock.

On a more basic level, after World War One, the settlers sought to alter the initial pattern of mutual interdependence with their squatter labour by holding that independent and extensive squatter production in the White Highlands was incompatible with the interests of the settler economy. Chapter Two examines the development of this conflict of interests in the inter-war period. Among other things, the conflict was heralded by the introduction of the 1918 Resident Native Labourers Ordinance (RNLO), which sought to define both the legal status and the labour obligations of the squatter.[9] Henceforth obliged to give more labour hours in exchange for less cultivation and grazing, the squatter was now envisaged as a resident labourer basically dependent on a wage, but with limited cultivation and grazing providing a small wage supplement. By this time it was becoming clear that the settlers had only tolerated independent squatter production because of the labour it provided. But for the squatters, signing a labour contract was the only way of gaining access to land in the White Highlands.

The chapter also analyses the subtle and sometimes unsubtle strategies that the squatters adopted to resist oppressive labour laws and settler attempts to transform them from independent producers-cum-labourers into proletarians. Tactics such as withdrawal of labour, returning to Central Province, illegal squatting, illegal cultivation and grazing, maiming squatter stock, and strikes were some of the ways in which the squatters made their presence felt in the White Highlands and in which they refused to succumb to coercion. The *kifagio* assault, however, which drastically reduced squatter wealth, represented a highpoint in the settlers' campaign against the squatters and cast doubts on the viability of any long-term squatter settlement in the White Highlands.

The squatters endeavoured to make their stay in the White Highlands as comfortable as they possibly could, given the settlers' attempts to eliminate independent squatter production and to pro-letarianise the squatter labour force. Chapter Three looks at the social organisation of the squatter community. It examines how disputes and social issues were mediated through the elders' councils (*ciama*), how circumcision rites were continued as a basis of social acceptance and, most important, how squatter self-help organisations provided schools for their children. The chapter also highlights the blatant subordi-nation of labour to capital by illustrating how the education of squatter children was seen to interfere with the settlers' demands for child labour and how the settlers therefore ensured that the squatters' educational programmes were adjusted to accommodate what they considered their (the settlers') prior claim to the children's time.

The colonial government also placed unreasonable obstacles in the path of the squatters' educational endeavours. Permission to run schools was denied on the grounds that the required standards were not being met, or because they were suspicious of the organisers' political affiliations. And yet, until the late 1930s, the government made no provisions for the education of squatter children. In their educational endeavours the squatters had to contend with opposition of different kinds from both the settlers and the colonial government.

The settlers constantly pushed the colonial government into enacting more and more legislation to control labour, with a consequent progressive infringement of the squatters' freedom. But each measure, including the RNLOs of 1918, 1924 and 1925, failed in one form or another to satisfy the settlers who continued to clamour for ever more stringent measures.

The enactment of the 1937 RNLO,[10] however, surpassed all other labour legislation and dealt a deathblow to squatter and settler communities alike by virtually transferring responsibility for squatter labourers from the government to settler-controlled District Councils. It gave settlers extensive powers over squatters and their welfare. As Chapter Three illustrates, this Ordinance had far-reaching effects and its enactment was a clear indication of the government's abdication of its responsibilities towards the squatters. The Ordinance allowed settlers to restrict or eliminate the number of squatter livestock, the acreage of squatter cultivation and the number of squatters per farm. In effect, it empowered settlers to enforce draconian measures against their squatter labour. The chapter records the subsequent disruption of the squatter economy, with the resultant anger and frustration which led to massive squatter resistance and politicisation.

Squatter politicisation was greatly enhanced by the Olenguruone crisis.[11] A direct product of the 1937 RNLO, the Olenguruone scheme accommodated some of the squatters evicted under the provisions of the Ordinance. Olenguruone became a hotbed of Kikuyu squatter opposition to government measures and a rallying point for Kikuyu political mobilisation. Chapter Four tries to evaluate the significance of Olenguruone amidst growing squatter agitation and dissent. It was at Olenguruone that the use of the oath as a tool for massive mobilisation was initiated as squatters and Olenguruone residents accelerated their struggle against 'the slavery of the White Highlands'. This laid the foundations for the Mau Mau rebellion.

It is a firm conviction of this study that Kikuyu squatters played a crucial role in the initial build-up of the events that led to the outbreak of the Mau Mau war. Pushed to the wall, squatters became easy targets for political mobilisation and by 1950 most Kikuyu squatters in Nakuru District had taken both the Olenguruone oath of unity and the Kikuyu Central Association oath of loyalty. Both oaths demanded a commitment to opposing the government. On settler farms and estates, acts of sabotage, including maiming settler stock, intimidation and killing squatters opposed to anti-settler and anti-government activities, were on the increase prior to the declaration of the state of emergency. Chapter Five, which explains the socio-economic basis of Mau Mau amongst the squatters, argues that there was a strong correlation between a squatter's socio-economic status (within the farm labour hierarchy) and his or her response to the Mau Mau movement. It also reveals the expansionist aspect of the struggle in that squatter freedom fighters had anticipated appropriating the White Highlands from the European settlers. The squatters were not, however, the only people with a claim to the area, but their prowess, as evidenced in the struggle for the White Highlands, can partly be explained by their custodial attitude towards other groups with a stake in the region.

In the final chapter, a bird's-eye view of the decolonisation process provides the context in which the squatters experienced their ultimate disinheritance. The terms of the independence settlement were decided at the Lancaster House talks,[12] where it was agreed that land in the White Highlands would be released on a 'willing seller, willing buyer' basis. The question of a free distribution of land was covered by the talks only in so far as it could be used as a stop-gap measure to forestall the illegal occupation of settler land. Post Mau Mau political mobilisation among the squatters under the Kenya Land Freedom Army (KLFA) is of special interest because, although decolonisation was orchestrated in London away from the forest battlegrounds, KLFA members were committed to resuming the armed struggle should decolonisation fail to give them free land. Although some may view their stand as evidence of political naivety, it does at least indicate the determination of these people to attain the means with which to acquire a decent livelihood. Their sense of betrayal is well documented by the former freedom fighters.

By and large, this book is about squatters and labour. Oral data collected from former squatters were used extensively in reconstructing the history of the period and were particularly useful in revealing the aspirations, expectations, attitudes, motives and responses of squatters under settler domination. Such insights are obviously lacking in official documents, but these were nevertheless invaluable for establishing government and settler positions on various issues. They were also useful for substantiating some of the squatters' own accounts and provided sources of quantitative data, which is impossible to retrieve with any precision from oral interviews. Although it was difficult to locate people who had been among the pioneer squatters, once they were located these informants proved invaluable in describing early squatter-settler relations. Former squatters who moved to the White Highlands during and after the First World War were easier to locate and interview. Together, these informants were crucial in the writing of this book – a study of squatter experiences as recounted by the squatters themselves.

Notes

1. KNA, PC RVP 6A/16/4, Minutes of the meeting in the Ministry of Local Government, Health and Housing on 16 November 1955, between Representatives of the Government and Representatives of the Nakuru County Council.
2. For the nature and extent of land alienation see Sorrenson, M.P.K., *The Origins of European Settlement in Kenya*, London, OUP, 1968.

3. See, for example, Mwangi-Wa-Githumo, *Land and Nationalism: The Impact of Land Appropriation and Land Grievances upon the Rise and Development of Nationalist Movements in Kenya, 1885–1939*, Washington, D.C., University Press of America, 1981.

4. In general, the establishment of colonial rule in Africa necessitated the generation of labour both for the administration of the colony and for the maintenance of the economy therein. See Sandbrook, R. and Cohen, R. (eds), *The Development of an African Working Class*, London, Longman, 1975, p. 15. See also Mosley, P., *The Settler Economies: Studies in the Economic History of Kenya and Southern Rhodesia 1900–1963*, Cambridge, Cambridge University Press, 1983.

5. Clayton, A. and Savage, D. C., *Government and Labour in Kenya, 1895–1963*, London, Frank Cass, 1974, give a full account of the evolution of various categories of labour in the colony. Also, see especially Van Zwanenberg, R. M. A., *Colonial Capitalism and Labour in Kenya, 1919–1939*, Nairobi, East African Literature Bureau, 1975.

6. Interview, James Mumbu Muya, alias Kinuthia Muya, 14 October 1976, Elburgon.

7. Interview, Arphaxad Kiiru Kuria, 21 September 1976, Elburgon. The abundance of land was constantly mentioned by informants as having been a major determinant of squatter movement to the White Highlands.

8. For the majority of settlers, capital was scarce and farming in the White Highlands difficult. See, for example, Simpson, A., *The Land that Never Was*, London, Selwyn and Blout, 1937; and Whittaker, E. *Dimbilil: The Story of a Kenya Farm*, London, Morrison and Gibb, 1956, for an insight into the daily struggles the settlers faced.

9. Ghai, Y.P. and McAuslan, J.P.W.B., *Public Law and Political Change in Kenya*, Nairobi, OUP, 1971, pp. 83–4. From a previous average of 90 days per year, the squatter was required to do at least 180 days' work per year after the enactment of the 1918 RNLO.

10. ibid., pp. 95–6.

11. See Rosberg, C. and Nottingham, J., *The Myth of Mau Mau: Nationalism in Kenya*, Nairobi, EAPH, 1966, pp. 248–59.

12. Among other works, Wasserman, G., *The Politics of Decolonization: Kenya Europeans and their Land Use, 1960–1965*, Cambridge, Cambridge University Press, 1976 analyses how decolonisation was organised so as to give the upper hand in the deliberations to the settlers and colonial government.

One

The Genesis of the
Squatter Community, 1905–18

By the end of the First World War, the squatter system had become an established part of the socio-economic structure of European farms and plantations in Kenya, with Kikuyu squatters comprising the majority of agricultural workers on settler plantations.[1] This study shows how, contrary to settler and colonial government intentions, the squatter phenomenon was created as a response to the difficulties of settlers in securing labour power and of Africans in gaining access to arable and grazing land.

To some extent, the squatters did meet the settlers' labour needs, but on terms other than those preferred by the settlers. The squatters, trying to cope as best they could with pressures from their own society, which were intensified by land alienation and labour extraction by the chiefs, exploited the weaknesses and dependence of the settler economy to turn themselves precisely into the kind of independent community the settlers and government feared. The squatter and settler communities thus created two incompatible systems. This dichotomy reached successive crises during the *kifagio* period (when the squatters lost their livestock) and in the Mau Mau rebellion.

The development and success of the European settler plantation agriculture as the basis of Kenya's economy depended heavily on the availability of land, labour and capital. In a series of excisions, the government alienated about 7 million acres of land, including some of the most fertile in Kenya. This land comprised what came to be known as the White Highlands, or the Settled Areas, which were set aside for exclusive European agriculture.

As well as access to land, the settlers needed a cheap and abundant supply of labour. It was intended that Africans should be farm-workers on settler farms. The government proceeded to impose various legislative and financial measures to force Africans into the labour

market.[2] These measures included the introduction of the H
Taxes (1901 and 1910 respectively), the alienation of African l
the discouragement of African cash crops, especially in areas bo.
the White Highlands. These would ensure that Africans were una   J
become self-sufficient and would have to seek wage employment to
meet their cash needs. For a period, the government even procured
forced labour. The 1906 Masters and Servants Ordinance and an
identification pass known as the *kipande* (1918) were used to control the
movement of labour and to·curb desertion. At the same time, the
government sought to strengthen the settler economy by providing
various services. These included a rail and road network, subsidies on
freight charges, agricultural and veterinary services and credit and loan
facilities.[3]

The above measures were all designed to polarise the settler and
African economies, by subordinating the latter to the former.[4] The
process was protracted, violent and subtle, and unleashed numerous
conflicts and contradictions. Although they were progressively sub-
ordinated, Africans, particularly the squatters, sought to adjust, and in
some cases to outwit, the colonial machinations. The following
examination of land alienation among the Kikuyu attempts to illustrate
both the colonial government's disregard for African rights of
proprietorship in land, and the Kikuyu responses to the situation,
especially with regard to the emergence of the squatter community.

Land alienation among the Kikuyu

When the British government declared a Protectorate over what came
to be known as Kenya, Kikuyu settlement stretched northwards of
Nairobi to the slopes of Mount Kenya.[5] European settlement of the
White Highlands began in the southern district of Kikuyu country.[6] It
soon transpired that settlers intended to appropriate the more highly
cultivated areas, land that had already been broken in preference to
waste and unoccupied land.[7] Administrative officers entrusted with the
task of processing European applications for land usually gave settlers
immediate authority to occupy land, with the only condition being that
they pay the Kikuyu owners a meagre three rupees per acre
compensation for their loss of rights.[8] In the Kiambu-Limuru areas
about 60,000 acres of Kikuyu land were alienated between 1903 and
1906.[9] By 1933, 109.5 square miles of potentially highly valuable
Kikuyu land had been alienated for European settlement. A register
listed 50 Europeans who were expected to compensate the African
owners of the land they now occupied with a total of 3,848 rupees to be
shared between approximately 8,000 Kikuyu. A further 3,000 Kikuyu
living on the land at the time of alienation received no compensation
whatsoever.[10]

This indiscriminate alienation of African land rendered several thousand Africans landless. Those Kikuyu who had lost their land to European settlers in the Kiambu-Limuru areas were urged to stay on to provide labour for them. By July 1910, there were 11,647 Kikuyu on the Kiambu-Limuru settler farms cultivating approximately 11,300 acres of land then owned by European settlers. Some of these 'squatters' were the original owners of these same farms.[11]

The term 'squatter', which originated in South Africa, denoted an African permitted to reside on a European farmer's land, usually on condition he worked for the European owner for a specified period. In return for his services, the African was entitled to use some of the settler's land for the purposes of cultivation and grazing. In the case of the Kiambu-Limuru Kikuyu, this meant that those who continued to reside on the same land were transformed from landowners to squatters overnight. This first group also included Kikuyu families that had fled from the Kiambu-Limuru area to Muranga during the 1899 famine and had since returned. They too were encouraged to remain on their alienated land to provide for the labour demands of the settlers.[12] But this initial attempt to create an African labour force was largely unsuccessful. Africans were reluctant to work as wage-labourers except temporarily and at their own convenience. In many cases, wage labour meant having to work far from home. This, coupled with the various hardships of wage labour, including inadequate housing, low wages, long working hours and unfamiliar diets, precipitated unrest and desertion among the workers.[13]

Attempts to turn the Kikuyu into farm-workers were therefore highly unsuccessful. This was partly because Kikuyu society had an expansionist dynamic of its own, propelled by clan (*mbari*) expansion and competition, by the entrepreneurial ambitions of the cattle-owning *ahoi* (landless people amongst the Kikuyu), and by the pressures of colonial measures enforced by greedy and hostile colonial chiefs. In addition, the settler community was weak and, for the most part, especially in the beginning, could get no more than the rent they charged from these Kikuyu frontiersmen.

The Kikuyu expansionist dynamic

The acquisition of land in Kikuyuland operated through what was known as the *githaka* system.[14] Under this system, each clan established its ownership over a specified portion of land, with each clan member being entitled to land within the *githaka*. *Ahoi* from another clan could acquire the right to cultivate portions of the *githaka* in return for gifts to the clan elders. In this way, they were able to accumulate large herds of stock.

Land ownership among the Kikuyu was initially established either through prior cultivation, breaking up virgin land (known as *kuna*), or purchase. The first occupant or purchaser then founded an *mbari* comprising an extended family or clan. The founder of such a group had jurisdiction over this *githaka* and parcelled it out to his wives, married sons and *ahoi*. On his death the eldest son of the senior wife assumed the role of *muramati* (the trustee of the land). Subsequent subdivisions resulted in the development of several *ithaka* whose boundaries and manner of acquisition were known. If disagreements arose, members could leave their clan to buy land or clear virgin land and establish a new clan with a new *muramati*. New clan, or *mbari*, land could also be established while still maintaining allegiance to the old *muramati*.[15]

The establishment of colonial rule then blocked any further Kikuyu expansion either to the north or to the south. The pioneer migrants visualised the opening up of the White Highlands as a new frontier, in much the same way as the southern Kiambu area had been in the closing years of the last century.[16] The availability of extensive virgin land in the White Highlands enabled squatters to continue their pre-colonial cultivation and stock-keeping on a much larger scale than was possible in Central Province.

In the following pages, I will show how squatters were not only drawn to the White Highlands by dreams of wealth, but were also pushed there because of land shortages and the oppression of chiefs. Initially the Kikuyu squatters merely took advantage of the suitable conditions presented to them but later, capitalising on administrative incompetence and inability to arrest their activities, they occupied and used vast areas of the White Highlands, bringing into existence an economic system that operated within and in competition with the settler economy.

Factors behind Kikuyu migration
Land shortage

Although there was definite evidence of land shortage in Kenya even before 1914,[17] during this period the application of the term 'land shortage' was relative. While some clans in Kiambu District owned enough or even surplus land, land alienation had rendered many families in the same area completely landless, especially in the Limuru area. As a result, there had already been a wave of Kikuyu movement to the White Highlands in search of land as far back as the early 1910s. One of these early migrants was Wanjiku wa Kigo. She moved to the Rift Valley with her stepmother before the First World War.[18] Her father had initially been left behind to look after the family's livestock. Wanjiku said that her family moved because their land in Central

Province was inadequate. They 'hated their plot (*shamba*) at home because the soil was "red" – it lacked fertility'.[19] This land compared poorly with the Rift Valley where 'the *shambas* were not measured'[20] and were fertile.

Wanjiku and her mother first settled in Ndunyu Buru near Elmenteita, where they had gone to join Wanjiku's brother, who had moved to the area earlier and become a squatter. There was a strong kinship basis to the squatters' migration pattern.[21] Ernest Kiberethi Kanyanja and his father went to the Rift Valley in 1917 'because of poverty in Kikuyu'.[22] Although his family had owned land in Githunguri, their plot was infertile and too small. His father therefore decided to move to the Settled Areas where he initially found employment as a 'forest cleaner' in Elburgon. As a forest squatter, Kiberethi's father would clear and cultivate an area, usually for about three consecutive years, after which it would be planted with young trees. He could then continue to plant his crops between the rows of trees for a while before moving on to clear fresh bush and repeat the process.

Some of the squatters who moved to the Rift Valley before 1918 were large stock owners who needed more land for their livestock.[23] As Hannah Njoki recalled: 'My father was a rich man so he hired his own bogie and got other people to board with all their luggage and livestock.'[24] The availability of good quality grazing land in the White Highlands was a great incentive for migration. Because of their impecunious state many settlers could only afford to pay meagre wages to these migrants and met the deficit by making part of their excess land available to the squatter. In this way the settler got cheap labour and the squatter access to prime land in return for minimal labour. In Njoki's case, her father grazed his stock while his son worked for the settler. It has been asserted that squatters leased out their landlords' grazing lands to their Kikuyu friends,[25] so that some of the squatters were grazing not only their own herds, but also those of friends and relations in Central Province.

Other early squatters had been *ahoi* who had lost their rights to use land in Central Province: a situation prompted on the one hand by an expansion of cultivation in Central Province and on the other by the alienation of lands for European settlement and consequent block on any further Kikuyu expansion. Under such pressures, *githaka* holders withdrew *ahoi* rights until the 1940s,[26] which forced the *ahoi* to look for land in the White Highlands.

Taxation

If the possibility of evading taxes provided an incentive for some Kikuyu to move to the Settled Areas,[27] they would have gained only temporary relief. This was because, apart from being employers, the settlers also acted as tax-collectors. Indeed, some squatters hoped to earn their tax money by moving to the Settled Areas. As Gitau stated, 'Some people had no money for the head-tax so they came here where the European would pay the tax for them. He [the settler] would only present the people with the receipts.'[28] In this respect, the 1910–11 Annual Report for Naivasha District noted that, since the Assistant Commissioner was confined to his office most of the time, the collection of taxes depended 'almost entirely on the willingness of the employer to pay the tax for their boys as an advance of wages or to collect and send it in on pay day.'[29] In most cases, the employer obliged in the latter manner.

The chiefs' oppression

The White Highlands were regarded as a haven for people wishing to escape conscription into the Carrier Corps during the First World War. Like several other informants, Shuranga Wegunyi had been captured for the Carrier Corps from his home in Muranga. His father redeemed him by paying in kind, one *ndigithu* (gourd) of honey and a ram to the local chief. On release, Shuranga and his father decided to move to the safety of the White Highlands. Here, the settlers protected their employees from conscription into the Carrier Corps for fear of losing what remained of their resident labour.[30] Some people moved to the Settled Areas to avoid the chief's authority, for in the reserve the chief and his headmen were entrusted with the task of providing labour for communal and public projects. People detested this form of forced labour, failure to do which could be punished by the confiscation of livestock. Mithanga Kanyumba's move to the Rift Valley was a direct attempt to escape the chief's authority. As he himself recalled:

> My father was rich. The chief used to choose young men who would be taken to Fort Hall. We [Mithanga and one other] stayed there for two days without knowing our fate. The European [who was to hire them] was at location 2 at Chief Njiri's. We were told by the Askari Kanga [the chief's soldiers] to wait for the European who would give us money for travel. We refused the money and went back. I left Kikuyu due to the chief's trouble. I went to Nightingale's place where I was employed.[31]

Other reasons, such as fear of witchcraft, hostile neighbours and family feuds also played a part in making individuals move to the Rift Valley,[32] but, in most cases, the move was the result of a combination of reasons.

Early labour recruitment

Naivasha and Nakuru, where the bulk of the work-force was Kikuyu, were among the districts least affected by labour shortages in the period before 1918. By 1918 there were about 8,000 squatter families in the Nakuru District alone. Of a population of 9,116 Africans in the Naivasha District, 6,600 belonged to almost exclusively Kikuyu squatter families.[33] Although salaries were low, between three and six rupees per month, because land was plentiful the two areas were exceedingly popular among Kikuyu squatter-labourers and attracted a number of illegal squatters. Incidentally, by 1905, one rupee was equivalent to 1/4d, or 15 rupees to one pound sterling. However, by 1920, one rupee was valued at two shillings (2/-).

The first settlers to recruit labour in Kikuyu country promised their prospective squatters large tracts of land for grazing and cultivation. An initial quantity of livestock, including cows and goats, was also promised and actually given to some of the pioneer Kikuyu 'labourers'. This all helped towards starting them off on a sound footing towards their ultimate goal of amassing wealth. In return, the Kikuyu were required to herd the settlers' livestock.[34] Later, especially after the First World War, this obligation was extended to jobs relating to the commercial cultivation of settler crops, but in the meanwhile the labour demands imposed on pioneer immigrants were minimal.

The early settlers capitalised on the depleted state of Kikuyu lands by offering prospective immigrants larger and more productive plots in the Rift Valley than were available in certain parts of Central Province. As a number of ex-squatters pointed out, it was not actual landlessness that made them decide to move to the Rift Valley, but rather the inadequate size and infertility of their own lands. Some of the Kikuyu who migrated to the Rift Valley in the period before and after 1918 were, however, completely landless, either as a result of direct land loss through land alienation or because they had been evicted by their Kikuyu landlords.

Unlike the Luo, Luyia and Abagusii contract workers, the Kikuyu labour-force brought their women and children to the settler farms, as well as certain items such as livestock and beehives, which could be regarded as indications of the permanent nature of their migration.[35]

Prospective migrants were initially offered free transport and this continued until the outbreak of the First World War. The Kikuyu, Limuru and Kijabe stations served as departure points, especially for squatters from the southern Kiambu area. One of my informants, Kiiru, who was among them, spoke about these journeys as follows:

> People began coming to the Rift Valley in 1909. Most of them were brought by Delamere. People would be put in a 'bogie' with their

beehives, livestock and skins (*ndarwa*) for sleeping on. All alighted aι Njoro where they would be taken to places where they could graze and cultivate freely without restriction. They were shown large fields which belonged to Delamere, who wanted them to look after his stock.[36]

Although Delamere's name was the one most frequently quoted by the ex-squatters, other settlers also made labour-recruiting journeys to Central Province and elsewhere.[37] Njoro was clearly not the only terminus for squatters thus recruited. The destinations of such labourers were as varied as the extent of European settlement.

The squatter system

As the squatter system evolved, it began to show a number of characteristics that revealed weaknesses in the settler community and colonial government's attempts to create an African work-force. For a start, not all the squatters were settler employees. Illegal squatting and what was rather derogatorily referred to as 'Kaffir farming' were integral to the squatter system and persisted until the settler presence in Kenya drew to a close in the early 1960s. It was largely from Kaffir farming that Kikuyu squatters acquired the socio-economic values of independent production, which they strove to maintain in the inter-war years amidst intensive opposition from the settlers and colonial administrators.

Kaffir farming

Kaffir farming, which like the squatter system derived its name from South Africa, referred to the practice whereby a large European landowner would allow Africans to use his land for grazing and cultivation in return for payment in cash or kind, the latter in the form of milk, manure, stock or crops.[38] As we shall see later on, various versions of Kaffir farming coexisted alongside the squatter phenomenon and evaded the scrutiny of the administration. By 1910, there were about 20,000 Kikuyu Kaffir farmers representing approximately 5,000 families.

In Kenya, the development of Kaffir farming was blamed on the small impoverished European settlers who, through financial impecuniosity, were prevented from engaging in productive agriculture on their farms.[39] But some forms of Kaffir farming seem to have been practised by a majority of European farmers throughout the colonial period.[40] The Ukamba Quarterly Report of December 1910 noted 67 villages of African tenants on one farm in the Province. For the right to use land, these tenants either paid between 8 and 30 rupees, or handed over part of their crop or the profits from its sale. These squatters did not normally work for the European landowners.[41] Even after the institution of the 1918 Resident Native Labourers Ordinance (RNLO), which was set up to convert squatter residence in the Settled Areas from a tenancy into a labour contract, some European settlers continued to demand a certain amount of squatter maize crop, milk or manure as part of their labour contract. Njoroge Mambo, Gacheru Manja, and Bethuel Kamau, all spoke of how their settler employer had demanded a minimum of six *gunias* (gunny-bags) of maize per year from each of his employees.[42] This was despite traders from Central Province offering better prices for maize than the settlers to whom they were forced to sell their crop.[43]

Many European Kaffir farmers were absentee landlords. The Africans who utilised their lands grew and marketed their produce both within and outside the White Highlands. The more successful European settlers and colonial administrators saw Kaffir farming as negating the whole purpose of European settlement. Since the White Highlands had been alienated for a European commercial agriculture dependent on African labour, the emergence of a flourishing peasant economy in the area was seen as an obvious and undesirable threat to settler hegemony. Interestingly, as will be illustrated later, the squatters' analysis of the plantation economy portrays a similar but opposite observation. As Kimondo, an ex-squatter observed: 'When the Europeans saw that people [squatters] were becoming rich, they began to reduce the size of the *shamba*.'[44]

It was feared that cultivation by Africans of large parcels of land in the White Highlands would, in time, create *de facto* African rights to land under their use.[45] Colonial administrators were concerned that settlers who did not engage in any production on their farms were failing in their obligation to contribute to exports, which were necessary for the economic development of the country.[46]

The settler Kaffir farmers, on their part, considered the practice a good way of building up settler stock, while at the same time keeping pasture under control and bringing in an income. Also, land that had already been worked by squatters was much easier to cultivate once the settler was ready to expand his own production.

Kaffir farming involved a landlord-tenant relationship between the European settler and the African squatter, and some settlers were almost entirely dependent on the African producers who resided on their farms.[47] When settler agriculture came to a standstill during the First World War, the squatters virtually took over responsibility for agricultural production in the Settled Areas.[48]

The administration found Kaffir farming difficult to control. Since the tenants could not be classified as employees, they were protected from prosecution under the Masters and Servants Ordinance of 1906, and the authorities were reluctant to prosecute the European Kaffir farmers.[49] The tenants who did provide labour to the European settlers did so intermittently and under vague verbal agreements which lasted for only three months in any one year.[50] Administrative personnel did sometimes confiscate stock from the Africans on the European Kaffir farmers' land, but the government complained of inadequate personnel and insufficient finances to maintain a close watch on Kaffir farming.[51]

Kikuyu migration to the Rift Valley

Kikuyu migration to the Settled Areas was initially looked upon by the colonial administration as a good opportunity for harnessing labour. Though Kaffir farming was thought to stifle the flow of labour, squatting was believed to have the opposite effect. The 1912/13 Naivasha Annual Report, for example, stated that 'squatting . . . might mitigate the labour difficulty'.[52] A year later, the 1914/15 report of the same district could boast that, 'there was no shortage of labour in the district',[53] and that '80 per cent of it was Kikuyu'.[54] The rest was Maasai, Kipsigis, Luo, Luyia and Baganda.

Unlike Naivasha, where the Kikuyu had established themselves as farm-labourers from an early period, in Nakuru District, the 'kavirondo [sic.] as farm hands were [initially] much preferred by the settlers'.[55] It did not take long for this situation to change, however, as the figures in table 1.1 indicate.

TABLE 1.1

Nakuru District Population 1915–16

Labourers on farms	1,800
Labourers on railways	400
Labourers in Nakuru Township	500
Kikuyu squatters	2,648
TOTAL	5,348

Naivasha District Population 1915–16

Europeans	147
Asiatics	13
Natives	3,289

Source: KNA, Nakuru District Annual Report, 1915–16, pp. 2, 3.

This early Kikuyu movement to the Settled Areas was initially profitable for both parties, the settlers and the Kikuyu squatters. The settlers were supplied with minimal but much needed labour, while the Kikuyu immigrants, for a period of at least two decades, evolved a lucrative peasant economy in the White Highlands. Both the squatters and the settlers anticipated continuous and permanent residence of the 'squatter' labour-force in the White Highlands. The government was especially concerned that the settlers should provide favourable conditions to encourage the workers to accept permanent employment. To this end, on 18 May 1910 the Governor, Sir Percy Girourd, issued a confidential memorandum to all Provincial and District Commissioners stating that: 'It is . . . in the interest of the employer to make him [the labourer] as comfortable as possible and try to persuade him to settle down and accept permanent employment'.[56]

Before 1918, the Kikuyu squatters had been able to withstand any pressures that threatened to thwart their endeavours. For example, any attempts by a settler to control the amount of 'squatter' cultivation, or the size of their herds, or even demands for more labour hours than the squatter considered necessary, were counteracted by the withdrawal of the squatters' labour. The squatters would simply move on to the next farm to continue their virtually independent existence. By changing 'masters', the squatters were thus able to establish and operate the labour pattern best suited to their major activities, namely extensive cultivation, herding and trading in crops and livestock. During this period, the Kikuyu 'labour-force' had thus created a beneficial socio-economic system, which they sought to retain in the wake of shifting relations in the economy of the Settled Areas.

Also during this *laissez-faire* period, the Kikuyu community began to feel very much at home in the Settled Areas: a feeling generated and reinforced by the relative prosperity that accrued from cultivation and livestock keeping in the region. And, in that this initial period was characterised by unregulated squatter production, squatter self-assertion was also enhanced.

Whatever notions the settlers held about their position in relation to the squatters, both groups were driven by the same dream of achieving a better life style through exploiting the rich Highland areas. But, to realize this dream, each group needed to exploit the resources controlled by the other. The settlers depended on African labour,[57] while 'squatters' capitalised on the availability of unused land in the White Highlands. As Muya Ngari, a pioneer ex-squatter, put it: 'I came because the Rift Valley was wide'.[58] However, whereas the squatter was a vital spoke in the wheel of the plantation economy, the settler presented an impediment to squatter activities in the area.

Squatter settlement patterns

Whereas Kikuyu squatters from the Kiambu and Muranga areas usually went to the Naivasha and Nakuru districts, those from Nyeri tended to move to settler farms in the Laikipia region. On arrival at European farms, squatters were free to locate their homesteads anywhere within the area the settler had set aside for them on his farm.[59] Thus, within certain limits, they were 'free to build where they wanted'.[60] This independence enjoyed by the Kikuyu in locating their place of residence contrasted sharply with the treatment meted out to contract labourers, who were housed in (or rather, herded into) wattle-and-daub labour camps (in lines), which the Kikuyu squatters derogatorily referred to as *maskini*[61] (poverty stricken). This consideration for the squatter's individuality played an important part in enhancing the Kikuyu's sense of self-respect.

The squatter's unrestricted use of land in the White Highlands before 1918 was aptly referred to as 'depending on one's hand'.[62] In other words, it was the squatter's industry, rather than the settler's restrictions, which determined how much land a squatter brought under cultivation and how much livestock he came to own. Unlike the settler economy, squatter agriculture did not depend on financial investment or on a fluctuating labour-force. With ample labour for cultivation and grazing, the squatters thrived at a time when the settler economy was still trying to gather enough momentum to take off.

Until 1918, labour requirements were minimal. A 'squatter and his wife might be expected to work for five months in the year between them: he would be required to work for three and a half months a year at least'.[63] This gave the squatter ample time to pursue his own productive activities. Although there were times when the settler's labour requirements coincided with the squatter's schedule for opening up new fields, sowing, weeding or reaping, the composition of a squatter's homestead was such that it could ensure that these labour demands were met. Wives, older men, women, any children not at school, and visiting relatives were all mobilised to cultivate the squatter's *shamba*. Since, in contracting as a labourer, the head of the family acquired the right to cultivate part of the settler farm for the rest of the family, it was really their responsibility to cultivate and graze the land.

Large tracts of unused settler land were cultivated by squatters for planting with maize, their major food and cash crop. Sometimes these squatters would need to seek additional labour from fellow squatters and their families, casual and contract labourers, or relatives from Central Province, for the production of a surplus maize crop was of prime importance to them. Most of the grain would be sold to the

European settlers, or to Indian and African traders at the various trading centres that had sprung up in the Settled Areas.[64] A certain amount of maize was sold to labourers who did not cultivate and at times found their *posho* (maize-meal) rations inadequate.[65] Some of the settlers insisted 'on a compulsory purchase, at a poor price, of the squatter's own produce'.[66] Even when squatters sold to the settler voluntarily, it was always at a lower price and the settlers sometimes resold the maize at a profit. In this respect, it was obvious that the squatter economy was subsidising the settler economy and in some cases, as in Naivasha before 1918, settlers were completely dependent on squatter produce: 'As the farms in the District are practically entirely stock farms, the resident labour is largely employed in growing foodstuffs which are as a rule sold to the employers, the rate for maize and beans being one rupee a load'.[67] As the figures in table 1.2 show, even as early as 1916–17, the extent of squatter cultivation was considerable.

TABLE 1.2

Native Produce Sold by Natives in the District: Approximate
Potatoes 200 tons at 50 cents per load of 60 lbs
Maize 180 tons at Sh. 1/- per load of 60 lbs
Beans 40 tons at Sh. 1/- per load of 60 lbs

There were about 3,330 Kikuyu in Naivasha at this time.

Source: KNA, Naivasha District Annual Report, 1916–17, pp. 2, 11.

While only some settlers produced enough maize for export, they all needed large quantities of it for milling into *posho*, which provided the main ration for their contract workers, mostly Luo, Luyia, Kisii, Maasai and some Kalenjin. *Posho* was also given to squatters during their first year of engagement before their crops matured.

Squatters found it surprising that contract labourers would willingly engage in labour contracts that forbade them to produce their own food crops, especially since the food rations were sometimes inadequate. Despite this, the contract labourers never put any pressure on the settlers to allow them to cultivate.[68] As Karanja Kamau recalled:

The *nduriri* [non-Kikuyu especially from Western Kenya] labour had no *shamba*. They only got *posho* because they were monthly employees. They did not want *shambas*. They would even buy maize from the Kikuyu because the European *posho* was not enough. Yet it did not occur to them to dig the *shamba*.[69]

The Kikuyu squatters were bewildered by these contract workers who had only come 'to work for their stomachs'. The odd contract worker might cultivate a vegetable garden, but on the whole, non-squatter labour did not cultivate land in the White Highlands. They had nothing to show for their efforts out there, which was what Kikuyu squatters found hard to understand. The bulk of these labourers were actually migrant target workers who signed on periodically when they wanted to raise money for specific cash needs at home, which might include items such as livestock for bride-wealth, taxes, school fees, or even a hoe (*jembe*). Once the labourer had accumulated enough money, he would return to his village 'to rest' and to attend to his personal and communal duties.[70] Rest periods varied as much as the periods of contracted labour, although, with time, these labourers spent longer and longer periods at work, either on settler plantations or in urban areas, while their wives and families tended the family *shambas* in the village.[71]

In the period before 1918, an average squatter family cultivated between six and seven acres of land, which meant that a surplus was almost invariably available for sale. Since the African market provided a more profitable outlet for squatter produce than the settler buyers,[72] most transactions were conducted at the various trading centres. Among those in Nakuru District were Subukia, Bahati, Ndundori, Njoro, Elburgon, Turi and Molo, where regular weekend markets were held, and large amounts of produce bought and sold. Urban proletarians from the various mushrooming townships in the White Highlands, especially Nakuru, were among the African customers for the squatters' produce.

Asian traders would purchase squatter produce in bulk to dispose of, either wholesale or retail, in the various urban areas. 'The best buyers, however, were those Kikuyu who came from Central Province'.[73] These would include the new arrivals to the Settled Areas who had not yet gathered their first harvest and therefore were in a poor position to bargain. But, the most profitable trade was undoubtedly with individuals or traders from hunger-stricken Central Province.

Despite the availability of abundant land, squatter production was occasionally reduced to subsistence levels because of the low prices offered for the produce.[74] Under these conditions, flooded markets discouraged the production of a surplus, and squatter produce would either be given to needy friends and relations from Central Province, or sold to them 'at the same price as the Europeans'[75], i.e. cheaply.

Squatter accumulation: livestock

In addition to growing maize and other surplus crops for sale, including cabbages, potatoes and peas, the Kikuyu squatters sought to accumulate livestock. In certain instances, they directly exchanged their foodcrops for livestock with the Dorobo, Tugen, Somali, Turkana or Maasai people.[76] More often, however, goats and sheep were purchased at trading centres from their Somali, Tugen or Maasai owners.[77] Sometimes squatters travelled long distances to purchase livestock: for example, from Nakuru to the Baringo District or from Naivasha to Maasailand.[78] There are even references to purchases of livestock from Maliboi in the Londiani-Kisumu region.[79]

The amount of livestock, especially of sheep and goats, increased rapidly in the White Highlands, and after a while the Rift Valley came to be referred to as *weru*, or pasture-land. Although it is difficult to establish the exact cost of livestock at this time, pioneer squatters obviously found the prices more competitive than in Central Province. At one time, two *debes* (tin containers) of *posho* were said to fetch two goats from the Turkana,[80] whereas the Somali and Dorobo would sell a cow for about two rupees.[81] At least seven other prices were quoted by these early pioneers, but, although there are minor differences and problems in translating into the cash equivalent the goods in kind given in exchange for livestock, the important factor is that these Kikuyu squatters saw these deals as competitive. Wangoi stated that three months' pay went a long way towards helping to accumulate 'a hutful of goats'.[82] This rapid accumulation of stock, first by cheap purchases and later by natural increase, served to popularise the Settled Areas among the Kikuyu, not only among those who were resident in the area but also those in the Kikuyu homeland. Livestock, the symbol of wealth the Kikuyu had consistently sought to acquire from the Maasai, was now readily available, at a price, in the Settled Areas. Herding the animals became the responsibility of the young boys and old men.[83]

One reason why the squatters were so keen to accumulate livestock was because of its importance in the social and economic lives of the Kikuyu. Sheep and goats were required for a multitude of ceremonies and rituals and for various other forms of social intercourse. L.S.B. Leakey[84] ventured to enumerate these occasions and identified 172 of them between the birth and death of each average individual (Kikuyu), each of which demanded the slaughter of a beast and the eating of meat. In addition, the acquisition of livestock was viewed as a way of saving; it could easily be converted into hard cash when necessary for the various expenditures that accompanied the establishment of colonial rule, such as taxes, school fees and the purchase of consumer goods. Though livestock still remained central to the payment of bride-wealth, other rituals, such as circumcision, required cash, with surgeons increasingly preferring to be paid in cash rather than in kind.[85]

In the Settled Areas, as in Central Province, the possession of livestock was concomitant with social status. It was always '. . . the rich people who spoke while others listened'[86] at important squatter gatherings like beer-drinking parties. High social standing (*igweta*)[87] among the other squatters was acquired by accumulating stock, and this led squatters to resist the added labour obligations and restrictions which were imposed by the settlers even before 1918. Squatters were reluctant to expend the bulk of their energy on settler farms as members of the labouring community. They aimed to earn their income from their own productive activities. As one ex-squatter's wife recalled, 'Wealth did not come from salaries, no, it came from *shamba* produce and exchange'.[88]

Squatters' wages were meagre, even in comparison with those of the contract labourers. To the squatters, however, especially in the pre-1918 period, the cash proceeds of their labour contracts were of little or no economic significance.[89] Wage differences did not determine whether or not a squatter agreed to make a contract. Although the money could be put to use, the squatter's major concern was the availability of sufficient land for cultivation and grazing. As Lucia Ngugi declared, 'People used to be paid in rupees and were also given *shambas*. But they preferred the *shamba*. The rupees could not do anything'.[90] Though the money was useful, access to land guaranteed a better basis than a salary for generating wealth.

By the end of the First World War, the settlers had got rid of squatter cattle, so from then on goats and sheep assumed central place in the squatters' social, economic and political life.[91]

Goats became the most important item in the payment of bride-wealth. But, because of their ready availability and high level of accumulation among the squatters, more goats were needed to pay for bride-wealth in the Rift Valley than in Central Province.[92] The standard bride-price between the late 1920s and early 1930s, when the squatters were at the height of their prosperity, averaged between 80 and 100 goats.[93] Although this price held during the *kifagio* (broom – signifying the sweeping away, or elimination, of livestock) period, it is necessary to recognise that this came at the height of squatter wealth and that, rather than sell their large herds, the squatters preferred to increase the size of the dowry as they married more wives.[94] Ngoci Ndegwa married two wives during *kifagio* and paid 120 goats for each of them. Wanyoko Kamau paid 120 goats for each of his *kifagio* brides and 80 for a third.

The immediate success that had given the squatter immigrants their sense of arrival in the early period was to be thwarted by the settler community in the period after 1918. But, in the meanwhile, in Central Province, the *kihiu-mwiri* circumcision initiates of between 1914 and 1918 drew attention to the opportunities to be found in the Settled Areas in their song entitled '*Ndingiria Gikang'u Njugu Iremeire Ndimu*'[95] (I cannot continue to eat maize only, when there is a surplus of beans at Njoro). The female initiates in the same age-group also formulated a song about the productivity of the Rift Valley; in which they expressed their desire to settle in this land of plenty:

> *Ngwithiira Ruguru,*
> *Ngahituke Mutamaiyo,*
> *Kuria Ngwaci cia Nyakiburi*
> *Ciaturagwo na rwamba.*

> *Ngwithiira na ruguru,*
> *Ngaikare murangoine*
> *Haria burugu uhihagiria marigu*
> *Wanjiarire ukunjuria thigagwo ku*
> *Na thigagwo kibui mucii*
> *Munene wi mburi na ngombe.*

> *Wanjiarire Unjuragia thigagwo ku,*
> *Ukiuga ni itheru wanjiarire*
> *thii kibui ukarorie.*[96]

I will go to the West [Rift Valley Settled Areas],
Beyond the Brown Olive Tree,
Where the *Nyakiburi* sweet potatoes
Are split with a sharpened stick.

I will go to the West
And sit at the entrance,
Where the *purko* [Maasai] roast bananas
Father you ask me where I will be married,
I will get married at Kibui the big
Homestead which has goats and cattle.

Father you ask me where I will be married,
You think it is a joke,
You had better go to Kibui
And find out (confirm).

Former squatters spoke of how the Kikuyu in Central Province homelands would try to marry their daughters to Kikuyu men in the Rift Valley, in an attempt to boost their wealth of stock with the anticipated bride-price.[97] There were also instances of women married in Central Province being freed from their marital ties and brought to the Rift Valley to remarry. This happened if the woman in question was being ill-treated by her husband. Her relatives in the Rift Valley would return the equivalent number of goats and other livestock paid for her dowry to her husband's family. Once redeemed, the girl would be brought to the Rift Valley where a better suitor would be found for her to marry.[98]

These discrepancies even extended to the circumcision fee. Although this later came to be paid in cash, here again the traditional surgeons (*aruithia*) agreed that rates of remuneration were higher in the Settled Areas than in Central Province. While in 1920 one *debe* (tin container) of honey was an acceptable surgeon's fee in Central Province, in the Rift Valley the surgeon received a gourd of beer, one half calabash of black peas (*njahi*), one gourd of fermented porridge and about ten shillings in lieu of the *gituiku*, the handleless blade then widely used as a circumcision fee.[99]

Up until 1918, little was done to regulate the legal relationship between European settlers and their African counterparts. It was difficult to distinguish between a squatter who was supposed to be an agricultural labourer and one who merely paid rent. Both were engaged in the same productive activity and over time each developed the same rationale to explain his presence in the White Highlands, i.e. settlement in the pursuit of wealth. In this respect, the constant references to the squatters' evasion of duty or reluctance to work for the settlers[100] were indicative of the dichotomy in the squatters' status as labourers on the one hand, and, colonists on the other. The latter was more apparent in the period before 1918, and although not publicly defended by the squatters or acknowledged by the settlers, it was an ever present phenomenon which posed a real threat to settlerdom.

This threat was instrumental in, indeed fundamental to, the formulation of the 1918 Resident Native Labourers Ordinance which, much to the disappointment of the settlers, emphasised the squatter's labour obligations without stipulating that his status in relation to the settler was that of a labourer rather than co-owner of the White Highlands. Some of the more self-sufficient squatters completely severed ties with their areas of origin. For others, the occasional visits of relatives from the country continued to increase and perpetuate the wealth of the Settled Areas. This, in turn, resulted in the Kikuyu migrating to the Rift Valley.

Like the European settlers, a generation of Kikuyu came into existence who moved from one area to the next in search of 'a place to feel at home'.[101] This worked against the colonial plan and led to the dual problem of labour shortages on the one hand, and increasing numbers of illegal squatters on the other. The colonial government was caught in the position of trying to maintain a balance between these two conflicting productive patterns. The much discusse⌐ ¯ ¯

shortage was attributed to a lack of manpower, but the irony of the situation in the White Highlands in the period before 1918 was that this badly needed labour-force was actually resident in the Settled Areas as illegal squatters. Employers merely failed to offer the kinds of conditions that would attract their labour.

The paradox of a labour shortage: squatter self-perception

Settlers and colonial officials assumed that African labourers in the Settled Areas would constitute a 'migrant labour force' which would leave once the contract expired, or at six months notice if the settler so desired. Kikuyu migrants viewed their presence in the Settled Areas in a different light. They sought to establish a 'dwelling place' (*utuuro*)[102] and to evolve a viable socio-economic system within the White Highlands.

One way of trying to understand how the squatters perceived their own situation is to look at them in their role as *ahoi*, as they understood it, in their own society.[103] Among the Kikuyu, at the time when migration and settlement were taking place, it was common for *ahoi* to help, not only in the task of defending the acquired land, but also in acquiring more land. The *ahoi* '. . .readily accepted such an invitation because the *rutere* (frontier) was regarded as the land of opportunity where an industrious person expected, sooner or later, to acquire wealth of his own to enable him to buy his own land'.[104] To the pioneer squatters, the Rift Valley was a new frontier which in many ways promised to be more rewarding than Central Province.[105] The early settlers were themselves instrumental in the crystallisation and consolidation of what became a widespread theory about the abundant opportunities that accrued from settling in the White Highlands. In other words, 'advertisements circulating in the reserves led Africans to believe that life on European farms would be a "paradise" for them'.[106] Like the European settlers, prospective African migrants anticipated easy and immediate prosperity in the White Highlands.

To this end, the migration of some squatters, especially those who abandoned their lands in Central Province[107] and moved to the Rift Valley, was a calculated risk. An unknown, but probably a considerable proportion of these migrants were large stock owners who were attracted to the Rift Valley because of the quality and extent of the grazing land available.[108] For these squatters, the White Highlands offered an opportunity not only to continue their pre-colonial mode of production but to do it on a larger and more rewarding scale. As an ex-squatter put it, 'During the earlier squatter days, the *shamba* belonged to both the squatter and the European settler'.[109]

Hopes of retaining this wealth (for the earlier squatter) or of acquiring wealth (among prospective migrants) began to fade once the settlers started restricting squatter cultivation in the early 1920s. Till then, Kikuyu squatters looked upon themselves and the settlers as the joint heirs to the Settled Areas.

The other squatters

Though predominantly a Kikuyu practice in Nakuru and Naivasha, squatting was by no means restricted to these two districts, nor to the Kikuyu people alone. There were also Akamba, Nandi, Kipsigis, Marakwet, Keiyo and Tugen squatters, even in these two areas, and after the First World War the Luo, Luyia and Kisii squatters made their appearance in the region as well.

Nandi and Kipsigis with insufficient pasture for their livestock would squat on European farms mainly in the Uasin Ngishu and Songhor areas. By 1921 they had begun to work as hired labourers for the meagre sum of four shillings per month in return for unlimited grazing rights.[110] Alternatively, they grazed on settler farms and paid their rent in livestock.

The earliest group of Nandi squatters came from the northern part of the Nandi homeland to serve as squatters on farms in the southern Uasin Ngishu District, to which they were brought in 1906. Many of them were born in the area and believed they were 'fully entitled to live in the Settled Areas, because it was formerly owned by them'.[111]

By 1912, settlers were making requests for labour to Nandi chiefs.[112] In that year it was observed that the cattle population in the Nandi reserve had fallen to about 12,000, as the bulk of the cattle had gone with the squatters to the neighbouring settler farms. Nandi headmen, when consulted, did not want their followers to leave, especially when they wanted to take their stock with them.[113] On the other hand, by 1916, settlers were complaining about 'the restrictions forbidding Nandi squatters to take their cattle on to farms',[114] for the Nandi refused to contract as squatters unless they were allowed to take their cattle with them. When the Veterinary Department granted temporary concessions allowing them to take a few milk cows, 'hundreds of Nandi registered for work on the farms'.[115]

Immediately after the War, about 100 square acres of Nandi land were alienated, including salt-licks. This resulted in further migration to the Uasin Ngishu and Trans Nzoia farms and by 1920 there were about 1,500 Nandi squatter families. Placing the Nandi reserve under quarantine for pleuro-pneumonia, rinderpest and East Coast fever during the period 1908–24 not only prohibited the movement of stock to and from the Nandi homeland, but also limited the possibilities of trade in cattle.[116] This meant that the Nandi had little or no means of obtaining cash, a basic necessity to many people during the colonial period, with the consequent result that some Nandi families drifted to the Settled Areas in search of work.

The Kipsigis too were short of land, mainly as a result of colonial machinations. In the southern part of their reserve, 130,000 acres (52,000 hectares) had been alienated for European settlement.[117] Some of this land was occupied by settlers and some converted into Crown Land. When the Maasai were pushed out of Laikipia to make room for European settlers, some of them came and settled on the Kipsigis land, which had already been partly penetrated by Abagusii.

The Kipsigis found the loss of the Sotik land and salt-licks particularly hard to bear. The administration operated under a self-imposed civilising mission of endeavouring to create agricultur-ists out of the 'backward' pastoralists. This was used as a good excuse for alienating large parcels of African-owned land which was then given for European settlement,[118] forcing the unlucky Africans to resort to wage labour in the White Highlands or elsewhere. This was the fate of a sizeable number of Kipsigis. The first Kipsigis squatters were registered in 1913 and by 1917 their numbers had increased to 1,800. The introduction of the Kericho tea estates demanded further alienation of Kipsigis land, resulting in the subsequent thrust of more Kipsigis into the labour market. Like the Nandi, the Kipsigis opted for squatter labour which afforded them grazing rights.

By the mid-1920s, the Keiyo and Marakwet[119] had also found it necessary to resort to squatter labour. As the victims of pre-colonial and colonial factors, they had occupied the eastern rim of the Uasin Ngishu plateau even before 1890. In 1922 they lost 328 square miles of forest land, which was alienated for E.S.M. Grogan Ltd. This was a substantial land loss and, over time, overstocking became a major land problem, leaving the residents no alternative but to sign on as resident labourers on European farms. Living in a marginal area sometimes forced the Keiyo and Marakwet to seek employment on European farms, especially during periods of famine, which were usually brought on by the severe droughts common to the area. Signing on as squatters was thus also a way of obtaining pasture for their livestock.

The pattern of squatting among other ethnic groups was to some extent different from the trend prevalent among the Kikuyu, for whom settlement in the alienated areas was often thought to involve (though was not invariably accompanied by) a complete severing of physical ties with their original homelands.[120] While the majority of Kikuyu agricultural labourers were emigrants, those from other ethnic groups were migrants who had their feet in two camps, their places of work and their areas of origin.

After the squatters, the second largest category of Africans in the colonial labour force in both settled and urban areas comprised the Luo, Luyia and Abugusii people. Although regional preferences were not exclusive, Luyia squatters tended to settle on Trans-Nzoia and Uasin Ngishu farms, Luo squatters contracted in the Muhoroni, Koru and Londiani areas, while the Abagusii were found on the Kericho tea estates. In terms of agricultural labour, especially in Nakuru District, the Luo, Luyia and Abagusii provided mostly casual labour. Abagusii, Luo, Maragoli and Banyore labourers contracted as squatters on the Kericho tea plantations for periods lasting about three years.

Apart from a concern to regulate the extensive independent Kikuyu production and presence in the White Highlands, by 1918 the government was also determined to create an abundant and controllable supply of labour for the settler plantations. Until then, the squatter system had little to do with wage employment. It was merely the product of settler undercapitalisation and of the abundance of fertile land in the White Highlands, which had satisfied squatters' needs for land but not the settlers' demand for labour. The squatter was an accident, a mark of the settlers' failure to obtain labour in any other way. The next chapter examines the government's attempts to turn squatters into labourers, a cheap source of labour, and shows how the squatters reacted to this initial assault.

Notes

1. By 1945, there were about 200,000 squatters, the majority of whom (122,000) were Kikuyu. See Leys, C., *Underdevelopment in Kenya: The Political Economy of Neocolonialism, 1964–1971*, London, Heinemann, 1975, p. 47.
2. For the evolution of labour during this early period see for example Clayton, A., and Savage, D. C., *Government and Labour in Kenya, 1895–1963*, London, Frank Cass, 1974; Leys, N., *Kenya*, (fourth edition), London, Frank Cass, 1973 (first published 1924); Ross, W.M., *Kenya from Within*, London, Frank Cass, reprint 1968 (first published 1927); and Dilley, M.R., *British Policy in Kenya Colony*, New York, Praeger, reprint 1966 (first published 1937).
3. Brett, E. A., *Colonialism and Underdevelopment in East Africa: The Politics of Economic Change, 1919–1939*, London, Heinemann, 1973.
4. See Dilley, *British Policy*, pp. 213–23.
5. Wrigley, C. C., 'Kenya: Patterns of Economic Life 1902–1945' in Harlow, V., Chilver, E. M. and Smith, A., (eds), *History of East Africa*, Volume II, Oxford, Clarendon Press, 1965, p. 212.
6. For an account of European settlement in Kenya, see Sorrenson, M.P.K., *The Origins of European Settlement in Kenya*, London, OUP, 1968.

7. ibid., p. 181.
8. Sorrenson, *Origins of European Settlement*, p. 179.
9. Rosberg, C. and Nottingham, J., *The Myth of Mau Mau: Nationalism in Kenya*, Nairobi, EAPH, 1966, p. 19.
10. ibid.
11. Sorrenson, *Origins of European Settlement*, p. 184.
12. ibid.
13. See Report of the Native Labour Commission, 1912–13, for a discussion of problems related to labour before the First World War.
14. See Sorrenson, M. P. K., 'The Official Mind and Kikuyu Land Tenure, 1895–1939' in the EAISR Conference, Dar Es Salaam, January, 1963. See also Muriuki, G., *A History of the Kikuyu, 1500–1900*, Nairobi, OUP, 1974, pp. 13–81.
15. Sorrenson, 'Official Mind', p. 6. See also Muriuki, *History of Kikuyu*.
16. See Tignor, R. L., *The Colonial Transformation of Kenya: Kikuyu and Maasai from 1900 to 1939*, Princeton, Princeton University Press, 1976, p. 107.
17. Van Zwanenberg, R. M. A. and King, A., *An Economic History of Kenya and Uganda, 1870–1970*, Nairobi, EALB, 1975, p. 35.
18. Interview, Wanjiku wa Kigo, 2 October 1976, Rongai.
19. Interview, Wanjiku wa Kigo, 2 October 1976, Rongai; Njoroge Kahonoki, 1 October 1976, Rongai, and Muya Ngari, 6 October 1976, Njoro. 1976, Njoro.
20. Interview with Muya Ngari, 6 October 1976, Njoro.
21. This was evident in the employment of relations on one farm and the prevalence of people from the same locality in Central Province to squat in the same neighbourhood. As Wangoi remembered: 'Employment was on [a] kinship basis'. Interview, Mary Wangoi Macharia, 6 October 1976, Njoro. People moved to areas where their relations had settled and initially lived with them as they sought employment. Impressed by the livestock his relation had accumulated at Olkalau, Munge moved to the Settled Area before the First World War. Interview, Munge Mbuthia, 8 October 1976, Subukia, oral interview with Njau Kanyungu, 2 October 1976, Rongai, and Nganga Githiomi, 2 October 1976, Rongai.
22. Interview, Ernest Kiberethi, 13 October 1976, Elburgon.
23. Kitching, G., *Class and Economic Change in Kenya: The Making of an African Petite Bourgeoisie*, London: Yale University Press, 1980, p. 18.
24. Interview, Hannah Njoki, 10 September 1976, Turi.
25. KNA, Naivasha District Annual Report, 1922, Special Report, p. 1.
26. See Tignor, *Colonial Transformation of Kenya*, pp. 307–8; Sorrenson, M. P. K., *Land Reform in Kikuyu Country*, Nairobi, OUP, 1967, p. 78.
27. Van Zwanenberg and King, *Economic History*, p. 222.
28. Interview, Gitau Gathukia, 16 September 1976, Njoro.
29. RH, Microfilm AR 895, Naivasha District Annual Report, year ending March 1911, plate nos. 000908–000909. Interview, Shuranga Wegunyi, 25 October 1976, Nakuru.
30. KNA, Naivasha District Annual Report, 1916–1917, p. 2. After many appeals, the settlers did, however, release their surplus labour to the Carrier Corps.
31. Interview, Mithanga Kanyumba, 14 September 1976, Molo.

32. Interviews, Kuria Kamaru, 2 October 1976, Rongai and Muchemi Kimondo, 8 October 1976, Subukia.

33. KNA, Naivasha District Annual Report, 1919–1920, p. 2.

34. Interview, Arphaxad Kiiru Kuria, 21 September 1976, Elburgon. The Naivasha Annual Report for 1911–1912 noted that there was no arable farming in the district and that the energies of the settlers were directed toward livestock farming.

35. See Kanogo, T.M.J., 'A Comparative Analysis of the Aspirations of the Kikuyu, Luo and Luyia Workers in the White Highlands, 1900–1930', unpublished article, Department of History, University of Nairobi, No. 18, 1977/78.

36. Interview, Arphaxad Kiiru Kuria, 21 September 1976, Elburgon.

37. Lord Delamere, a pioneer settler who gained prominence as a champion of settler interests, seems to have achieved a mythical image among the squatters. He seems to fulfil the same mythical function as *Gikuyu na Mumbi* who are seen as the founders of the Kikuyu tribe.

38. Van Zwanenberg, R. M. A., *Colonial Capitalism and Labour in Kenya, 1919–1939*, Nairobi, EALB, 1975, p. 257. See also Sorrenson, *Origins of European Settlement*, p. 185.

39. Sorrenson, *Origins of European Settlement*, p. 185.

40. For a brief discussion on Kaffir farming see Van Zwanenberg, *Colonial Capitalism*, Pp. 257–60, and Tignor, *Colonial Transformation*, pp. 106–10, 160–4 and 192.

41. KNA, PC RVP 6A/25/3, 'Squatters 1931–38: A Note on the Squatter Problem' by Fisher, V.M., Principal Inspector of Labour, June 1932.

42. Clayton, A. H., 'Labour in the East African Protectorate, 1895–1918', Ph.D. thesis, University of St. Andrews, 1971, p. 193.

43. Interviews, Njoroge Mambo, Gacheru Manja, 4 October 1976, Elburgon, and Bethuel Kamau, 8 October 1976, Subukia.

44. Interview, Muchemi Kimondo, 8 October 1976, Subukia.

45. Van Zwanenberg, *Colonial Capitalism*, p. 257.

46. ibid.

47. Clayton, 'Labour in East African Protectorate', p. 104. See also Ghai, Y.P. and McAuslan, J.P.W.B., *Public Law and Political Change in Kenya*, Nairobi, OUP, 1971, p. 83.

48. KNA, Naivasha District Annual Report, 1916–1917, p. 2.

49. Clayton, 'Labour in East African Protectorate', p. 193.

50. ibid.

51. KNA, PC RVP 6A/25/3, P.C. Ukamba, Mr Traill, to Chief Secretary, 7 May 1915 on 'Native Cattle on European Farms', A.19/5.

52. KNA, Naivasha District Annual Report, 1912–1913, p. 2.

53. KNA, Naivasha District Annual Report, 1914–1915, p. 13.

54. ibid., p. 14.

55. KNA, Nakuru District Annual Report, and Quarterly Report 1910–1911, p. 3. Kavirondo was a colonial misnomer for the Luyia, Luo and Abagusii people who inhabit the Nyanza and Western regions of Kenya.

56. KNA, DC NVA 4/1, p. 5.

57. Clayton and Savage, *Government and Labour*, p. 20.

58. Interview, Muya Ngari, 6 October 1976, Njoro.

59. Interview, Kihiko Mwega, 25 October 1976, Nakuru. See also Shuranga Wegunyi, 25 October 1976, Nakuru, and Muchemi Kimondo, 8 October 1976, Subukia.

60. Interview, Icogeri Nyaga, 6 October 1976, Njoro.

61. Interview, Muta Njuhiga, 1 November 1976, Bahati. These camp houses were poorly constructed and most likely overcrowded as the labourers had to share accommodation.

62. Interview, Munge Mbuthia, 8 October 1976, Subukia.

63. Mbithi, P. and Barnes, C., *Spontaneous Settlement Problems in Kenya*, EALB, Nairobi, 1975, p. 45.

64. Interviews, Njoroge Mambo, 4 October 1976, Elburgon, Gacheru Manja, 4 October 1976, Elburgon, and Bethuel Kamau, 8 October 1976, Subukia.

65. Interviews, Joseph Matahe, 30 September 1976, Bahati; Karanja Kamau, 21 October 1976, Nakuru.

66. See Clayton, and Savage, *Government and Labour*, p. 5, and interviews with Solomon Muchangi, 16 September 1976, Njoro; and Wilson Mwangi Njau, 13 October 1976, Elburgon.

67. KNA, Naivasha District Annual Report, 1916–1917, p. 2.

68. See Kanogo, 'Comparative Analysis'.

69. Interview, Karanja Kamau, 21 October 1976, Nakuru.

70. Interviews, Ochama Omolo, 17 October 1976, Kericho, and Jackton Oyoo, 14 October 1976, Kericho.

71. See Kanogo, 'Comparative Analysis'.

72. Interview, Gacheru Manja, 4 October 1976, Elburgon.

73. ibid.

74. Interviews, Wanjiku wa Kigo, 2 October 1976, Rongai, Kuria Kamaru, 2 October 1976, Rongai, Gacheru Manja, 4 October 1976, Elburgon, and Muchemi Kimondo, 8 October 1976, Subukia.

75. Interview, Gacheru Manja, 4 October 1976, Elburgon; Njoroge Mambo, 4 October 1976, Elburgon; Bethuel Kamau, 8 October 1976, Subukia.

76. Interview, Mrs Kamau Wanyoko, 13 September 1976, Londiani; Mary Wangui Macharia, 16 September 1976, Njoro.

77. Interviews, Muta Njuhiga, 1 November 1976, Bahati, Wangari Thuku, 3 October 1976, Njoro, and Njau Kanyungu, 2 October 1976, Rongai.

78. Interview, Shuranga Wegunyi, 25 October 1976, Nakuru.

79. Interview, Wanjiku wa Kigo, 2 October 1976, Rongai.

80. Interview, Mary Wangui Macharia, 16 September 1976, Njoro.

81. Interview, Kamau Wanyoko, 13 September 1976, Londiani.

82. Interview, Mary Wangui Macharia, 16 September 1976, Njoro.

83. Interview, Kuria Kamaru, 2 October 1976, Rongai.

84. Leakey, L.S.B., 'The Economics of Kikuyu Tribal Life', *East African Economic Review*, Vol. 3., No. 1, 1956, pp. 158–80.

85. Interview, Gacheru Manja, 4 October 1976, Elburgon.

86. Interview, Bethuel Kamau, 8 October 1976, Subukia; Nganga Githiomi, 2 October 1976, Rongai.

87. Interview, Bethuel Kamau, 8 October 1976, Subukia.

88. Interview, Mrs Kamau Wanyoko, 13 September 1976, Londiani.

89. Mrs Kamau Wanyoko, 13 September 1976, Londiani, Kuria Kamaru, 2 October 1976, Rongai, and Nganga Githiomi, 2 October 1976, Rongai. Squatters expressed surprise at the Luo, Luyia and Kisii workers who 'did not come to cultivate. . .but came [to the Settled Areas] for salaries'.

90. Interview, Lucia Ngugi, 10 September 1976, Turi.

91. Interview, Nganga Githiomi, 2 October 1976, Rongai.

92. Interview, Shuranga Wegunyi, 25 October 1976, Nakuru.

93. Interviews, Gacheru Manja, 4 October 1976, Elburgon, Ernest Kiberethi, 13 October 1976, Elburgon, and Kihiko Mwega, 25 October 1976, Nakuru, for figures quoted as bride-wealth during this period. Riiyu Ngare, 30 December, Nakuru.

94. Interview, Ngoci Ndegwa, 29 October 1976, Nakuru.

95. Interview, Arphaxad Kiiru Kuria, 21 September 1976, Elburgon.

96. Interview, Wanjiru Nyamarutu, Njoki Mucaba, 18 December 1976, Nakuru.

97. Interviews, Njoki Mucaba, Wanjiru Nyamarutu, 18 December 1976, Nakuru, and Njau Kanyungu, 2 October 1976, Rongai. Njau indicated that bride-price was much higher in the Settled Areas than in Central Province.

98. Interview, Wanjiku wa Kigo, 2 October 1976, Rongai.

99. Interview, Kihiko Kimani, 2 October 1976, Nakuru; Gacheru Manja stated that at a time when *gituiku* was the equivalent of two shillings in Central Province it was six shillings in the Rift Valley.

100. The settlers believed that the African was inimical to work and needed to be taught the dignity of labour. See, for example, *Leader of British East Africa*, 13 April 1912 and Huxley, E. *White Man's Country, 1870–1914*, London, Macmillan and Co., 1935, pp. 214 ff., where the 'uncivilised' nature of the African and his obligation to provide the much needed labour are stressed. With time, however, the African labourer became sufficiently sophisticated to know that he could go and work where and for whom he desired and did not have to comply with administrative directives. See KNA, DC NZA 3/20/4/2, DC Kisii to Senior Commissioner, Nyanza, 7 January 1925.

101. Interviews, Bethuel Kamau, 8 October 1976, Subukia, and Muya Ngari, 6 October 1976, Njoro. The latter stated that once in the Rift Valley, squatters did not anticipate a return to Central Province. As if to clinch the point, Ngari recollected the Biblical story in which Noah sent a dove to survey the possibility of locating dry land. On spotting the land, the dove remained on the dry land (to eat of it) and did not relay the message to Noah. See Genesis 8: 6–12.

102. Interview, Arphaxad Kiiru Kuria, 21 September 1976, Elburgon.

103. As early as 1910, however, the *ahoi's* traditional rights to cultivate and occupy land were already decreasing, largely because of land shortage. See Muriuki, *History of Kikuyu*, p. 174.

104. ibid., p. 78.

105. Interview, James Mumbu Muya, alias Kinuthia Muya, 14 October 1976, Elburgon. Muya summed up the White Highlands as offering 'satisfaction of the stomach and livestock'.

106. Mbithi and Barnes, *Spontaneous Settlement*, p. 147.

107. Interviews, Kihiko Mwega, 25 October 1976, Karanja Kamau, 21 October 1976, Nakuru, Njuguna Kiorogo, 12 October 1976, Nakuru, and Bethuel Kamau, 8 October 1976, Subukia.

108. Kitching, *Class and Economic Change*, p. 294.

109. Interview, Kimondo Muchemi, 8 October 1976, Subukia.

110. Van Zwanenberg, R. M. A. *Colonial Capitalism and Labour in Kenya*, p. 231. A 25 per cent drop in wages had reduced their salaries to this low level.

111. ibid, p. 230.

112. KNA, DC NDI 5/2, 'Returning Squatter Stock from Uasin Ngishu', Notes from Nandi Political Record Book.

113. KNA, Nandi District Annual Report, year ending 31 March 1914, p. 1.

114. KNA, Nandi Political Record Book, 1916, p. 35.

115. KNA, Nandi Political Record Book, 1916, p. 36.

116. KNA, DC 3/2. Nandi Political Record Book, 'Cattle Diseases, Veterinary Department Activity among the Nandi Cattle, 1908–1942'.

117. For a discussion of land alienation among the Kipsigis, see Korir, K.M., 'The Tea Plantation Economy in Kericho District and Related Phenomena to Circa1976', BA dissertation, Department of History, Nairobi University, 1976.

118. See *Kenya Land Commission: Evidence and Memoranda*, pp. 3438, 3441 and the Memorandum from C.M. Dobbs, paragraph 1152.

119. Van Zwanenberg, *Colonial Capitalism*, p. 234.

120. Interview, Ngugi Kuri Kamore, 10 October 1976, Turi. This should not be taken to mean that all Kikuyu squatters severed all ties with Central Province. The parallel is only a relative one.

Two

Settlers and Squatters: Conflict of Interests 1918–37

No native should be allowed to settle on land held by Europeans, unless *bona fide* employed by the owner. . ... No renting of land in European occupation should be allowed.[1]

The European settlers who have invested their fortunes in the country at the invitation of the British government cannot be blamed for demanding native labour. Put in the same situation, the twelve apostles would not have acted otherwise.[2]

The previous chapter looked at how the European settler demand for labour was to a large extent satisfied through squatterdom rather than wage labour. The evolution of this squatter community was shown to be only marginally related to the labour problem, with the Kikuyu influx to the Settled Areas being mainly in search of sufficient land for grazing and cultivation. As time passed, it became increasingly obvious that the settlers were tolerating squatter cultivation and grazing only as a convenient arrangement while tropical agriculture was in its pioneering stage. But unlike settler agriculture, squatter production was not dependent on capital and therefore thrived while settler agriculture foundered.

In the inter-war period, however, the settlers emerged as a much stronger community determined to consolidate their hold on squatter labour and the productive machinery in the White Highlands. The period marked the beginning of a protracted and overt conflict between settlers and squatters. The settlers believed that, if their economy was to develop, then the government and the squatters must rally behind them. Their priority was to ensure that they had at their disposal a cheap, adequate and controllable supply of labour and this called for the introduction of various labour regulations. In this chapter an attempt will be made to examine how, with the help of the colonial government, the settlers tried to 'regulate' squatter labour and how the squatters reacted.

Inherent in the settler programme was the determination to curtail the extensive squatter cultivation and grazing to the immediate needs of squatter households. As well as limiting squatter usage of land in the White Highlands, this would release the squatter for his labour obligations. The measures applied threatened both the economic and the social viability of the squatter community. By overlooking the fact that they only paid minimal wages to squatters, who therefore supplemented their income by cultivation, grazing and trading, settlers dismantled an earlier mutually beneficial relationship and sought to replace it with a set-up which the squatters felt undermined their very *raison d'être*. Their response was both adamant and tenacious. It comprised outright resistance by way of strikes and illegal squatting, refusal to sign on again, and withdrawal of labour to Central Province and elsewhere.

As early as 1918, in an address to the Acting Chief Secretary on the subject of native cattle on European farms, the Acting Provincial Commissioner for Ukamba doubted 'if the labour which settlers hope to acquire by means of this inducement, will prove satisfactory'.[3] He also feared that Kaffir farming would be practised at every opportunity and that while the sole object of the measure was to provide labour for farms, in his opinion the price was too high. As he put it, 'There may be some temporary relief but I cannot bring myself sincerely to believe that the policy is one which will prove of ultimate benefit to the country'.[4]

As well as facing insecurity of tenure and lack of land in the reserves, he viewed the squatters as a great danger. He held that for the 16 years that 'promiscuous uncontrolled squatting'[5] had existed it had been a bad thing but that any attempts to control it by amending legislation would be 'another sop to Cerberus'. The most permanent solution to the problem would be to pack up the squatters with their families and livestock and send them away from the farms. But since it was unlikely that anybody in the field of practical politics would agree to sponsor such an alternative, he made two other recommendations. The first was that the supervision of squatters and their stock by the then inadequate supply of police and veterinary officials be increased without any need to amend legislation, and the second that a *laissez-faire* policy be adopted whereby each farmer controlled his squatters as he pleased. The local option would allow the District Council to decide on the number of squatters per farm, whether or not any stock be allowed on the farms, and if so, what kind. Records of these could be kept and provisions made for the branding of squatter stock. The above powers would be enforced by the criminal code, and squatter and occupier could enter a civil contract agreeable to both and attested by the District Commissioner if equitable. The result would be that any breach of contract could be dealt with.[6] Throughout the 1920s and early 1930s settlers grappled with the problem of squatter stock, applying variations of Mr Traill's recommendations in varying proportions, depending on the local conditions and the individual settler occupier. The first regulation provided a legal context for the squatter community.

The 1918 Resident Native Labourers Ordinance (RNLO)

To create a stable and malleable supply of labour for the White Highlands, it was thought necessary to introduce a publicly supervised contract of agricultural labour. This was embodied in the RNLO of 1918, the preamble of which declared that: 'It is desirable to encourage resident native labour on farms and to take measures for the regulation of squatting or living of natives in places other than those appointed for them by the government of the protectorate'.[7] The Ordinance did not create the institution of squatterdom, but rather sought to legitimise it and to provide a legal framework for its social control.

The fundamental provision of the Ordinance was the squatter's obligation to provide not less than 180 working days per year on a farm. In return for this, the worker and his family were allowed to live on the farm and cultivate a part of the settler's land for his own use. A minimal wage would be paid for the work done. The Ordinance did not specify the acreage or number of stock allowed per squatter.

To enforce the Ordinance it was necessary that Kaffir farming be abolished and replaced by labour tenancy. Except for labourers on monthly contracts, the Ordinance stipulated that residence for Africans in the White Highlands should be restricted to Africans with squatter contracts, thus prohibiting illegal squatting. The adoption of this new set-up helped to limit the employers' cash remunerations to the labourers. The labourer was expected to feed and house himself and his family.

More importantly, resident labourers would ensure the supply of sufficient and easily available labour to the farmers, for the squatters' wives and children could be called upon at peak labour periods, especially during the harvesting season. Nonetheless, as will be shown later, labour shortages remained rife until the late 1920s, when labour requirements were eased by the depression.

In the meantime, ways and means were discussed as to how to compel 'idlers', i.e. 'men who have not recently been in employment and who are not adequately engaged upon definite agricultural or other economic enterprise in their reserves', to work.[8] In the Settled Areas, labour shortages were juxtaposed with the problem of illegal squatting. Not only were the illegal squatters reluctant to sell their labour at all, but there were also incessant complaints about the contracted squatters' failure to provide adequate labour. This confirmed the settlers' contention that the native had no conception of the dignity of labour.[9]

Though designed to generate and control labour by emphasising the squatter's labour obligations, the RNLO of 1918 largely failed to ensure the development of an adequate labour supply. The squatters continued to pursue activities that undermined and evaded the colonial government's sole reason for allowing them into the area. Right from the beginning, then, there had been an ambivalence between the motives of the squatter community on the one hand, and the settler government on the other. But in so far as settlers could now evict any excess or illegal squatters they did not wish to sign on, the Ordinance could be said to have provided a legal framework within which the settlers could exercise some control over squatting. But in itself the Ordinance was insufficient.

Additional labour legislation

Settlers had hoped that the 1918 RNLO would be reinforced by the existing Masters and Servants Ordinance of 1906, under which workers were liable to heavy penalties for negligence of, or absence from, work. However, since squatters belonged to the category of labour-tenants rather than servants, they were able to avoid prosecution, even under the amended 1919 Masters and Servants Ordinance.[10] The settlers continued to clamour for the inclusion of squatters under the Masters and Servants Ordinance of 1924,[11] which would make the squatters liable to prosecution for negligence of duty. The settlers maintained that it was necessary to define the word 'squatter' to emphasise that the status of a resident labourer was that of a servant rather than tenant.[12]

With the 1918 RNLO's obvious limitations, other enactments to control labour were also used. From 1919 onwards, labourers were required to carry an identification certificate (*kipande*), on which the owner's previous and current labour history was entered, including the nature of employment, date of engagement, length of contract and wages paid.[13] The *kipande* system was a vicious imposition on 'native' labour. It made desertion very difficult, helped to keep the labourers' salaries static, and turned the labourer into a virtual prisoner until such time as his contract came to an end and he was discharged. Even then, the squatter stood few chances of getting a better paid job unless he risked destroying his identity card, along with all the revealing information it contained. The combination of the *kipande* and the 1918 RNLO in effect meant that the squatter contract ceased to be a civil and mutual agreement between two people and became a 'publicly supervised and enforced enterprise'.[14]

By 1920, it was evident that for a squatter the acquisition of a labour contract was little more than a means to an end. Settlers were forced to 'police' the attested squatters to ensure that they provided adequate labour. Uncontracted Kikuyu continued to reside illegally on occupied and unoccupied land in the White Highlands.[15] In as much as both categories of squatters – legal and illegal – failed to comply with settler expectations, they were seen to constitute the much detested 'squatter menace'.

To reduce the shortage of labour, settlers continued to welcome more squatters from the Reserves, even though those whose contracts had expired seldom returned home, preferring to stay on in the Settled Areas. New generations of squatters' children also remained in the Settled Areas, though not always employed on the farms. Although the owners of large farms were seen to be particularly vulnerable to illegal squatters, it was the poorly-supervised unoccupied and Crown lands that literally teemed with uncontracted Kikuyu. The manner in which the Kikuyu encroachment took place made detection especially difficult, as an exasperated administrator remarked:

> They creep on all unbeknown; first of all living with a friend or relation, then occupying the hut of a deceased person. Later a wife appears and a few handful of maize are planted. If enquiries are made it is stated by all that the person concerned is only on a short visit and was kind enough to give a hand in the hosts' garden.[16]

According to the laws in operation in the mid-twenties, it was neither possible nor considered tactful to prosecute the occupier. But, as the administrator concluded, the 1918 RNLO also made it impossible to prosecute an African who encroached on such land:

> Nothing exists in the law to prevent a native from going to a European farm, cultivating a crop and later when called upon to work sliding off and doing exactly the same thing. He gets virgin soil, the price of a good crop and no work. If fact we seem to have encouraged in the Kikuyu just what we wanted to put a stop to.[17]

Even when the demand for labour fell, exodus to the Settled Areas continued. This was most noticeable in the Naivasha, Nakuru, Eldoret and Trans-Nzoia Districts where 'numbers of natives residing on farms continued to increase during the year (1923) somewhat out of proportion to the actual labour requirements'.[18] In both the Naivasha and Nakuru Districts the African population, which was largely squatter, increased markedly.[19] If we compare table 1.1 in Chapter 1 with the figures in table 2.1, we can see just how much the squatter population did increase in only one decade.

TABLE 2.1

Population in Nakuru and Naivasha, 1927		
	Nakuru	Naivasha
Europeans	1,137	380
Goans	143	24
Indians	926	152
Other races	67	25
Africans	29,258	15,500
TOTAL	31,531	16,081

It was felt that existing legislation was inadequate for coping with this sharp rise in the squatter population, and new Ordinances were therefore adjusted to take this into account. For example, the RNLOs of 1924 and 1925 provided for the punishment of a labourer who failed to carry out his duties, or who resided on a farm other than as a squatter under a labour contract. The 1925 Ordinance also stipulated that, when a farm changed hands, the contracts were automatically transferred to the new owner. In return for their increased powers over the squatters, the settlers were obliged to provide the squatter with building materials, in addition to land for grazing and cultivation.[20] Even these increased powers, however, failed to curb squatter resistance and the administration had to intervene by forcibly removing illegal squatters from unoccupied or badly supervised farms to those that needed labour.[21]

Settlers and squatter stock

Existing legislation was also inadequate for dealing with the large numbers of squatter stock and the detrimental effect this was believed to be having on the settler economy. In the 1920s, high commodity prices encouraged settlers to diversify the largely maize monoculture economy into the stock and dairy industry. Settlers imported herds of expensive grade cattle and sheep, some of which they interbred with local stock. The settlers maintained that the stock industry could prosper only if squatter stock were eliminated. Squatter stock were carriers of such tick-borne diseases as redwater, blackwater and East Coast fevers – which might infect settler stock.[22] They also suffered from rinderpest and bovine pleuro-pneumonia. It was argued too, that the presence of squatter stock would encourage stock theft from settler herds.[23] The constant movement of African stock between the White Highlands, Central Province, Maasai Reserve and other African areas only compounded the problem.

But it is important to remember that the squatters regarded their stock as their main form of saving and investment. By the 1920s, the number of squatters and their cattle had increased tremendously. Squatters had concentrated all their energies into accumulating stock, which, until then, had provided the settlers with milk and manure. Some settlers had even built their herds from squatter livestock. In some ways, this arrangement was mutually beneficial to the settler and the squatter. The rapid increase of squatters and their herds was to a large extent an index of squatter autonomy in the White Highlands. Settler attempts to alter the relationship by demanding that the squatters de-stock overlooked the economic and social significance of livestock to squatters' livelihoods. They were, in fact, far more dependent on their crop yields and livestock than they were on wages, and any money from the sale of surplus crops was almost invariably used to purchase more livestock. The settlers had, so to speak, hit the squatters below the belt.

Despite this, in many areas there was no corresponding rise in squatter wages, which remained static from the mid-1920s to the early 1940s. This was mainly because the ticket system of squatter contracts which was in operation at the time limited how much a squatter could earn. The average wage was eight shillings for a 30-day ticket, but it took an average of 45 days, much longer in some cases, to complete a ticket. Again, on average, a squatter completed only seven tickets per year, even though he might well have worked for the greater part of the year. When an individual squatter's tax burdens are taken into account, not to mention the various cash fines for 'crimes' committed on the job, such as negligence of duty or petty theft, then it becomes clear that even at the best of times a squatter's income from wages was irregular and minimal. Evidence of these constraints can be found in the labour records of individual squatters, of which three, those of Waweru Wa Munge, his wife (*bibi*)[24] and Kachego Wa Chege,[25] are reproduced in tables 2.2 and 2.3.

Kachego Wa Chege's ticket in the Nakuru area portrays less contingency expenditure but is indicative of how long it took to complete a 30 day ticket. His income between 1926 and 1929 is shown in table 2.3.

There were two major reasons for the tickets taking so long to complete. In the first place, settler labour demands were staggered throughout the year so that a thirty-day contract did not run consecutively, but

TABLE 2.2

Waweru Wa Munge, Registration Number NKU 24078860.
Engaged as squatter at shs. 8 per ticket. Ticket No. 424

Start Date	Finish Date	Paid (shs.)	Remarks	Days taken to complete
21.02.27	07.05.27	8		75
08.05.27	09.07.27	8		124
08.09.27	14.10.27	8		36
15.10.27	20.12.27	8	One ticket cut for theft	66
06.01.28	04.02.28	8		29
01.05.28	07.06.28	8		37
17.07.28	27.08.28	8	One ticket cut for Hut Tax	41
28.08.28	29.10.28	8	4 shs. cut for Hut Tax/4shs. cut for father's Hut Tax	63

Bibi's Ticket (Waweru's wife's ticket)

Start Date	Finish Date	Paid (shs.)	Remarks	Duration
09.08.28	15.09.28	6		37
30.10.28	13.12.28	8	One helper ticket at shs. 6	44
14.02.28	19.01.29	8		36

straggled over a much longer period. In the above case, the six tickets between 28 January and 21 December 1927 covered a period of 322 days, whereas six tickets (the squatter's minimum obligation to the settler) were only really supposed to comprise 180 working days per year. Second, the squatter might fail to complete what the settler had stipulated as a day's task within the day. In such cases, the day would not be recorded, thus increasing the days it took to complete a ticket. Njoroge Gakuha illustrated this point twice over. His father was employed at a settler's farm in Elmenteita. He was required to prepare 60 fencing poles a day. The task, according to Njoroge, required the joint effort of the informant, his father and his mother, if it was to be completed in one day. Failure to complete one's daily quota of work often meant no wages were recorded for that day.

The second example was drawn from the informant's own experience. Between 1929 and 1950 he worked as a field hand at Kampi Ya Moto. On a certain Bwana Kamundu's farm, each labourer was required to weed eight rows of maize plants per day. The task seems to have been an arduous one since it proved impossible to complete in a

TABLE 2.3

		Ticket no 437 at shs. 8 per 30 day ticket		
Start Date	*Finish Date*	*Paid (shs.)*	*Remarks*	*Duration*
04.09.26	15.10.26	8		41
16.10.26	08.12.26	8		53
09.12.26	27.01.27	8		49
28.01.27	19.03.27	8		50
21.03.27	14.06.27	8		84
15.06.27	02.08.27	8		49
03.08.27	20.09.27	8		48
21.09.27	03.11.27	8		44
04.11.27	21.12.27	8		47
22.12.27	03.02.28	8		43
04.02.28	15.03.28	8	1 bag *posho* advanced	70
07.03.28	11.05.28	8		65
18.06.28	27.07.28	8	Shs. 4 cut for Hut Tax	38
27.07.28	06.09.28	8		41
07.09.28	23.10.28	8		46
24.10.28	23.11.28	8	1 bag *posho* returned on 1 Nov	30
24.11.28	11.01.29	8		49
12.01.29	24.02.29	8		43
24.02.29	24.04.29	8	Shs. 4 cut	59

day, even with somebody else's help. In Njoroge's words: 'If you did not finish [cultivating] the lines, you got the day's *posho* but the day was not recorded [for payment]'.[26] On completion of some tickets, the squatter would have to go home with a completely empty pay packet, the settler having withheld the money for Hut Tax, fines for petty thefts or crimes, or other expenses.

It was widely acknowledged that squatters were a cheap source of labour and that, by cultivating and grazing on settler land, they were rightfully receiving payment in kind as a supplement for their low wages. Technically, this was contrary to the provisions of the 1926 Employment of Natives Ordinance, which forbade any payments in kind, but the legislation was flagrantly violated. On a Mrs Irvine's farm in Songhor Valley, for example, the labourers received no pay whatsoever, the only remuneration for their work being 'the liability accepted by the employer to pay their tax'.[27] Because Mrs Irvine grew coffee and needed as much manure as she could get, she allowed her squatters to engage in extensive grazing and refused to be bound in any way by the opinions of her neighbours. Squatters on her farm agreed to sign on at the rate of three shillings per ticket. The District Commissioner was hoping that the introduction of a new RNLO would correct the situation, but in the meantime, he could do nothing and squatters working six tickets earned 'merely 18 shillings of which 12 shillings (at least) goes to Hut Tax. If 1932 or 1931 taxes were not paid or the man has 2 huts, he has to work for more months without obtaining anything other than tax receipts'.[28] In a similar case, a Mr J. Wallace of Ol Arabel in Rumuruti signed squatters on at five shillings without *posho*. He asked the District Commissioner to sign on more squatters for him, but the District Commissioner refused to do so under Section 4 (5) Ordinance V of the 1925 RNLO until he had heard from the Provincial Commissioner 'as to whether you consider this a fair remuneration'.[29] The Provincial Commissioner responded that it was not, unless there were special circumstances like 'ploughing of squatter *shamba* and supply of seed by the employer',[30] which would still require the payment of a minimum of eight shillings minus the *posho* ration. The Provincial Commissioner was of the opinion that, if there were major disagreements over the minimum rate, the District Commissioner should discuss the issue with the District Committee.

The depression further affected squatter wages, which were then reduced to six shillings per ticket. Immediately before the depression, casual labourers earned between 12 and 16 shillings, as against the squatter's 8 shillings. In 1932, the earnings of casual labourers dropped to a new low of 8 shillings per month, which was complemented by a *posho* ration.[31]

It would be possible to enumerate many more cases to illustrate that squatter wage incomes were both minimal and inconsistent.[32] There is no doubt that, by playing the destocking card, the settlers were reducing the squatters' main source of income, and therefore threatening to dismantle the squatter community as it stood in the 1920s.

Settler differences over squatter stock

Settlers in different ecological and economic brackets held different opinions about keeping squatter stock. In general, settlers in the drier dairy and stock-keeping areas advocated the complete eradication of squatter cattle. This category of settlers functioned independently of squatter labour and could therefore afford to enforce stringent measures against squatter stock. Settlers in mixed-farming areas, where maize and wheat were grown, as well as those engaged in the plantation production of tea, coffee and pyrethrum, were heavily dependent on seasonal workers, especially during planting and harvesting periods, so could ill afford to antagonise their labour. Although willing to reduce squatter cultivation and stock-keeping, they were totally opposed to the complete eradication of the squatter and his stock.

A third category of settlers, undercapitalised and occupying marginal land for stock and dairy cattle and occasionally limited mixed farming, were heavily dependent on squatters in more ways than one. Apart from appropriating their labour, for which they could barely afford to pay, these settlers entered into mutually beneficial agreements with their squatters, through which they acquired milk, manure, livestock and other produce. For the very poorest of these settlers, the total eradication of squatters òr their livestock would result in the collapse of their agricultural undertaking. Also, in the more marginal areas where crop production was minimal even in good years, it was absolutely necessary that the squatters be allowed to keep livestock.

Even within the same district, settlers would vary in their opinions about squatter livestock and, unable to arrive at a consensus, would eventually evolve a policy embracing numerous local options. In the predominantly dairy and stock area of Naivasha District, however, there was consensus over the need to eliminate squatter stock. In the Trans-Nzoia district, where settler production ranged from dairy and stock-keeping to maize and wheat production, opinion was divided, and here, as elsewhere, the policy of local options was employed.

Nakuru District sustained a wide range of agricultural activities, which by the end of the inter-war period included pyrethrum, maize, wheat and coffee, as well as a certain amount of livestock. Although all these settlers were heavily dependent on squatter labour, the settler community at large did not see this as a mitigating factor and some of the settlers wanted the squatter community, as it existed in the White Highlands, to be completely replaced by resident wage labourers.

Apart from taking individual measures to reduce squatter stock on their farms, settlers started pushing for legislation to back up their actions. But a court decision taken over the issue at the time left the matter unresolved. The judge argued that keeping what might be considered excess squatter livestock could hardly be regarded as an officially punishable crime.

> There is no such offence as maintaining cattle on a farm in excess of the number allowed by the contract. The fact of having an excess may be a ground for rescission of the contract between the occupier and the squatter, but it does not render the latter liable to conviction.[33]

The judge proceeded to quash the conviction that had brought about the controversy and directed that the fine be refunded. But in the same breath, he went on to say that it was perfectly permissible for a settler to take it upon himself to carry out an arbitrary execution of justice.

full text of Mr Justice Sheridan's judgement under Section 5 of the 1925 RNLO (which incidentally was circulated for future guidance to all police officers in all the Rift Valley police units) shows how even the judiciary shied away from protecting the squatters and thus left their welfare open to the machinations of settlers. Thus, by Christmas 1927, although squatters could not be convicted for keeping excess livestock on settler farms, they could have their contracts withdrawn for the same reason. This state of flux over the control of squatter labour was characteristic of most of the colonial period and enabled settlers to exercise excessive powers over squatters and their livestock.

'Kifagio'

The arbitrary elimination of squatter stock reached a new high in 1929 when squatters talked of *kifagio* to refer to the drastic reduction of their stock. *Kifagio* is a Swahili word which literally means 'the broom' and the term was used to imply the 'sweeping away' of squatter stock. Government officials from the Ministry of Labour who at times participated in the de-stocking campaign were also referred to as *kifagio*. While some of the stock were butchered, the rest were shot or confiscated. No compensation was paid for the eliminated stock.[34]

This drastic reduction of squatter stock in the late 1920s from an average of several hundred per labourer to about five per family was a great blow to squatter income, especially since the reduction was not accompanied by an increase in wages. Some of the squatters' bewilderment is captured in the following description of the events, by Gachago, an old man who had lived through the ordeal:

> *Kifagio* found me in Ol'Joro Orok. Here some people had up to 300 goats. After a short time some areas were only allowed to keep 30, 15, or 5 goats per person. This was not according to the climate of the area, but according to the wishes of the European. If he had livestock, then he refused to allow Africans to keep livestock. We were told to keep 15 goats only. The rest were taken away and sold. We were not paid for these. Since these matters were decided at the meetings we had no choice. We would never raise the issue with the settler since it was he who called *kifagio*. In the forest areas as well as on the *shambas*, Europeans did not allow us to keep *migoma* (she-goats), they did not want us to drink the fat of the *thenge* (he-goat).[35]

Individual settlers also confiscated any squatter stock that happened to wander onto their farms.[36] Some of the squatters had accumulated large herds by the time *kifagio* struck. Wanyoko, for example, who had been a foreman (*nyapara*) on a farm in Londiani, had, with the help of his employer, leased land in the Londiani forest where he grazed some of his 800 goats.[37] Ngoci Ndegwa stated he had about 1,000 goats in the Naivasha area where he was a squatter. Some of these animals had been held on other farms by various members of the family. For example, Ndegwa entrusted 300 of his goats to a brother-in-law resident in the Kiambogo area on the western shores of Lake Naivasha. Ngoci also cultivated about 10 acres of land on the shores of Lake Naivasha where he mainly grew cabbages, which were collected by lorry for transportation to various destinations.[38] Riiyu Ngare said that he had owned 500 goats when *kifagio* struck.[39]

Although by no means all squatters achieved such large accumulations of livestock, it is true to say that on the whole the squatter community was economically more viable than the majority of urban proletarians and peasants in the reserves. Although the settlers had always regarded the squatters as a cheap source of labour, in real terms the squatter accrued more benefits from his employers than were visible.

Squatter resistance

The squatter began to develop strategies for trying to evade further harassment by the *kifagio*. Gachago, for example, moved from Nakuru to a farm in Rumuruti where the settler owner was prepared to accommodate squatter livestock. The farm grew maize and wheat, and also reared a few cattle. The settler's tolerance was explained by his farm being large enough to spare room for squatter cultivation and grazing.[40] Many squatters made similar moves.[41] While some settled for low prices for their stock, the more adamant among them refused to give in to the new order and either trekked away in search of more tolerant farmers, or took the more painful decision to go back to Central Province. But, because Central Province was already overcrowded, the latter option was almost invariably only temporary.

Not all squatters suffered the same fate under *kifagio*, for, even within the ranks of the settlers, there were some who considered it important to maintain allies among the squatters. Njuguna Kiorogo, who was a foreman during the *kifagio*, exemplified the lucky few. His master intervened on his behalf, so that for a time he maintained his flock until he could dispose of them profitably. He used part of the herd for his brother's dowry and sold the rest.

Moving to other areas, either within the Settled Areas or to Central Province, were not the only forms of squatter resistance to *kifagio*. Sometimes steps were taken to sabotage *kifagio* efforts right under the noses of Department of Labour personnel. The usual procedure in the elimination of squatter stock was for a Department of Labour employee to 'ask for all goats [to be displayed] and he would count them. The excess were slaughtered immediately'.[42] The squatter would often try to find ways out of this predicament. At times 'people [squatters] would go and hide the goats by the riverside'[43] before *kifagio* arrived, or they would 'hide the goats in other farms'[44] which had either been visited or were scheduled for later visits. In this manner, squatters would postpone or avoid the decimation of their stock.

Squatters argued that the settlers were jealous of their wealth and that this was really at the heart of their campaign to reduce it. Being denied their goats was perceived as the biggest single contribution towards their impoverishment and, as Mrs Wanyoko observed, the harbinger of 'perpetual slavery'.[45]

The *kifagio* ordeal was detrimental both to the squatters' sense of security and to their material well-being. Squatters perceived *kifagio* as an indication of the settlers' hegemony and of their ruthless and vicious lack of concern for Africans in the White Highlands.[46] This was overtly evident in the productive field. Nganga Kimani spoke of how 'the *mzungu* [white man, in this context settler] could destroy one's harvest in any way. He did not harvest the crops. Probably he knew it was a sin. At times the *mzungu* drove their animals to the labourers' *shambas* to graze therein, or they had the crops cut and fed to the animals'.[47] Another informant, Gitau Gathukia, stated in similar vein that 'the European could send you away any time. He could even burn your homestead.'[48] Squatters were sometimes sent away just when the maize crop was ready for harvest. 'No compensation would be paid for the crop. The white man was tough, he taught us to be clever.'[49]

Losses suffered by the squatters during the *kifagio* period were sufficiently severe to make them wary of any further government legislation relating to the squatter-settler relationship. In other words, even before its inception, squatters visualised the pending legislation as another plot, not only to legalise their subordinate position, but also to endorse a policy that would restrict them further. It was fear of these imminent restrictions that made squatters reluctant to sign new contracts, even though existing terms of employment left much to be desired. In their experience, new regulations would almost inevitably be more demanding.

In their campaign against squatting, the settlers believed that the future of the whole country was at stake, and that it was the government's responsibility to force Africans to cooperate in attempts to establish what the settlers considered a viable economy. Among the squatters, *kifagio* not only entailed the reduction of their livestock but, in some areas, also precipitated the beginning of child labour. This applied especially to areas where pyrethrum had been introduced by settlers in the late 1930s. Since children, who had up to that point been herding family livestock, were now needed for picking the pyrethrum flowers,[50] the squatters equated the introduction of this crop with the reduction of their stock. Some of these children were not even put on the payroll.

The call for the drastic reduction of their stock came as a rude shock to Kikuyu squatters in the Nakuru District, as undoubtedly in other areas as well. From the remarks of one informant, Gikunju Gakuo, that 'the white man did not want us to become rich, he wanted us to remain poor labourers and to work for him always',[51] it is clear that squatters understood that there was a conflict between the two modes of production. This was borne out by some settlers directly challenging the wealth of the squatters and the prosperity of the peasant option in the White Highlands,[52] rather than merely centring their complaints on the damage squatter activities had done to their land and water resources. No mention of increase in wages in lieu of squatter loss of income was made during the de-stocking campaign.[53]

The *kifagio* ordeal was compounded by the rumours that began to spread over the White Highlands in 1929, inferring that if squatters signed the labour contracts they would be forced to work for European settlers for 30 years, or even become permanently enslaved to them. While the exact origins of these rumours are uncertain, there is evidence that, for example, the Njoro Settlers Association was aware that the Paramount Chief from Kiambu, Kinyanju, had 'told his people round our district [Nakuru] not to put their thumb marks to any agreements with Europeans'.[54] Six months later, the Association noted that many squatters were returning to their reserves. Captain Graham, who first raised the issue in the meeting, stated that he would 'like an assurance from the government that should drought occur there [in Central Province], these natives would not be fed on public funds'.[55] Some people blamed poor rains in the Rift Valley for the squatter exodus back to Central Province, and believed that once the situation returned to normal, the squatters would come back to the White Highlands. But, if they failed to do so, this would certainly jeopardise labour.[56]

Like other such bodies, the Njoro Settlers Association was convinced that its problems emanated from the squatters' nebulous status and wanted the Attorney General to clarify his interpretation of the Squatter Ordinance. The squatters, however, were convinced that new labour contracts during the de-stocking campaign would only subordinate them further by curtailing their economic independence and increasing their labour obligations. The following extract from an interview with Shuranga Wegunyi gives an indication of the levels of anxiety reached by the squatters over the new labour legislation:

People refused to put the *kirore* [fingerprint in lieu of signature on contracts]. They said it was a *maisha* [lifetime] thing. They added that if one signed the contract, one would not be allowed to go on leave. One would not even be allowed to slaughter livestock. If one did, the settler too would slaughter some of the squatters' livestock. Even dowry paid for one's daughter would have to be shared with the settler.[57]

Although the above is perhaps a somewhat exaggerated account of the squatters' worst fears in the wake of the *kifagio* ordeal, it is at least indicative of the extent of their distrust. In Nakuru district, where the majority of labourers were Kikuyu squatters, a consequent and quite serious disruption of labour ensued. On the expiry of their contracts in 1929, a large number of squatters refused to sign on again on the grounds that they intended to return to Central Province and, for a period, many continued to make the journey home. This necessitated the convening of several public meetings (*barazas*) in Nakuru, at which administrative officers tried to dispel rumours and stabilise labour.[58] Similar meetings were held in Naivasha, at which the Resident Commissioner explained the squatter position. Registration under the Squatters Ordinance was temporarily difficult[59] and measures were being taken to ensure that the squatters either signed on or left the farms.[60] Although the general belief prevailed that 'natives employed on farms . . . [were] far more difficult to control from the aspect of labour'[61], the meetings were said to have had a good effect and to have reduced the propaganda that had given rise to the problems in the first place.

None the less, squatters continued to resist settler authority by leaving the farms, squatting illegally, staging strikes characterised by a refusal to perform tasks allotted to them, and engaging in other acts of sabotage, like maiming settler cattle and setting fire to settler crops. Rather than trying to understand the reasons behind the wave of squatter discontent, the administration merely labelled it as bolshevik. In the Naivasha District Commissioner's words: 'There . . . [had] been a growing tendency on the part of the Kikuyu labour to bolshevism manifesting itself in co-operation by strikes'.[62]

The settlers then took to policing their areas and checking on one another to ensure that the resolutions passed at the meetings on squatter cattle, or activities associated with Kaffir farming, were upheld. In Nakuru District, the various settler associations continued to take independent actions to deal with squatter livestock. The Njoro Settlers Association passed several resolutions on how harmful squatter cattle were to the cattle industry and reaffirmed its earlier decision to use its influence to 'expedite the removal of all native cattle from white farms' especially within Nakuru District.[63] At their 1929 annual general meeting, members of the Association decided to lobby settlers in their own area who were failing to implement the Association's wishes. The Secretary was instructed 'to write a tactful letter to the few landowners in the District (duly named) who allow squatter cattle, asking them if for the good of the district they would cancel any existing agreements authorising squatter cattle as soon as possible'.[64]

Some of the settlers and administrators recommended that squatters only be attested on condition they agree not to bring livestock to the White Highlands. Although a clause could have been inserted into the RNLO of 1925 to make the limitation of stock a precondition for signing on, the Ordinance would still have been inadequate in so far as it failed to include any penalties for exceeding the limit.

The District Commissioner for Elgeyo Marakwet recommended that 'as agreements expire the squeezing out process can be continued as circumstances dictate'.[65] On long term projections it was anticipated that, with improvement and expansion of settler agriculture, pasture for non-European stock would decrease.[66] Some of the settlers only tolerated stock as an adjunct to labour.[67] The administration's claim that the unrest among squatters was due to the activities of unemployed Kikuyu agitators from outside the District[68] underplayed the widespread nature of squatter discontent. Squatter reluctance to re-attest could be explained by the sense of insecurity that the settler assault had generated.

In the Nakuru and Naivasha Districts, most of the squatters remained, either on temporary one-year contracts or as illegal squatters. For the majority of these, Central Province did not offer a welcome alternative to the Rift Valley.[69] In cases where contact with Central Province had been maintained, few could claim land in the region. Those who had owned it previously had entrusted it to relatives who, over time, had come to regard it as their own. In other words, 'other right holders had extended the area of their cultivation and there . . . [was] no room for them'.[70] Since it would have been difficult for the squatters to have claimed their land back, some of them remained in the Settled Areas as a matter of expediency, where they could at least eke out some sort of living if they managed to evade the authorities. The Nakuru District Commissioner saw the situation as potentially explosive and warned that:

> There are too many unemployed natives who live on the farms and elsewhere in the District. They pay no taxes, do no work, live on their friends and are generally undesirable. There are, however, no means of dealing with these people; they come and go as they please, are subject to no discipline, tribal or otherwise, they will create a problem in the near future. *I am of the opinion that in a few years' time [a] strong claim will be laid by the Kikuyu to the land in this district.*[71]

According to one estimate, by 1931 squatters were using 1,061,833 acres for cultivation and grazing in the Settled Areas, which comprised about one-sixth of all alienated land or 40 per cent of the land under beneficial use in the White Highlands.[72] But this estimate was probably too low, for it was based on livestock figures given by squatters. 'It was counter-argued that in reality the squatters probably occupied as much as 1,850,000 acres, which was just over one-third of the owned alienated land or just under 70 per cent of the land in use'.[73] None the less, whatever the real figures, the District Commissioner's observation did echo what by 1930 had become a real fear among the settlers, who felt that the administrative machinery was totally inadequate for the social control of squatters. The real problem lay in the differential and contradictory advantages that the squatter system held for the squatters and settlers respectively. For the squatter, the importance of the labour aspect was insignificant in comparison with owning stock, whereas for the settler the only advantage of the system was in the labour it could provide.[74]

On most farms unauthorised squatting was being dealt with by police intervention and, as a consequence, it was becoming increasingly easy to control illegal squatters in the Eburu, Mau and Kinangop areas.[75] But in the Nakuru District, illegal squatters and other floating populations had become endemic and were seen as an 'unmitigated nuisance', for 'they pay no taxes and do no work'.[76] Constant battles were waged against them, which occasionally even required help from outside the District. For example, in a large-scale raid on the Elburgon area, the Assistant Commissioner of Police, 40 'native ranks' and two British officers from Nairobi were called in to help the local forces, who were also joined by Labour and Forest Officers from the area. The raid was considered successful in that it 'led to 156 arrests mostly of Kikuyu. Other unemployed Kikuyu also left the area (at any rate for the time being)'.[77]

As the de-stocking campaign continued, squatters were offered several dead-end options for getting rid of their stock. The lucky ones could sell their animals to the settlers, though they were only offered very low prices.[78] The option of repatriating their cattle to the reserves, which were already overstocked, was highly unpopular with local leaders in the reserves, especially in Central Province.[79] In the Settled Areas, the various District Councils and Settler Associations found it impossible to enforce their decision through the lawcourts before the new Ordinance had been enacted.[80]

While some settlers felt that the decision of the majority, at least over the issue of de-stocking, should be binding to all within the region, others expressed the opinion that because labour requirements varied considerably, even within the same district, local options should be allowed in the different areas. In this respect, Hoey's Bridge Farmers

Association resolved that because of the general shortage of labour in the area, the District Commissioner would be asked to use his discretion to amend the local squatter rules. This would allow both new and old squatters to possess a maximum of twenty head of stock instead of the allowed ten. The settlers also hoped that the Kapchekenda clan (previously barred from contracting as squatters as a punishment for stock thefts by their clan members) would be allowed to come out as squatters.[81] This contrasted with Associations like the Molo and Mau Summit ones, which called for the total elimination of all squatter goats and sheep, without any provision for local options. In Rongai, the settlers had agreed 'by mutual consent, to rid themselves of all squatter cattle, with contracts being strictly observed with respect to notice of termination.[82]

Although this troublesome question of squatter livestock was protracted by the differences of opinion amongst settlers even within the same district, draconian measures were anticipated by those settlers who wanted to see the complete elimination of squatter stock. For example, in their 1934 resolution, the Uasin Ngishu and Trans Nzoia District Councils agreed that:

(a) No squatter with stock was to be allowed from the reserve unless with special permission from the District Commissioner.

(b) No squatter would be allowed on Crown Land except on transition to the reserve. This must not last longer than one month.

(c) If the squatter had no recommendation from the past employer, he was not to be signed on unless with the District Commissioner's permission.

(d) New squatters were not to be attested with more than ten cattle including calves.

(e) It was necessary for a new squatter to have a statement from the previous employer on number of cattle owned.

(f) All Nandi out of the reserve would have a pass.

(g) Nandi squatter beginners were to seek the permission of their own District Officer and District Commissioner in Kitale and Eldoret, who would prove the squatter fit to reside outside his district and, having paid the necessary taxes in their home districts, they would be struck off the Native Tax Register.

(h) On leaving the farm, the squatter would be required to carry a pass from the farmer stating destination, duration and their name.

(i) Discharged squatters were to be sent to the reserve within one month of the expiry of their contracts, ensuring that no cattle were transferred to neighbouring land. Neither were squatters to be allowed on unoccupied land or land that was not in beneficial use.[83]

Some settlers hoped to get rid of their squatter stock, especially goats, by replacing their squatters with casual labourers.[84]

For the authorities in the Reserves, the imminent arrival in their areas of large numbers of squatters and their livestock was looked upon with mounting concern. The Provincial Commissioner for Central Province wrote to his counterpart in the Rift Valley seeking to know whether information from Chief Koinange to the effect that many Wakikuyu in Nakuru District and in all parts of the Rift Valley Province had been given notice to leave the farms with their stock was true.[85] Koinange was worried because there was no grazing land for additional stock in his area. In reply, the Provincial Commissioner for the Rift Valley confirmed that there would be a movement due to the reduction in number of squatters in Laikipia and Thompson's Falls. He did not, however, anticipate any abnormal return of squatters on a large scale in the near future, although any illegal squatters discovered would be returned 'with thanks'.[86]

It was quite obvious that the settlers anticipated an all out campaign against squatters and their stock and that they had evolved a multitude of measures designed to exercise greater control over them. The squatters, in return, expressed great anxiety about their future in the White Highlands. In the absence of land in Central Province, Kikuyu squatters drifted between unoccupied farms, forest reserves in the Rift Valley, urban centres and, as a last resort, Central Province.

Large numbers of squatters who found conditions in the Settled Areas incompatible with their expectations continued to trek back to Central Province. Late in 1936, about 1,000 Kikuyu returned to Kiambu District from the Naivasha area. The Colonial Secretary sought to know whether this exodus was due to the expiry of squatter agreements under the RNLO and, if so, had the squatters refused to renew their agreements? He also enquired whether it was the general policy in the Rift Valley to reduce squatter numbers and, if so, would more Africans return to the Reserves in the near future?[87] The issue of squatter exodus had been raised by Archdeacon Burns in the Legislative Council, where he represented African interests.

In response, the Provincial Commissioner dispatched copies of the Colonial Secretary's letter to the District Commissioners in Laikipia, Samburu and Nakuru and to the Police Superintendent and his assistants, with instructions to find out 'if there have been large squatter movements from your areas to Kiambu'.[88] The Superintendent of Police could throw no light on the issue since he could not find out any information concerning the squatter exodus. However, the Assistant Superintendent of Police in Naivasha, one of the most affected areas, came up with the truth about the matter. He reported that after enquiring at all the police stations in Thompson's Falls, it was evident that European stock owners in that area were endeavouring to improve their herds, and thus wished to reduce their squatters' stock. Consequently, 'there has been a considerable exodus of Kikuyu squatters from the South East Rumuruti area for the above reason'.[89]

Since the movement of squatters back to the Reserves was said to have been the outcome of employer rather than government policy, the possibility of more squatters returning to the Reserves depended on employers and not the government. The official position was 'one of neutrality'.[90] The District Commissioner calculated that the Colonial Secretary's figure of 1,000 men, women and children averaged 200 squatter families. This would be considered a considerable movement if it had happened within a short space of time, for example a month, but since it was spread over a year, as the District Commissioner stated, 'it was hardly out of the way', especially since, as he added, 'the balance of movement' was back to the Reserves to which the squatters had 'been in the process of repatriation since early 1935'.[91]

The above calculations were based on figures from the estates of Kipipiri, Hewill, Soysambu, Marula and E. Cole, all of which stated that they 'deliberately packed off squatters varying from 30 to 100 in each case in 1935 to 1936'.[92] The movement was still going on and the estates concerned did not 'as a rule replace current wastage in existing squatters, except by casuals'.[93]

This squatter repatriation to Central Province was not restricted to Naivasha District alone. In his reply to the Colonial Secretary, the acting Provincial Commissioner for Rift Valley Province, Mr S. O. V. Hodge noted that the squatter movement had been going on for a period of about 18 months and that areas affected included Naivasha, Gilgil, Thompson's Falls and Laikipia.[94] The majority of squatters who had trekked to Central Province found the situation unfavourable and were forced to move back to the White Highlands. Others moved on to the Maasai Reserve,[95] whereas others still stayed on in Central Province in the hope that some land might be freed from European farms adjoining the Reserves should a delegation to Moscow from the Kikuyu Central Association, a political party formed in 1924, among other things to challenge the alienation of African lands for settler occupation, succeed.[96] The settlers intended to convert those who remained in the Settled Areas into wage-labourers.

Squatter production in the inter-war years

Although the inter-war period was characterised by an increase in settler control over the squatter community, the latter in turn sought to consolidate their position in the Settled Areas. Some squatters moved from one farm to another in search of employers who were less restrictive about squatter cultivation and grazing. At times, squatter commercial agriculture provided considerable incomes, as Kiiru's experience of opening a bank account indicated:

> I went to Kericho in 1928 after our school at Elburgon was closed. I was employed as a cook at Mr R. T. Senity's [sic] coffee farm. The *shamba* had over 300 workers, only 4 of us were Kikuyu. We were given 10 people to clear a *shamba* for us. During the first year, I sold 600 bags of maize to the European. He wrote a cheque to me on Thursday and said he would show me where to keep the money – in a bank, not in the house. On Friday we went to Nakuru where he opened an account for me, using my identity card (No. ID/NKU.0402381).[97]

Kiiru's *shamba* adjoined the forested edge of his employer's farm. As such, he was in a position to expand 'his' acreage into the forest. He made use of the casual labourers in cultivating his *shamba*, because, as he put it:

> I was friendly to the other workers. So after two o'clock when they had finished [doing] the *mzungu*'s work, I would get about 40–50 workers to work in my *shamba*. I would slaughter [goats] and cook for these Kisii, and *Wamera* [Kikuyu slang for Luo] and they would finish [cultivating] the *shamba*.[98]

By 1933, Kiiru had moved back to Elburgon because:

> . . . the Kikuyu had increased in the *shamba*s around. Also, in the *shamba* where we were, the *Lumbwa* [Kipsigis] who would not cultivate ate [stole] the goats. Nine sheep were also stolen. I had no herdsman except my wife and sister; I feared they might be killed by the *Lumbwa*.[99]

This is an unusual example and certainly not typical of the annual gains Kikuyu squatters could expect to achieve in the Settled Areas. None the less, the fact that Kiiru found it feasible to grow such a large amount of maize at a time when settler onslaught on squatter agriculture was gathering momentum, gives some indication of how much the squatters could grow in the pre-1918 period when conditions were less strict. It also indicates that, despite increasing limitations, squatter production was not entirely crippled.

In some ways, introducing the Marketing of Native Produce Act to the Settled Areas was a profitable measure, especially when it was extended to Nakuru District where it was confined to maize grown by native squatters.[100] Before the inspection services were introduced, native-grown maize was never exported beyond African ports. This was because it was regarded as of inferior quality and was therefore shunned by all the large buyers. With the introduction of the above legislation, first in Central Province and later in Nakuru District, squatter maize was graded on similar standards to European grown maize. In concrete terms, this meant that the squatters got better prices for their maize. In a way, this was a positive incentive for the squatters to grow more maize irrespective of the many odds they faced. At a national level, however, it meant that squatter maize became subject to world market fluctuations.

The Kenya Farmers' Association had the monopoly as the sole buyer of maize in the country and this forced Africans 'to share the burden of the less profitable export market'.[101] This was in contradistinction to the lucrative internal markets in which squatter maize could only be sold to specified traders at organised markets, which, in turn, interfered with the fluidity of the squatter enterprise. With better prices for their maize crop, the squatters then tried to expand their production of maize. The District Commissioner for the Nakuru-Ravine-Naivasha Districts noted that:

> Among the natives, the Kikuyu, the majority are getting such excellent prices for their maize that their whole energies are bent on the production of this crop, leading to difficulties with the squatters, whose land hunger is more voracious than ever and a positive menace in the Elburgon area.[102]

This temporary prosperity among the squatters was reflected in an increase in African taxation in the area amounting, in 1937, to £11,362, which represented an increase of £2,239 or 24 per cent. Because the forest authorities had no objection to squatter cultivation, it was much easier for squatters contracted as forest hands to engage in large-scale cultivation and to extend their *shambas* at the forest edges.[103] Although this does not necessarily mean that squatters had a free hand in the forest reserves, production there was high. A total of 64,432 bags of maize were inspected under the provisions of the Native Produce Ordinance at native markets at Elburgon, Rongai, Solai, Gilgil and Kijabe.[104] Grazing, however, was strictly controlled in forest areas where young trees were being planted and cattle and goats were prohibited. Unlike other crimes, there was a steady increase in illicit grazing in the forest reserves, as the figures in table 2.4 indicate.[105]

TABLE 2.4

Crime	No. of Cases per Year			
	1935	*1937*	*1938*	*1939*
Illicit grazing	756	802	1035	1203
Theft of forest products	635	82	1101	970
Illicit honey hunting and careless use of fire	94	225	338	233
Damage to trees	94	264	167	318
Other	74	—	120	108

The success of any squatter enterprise, even in the forest, depended on taking subtle calculated risks. For example, a squatter might graze in the depth of the forest in the hope that the forester would not venture that far. A squatter might also encroach on forest land with the full knowledge that he risked having his crop either confiscated or burned. On settler farms, as in forest reserves, it was hard to predict the fate of any one year's crop, but none the less there was considerable trade, as might be gauged from the average attendance at the various market-places that developed in the Settled Areas. See table 2.5.[106]

TABLE 2.5

Market	Days Operating	Attendance	Items of Trade
Elburgon	Sundays	500	Snuff, gourds, potatoes, chickens, vegetables, bananas
Njoro	"	100	"
Rongai	"	300–400	"
Ravine	"	200	Snuff, ornaments, sheep, goats, maize, bananas, potatoes, vegetables, gourds, native pottery
Elmenteita	Thursdays	300–400	Native produce
Subukia	Sundays	150–200	"
Bahati	Wednesdays Sundays	300–400	"
Kulungu (T/Falls Road)	"	200–300	"
Ndundori	"	300–500	"
Olkalan	"	400–600	"
Gilgil	"	1000–1500	"
Naivasha	Every 3rd day	300	"
Kijabe	Mondays Thursdays	150–200	"
South Kinangop	Sundays	300	Native produce and second-hand clothing

In addition, the Nakuru municipal market traded daily in all sorts of produce brought in from squatters in the surrounding area.

At a time when more labour time was being demanded from the squatter, it became increasingly difficult for him to engage in trade in livestock. This was left to the uncontracted kinsmen to undertake. However, they were liable to arrest and prosecution for what came to be known as *kanyanga* (trespass) in the course of their trading journeys within the White Highlands. Despite this, squatters continued to accumulate livestock, a practice which was greatly dislocated, and in some areas completely eliminated by the protracted *kifagio* campaign.

The sanctity of the White Highlands versus squatter assertion: from squatters to wage-labourers

Even in 1934, after about 30 years of occupation, only 11 per cent of all the land alienated for settlers was under cultivation for settler export crops.[107] This represented a great anomaly in the government's policy on the utilisation of land. Earlier, the colonial government had justified its alienation of African lands on the basis that it was not under full utilisation. The Kenya Land Commission, part of whose responsibility was to examine the land needs of Africans, felt that:

> If . . . the possession of large undeveloped tracts of land by any tribe, person or class . . . [was] prejudicial to the welfare of a country, it would be a proper exercise of the function of the government, when it has armed itself with the necessary powers, to intervene and adjust the matter.[108]

The same principle did not seem to apply to the settler occupiers. Although there was only a limited amount of land they could use, they and the government were concerned to keep the White Highlands for the exclusive ownership of Europeans.

There was general consensus among the settlers and administrators about squatter avarice for more and more land for grazing and cultivation. The squatter had come to symbolise a destructive and economically irrational African who sought to utilise as much settler land as he could, regardless of the apparent depleting effects this had on the land.[109] The term squatter had also come to refer to an African who did everything possible to evade his labour duties and contravened every known labour obligation.[110] The squatters were said to have:

> the desire for a life wherein for a minimum of work and scanty wage they obtain almost unlimited areas for grazing and haphazard cultivation. . . . Unless closely watched they will bring in the stock of their friends and relatives, cut down forests, cultivate areas along the streams, *and proceed to eat the heart out of the land without putting anything back into it.*[111]

Apart from being a threat to the stock industry and destroying settler land, extensive squatter grazing and cultivation were seen to alter the status of the squatter from that of a labourer to an independent producer. To ensure that the squatter did not consolidate this self assertion, it was:

deemed necessary that any contract between the employer and the squatter should be a labour contract. This would allow the employee for his greater comfort to keep the number of cattle required for himself and his family. If however he is allowed to keep more than that number the character of that contract changes in effect until it is predominantly a tenancy contract, which, in our opinion, ought to be prevented as being contrary to the purposes for which the European Highlands have been reserved.[112]

One report had declared that squatters were undesirable to both employers and themselves and that, although they were vital to settlers who grew coffee, pyrethum, tea and sisal, they were 'very much more trouble than they were worth'.[113] Although they were seen by some settlers as a cheap source of labour, they did more harm than good, they 'did in' a large number of settler cattle through disease, 'did in' settler land, and were 'most frightfully difficult people to manage'.[114]

The fear that squatters might acquire rights to the lands they utilised fuelled the campaign further. Talk began in earnest of the need to transform the tenant-labourer squatter into a resident labourer whose status would be that of a servant.[115]

Unlike a squatter, a resident labourer would go out to work for a salary but would be allowed to supplement this by limited subsistence farming. Some settlers envisaged limited grazing for this new employee although some were opposed to it. The resident labourer was expected to be the antithesis of a squatter 'who receives little or no pay for his labour, and trusts to his making a livelihood out of the farm on which he squats by keeping stock, by growing crops for sale and by less reputable methods'.[116] It was considered preposterous that settlers had consistently 'squealed' for land only to 'give' it to Africans.[117] The European elected member for Nyanza, Mr Long argued that if the squatter wanted to farm seriously:

He should do it in the reserves where 47,747 square miles had been set apart for African use. On alien land, the African was expected to grow only enough for himself and his family and, should a surplus arise, it would be necessary for the squatter to inform his employers.[118]

A motion was put and carried to the effect that any native with surplus produce should notify his master of his intention to sell. Mr Long went on to explain that the squatters were invariably 'the most expensive form of labour that one can possibly imagine – certainly as far as Kenya is concerned'.[119] It can be assumed that many settlers never sat down to compute the relative cost of their squatter labour. They were, however, all aware of the drawbacks associated with squatter labour. For many settlers the prime conviction that squatters were vital for farming deterred them from supporting the motion on the need to abolish the squatter system. Mr Long, who had farmed for 25 years, 15 for somebody else and 10 for himself, did not agree with this belief. He stated: 'I have no squatters, and have never had any, except for a fortnight. I got rid of them, and their sheep and goats and everything'.[120] Given a good house and good conditions, Mr Long said it was possible to 'keep your labour without necessarily allowing him to bring stock with him on the farm.

Mr Long did not state what constituted 'good conditions'. No conditions that excluded the ·peasant option would have been acceptable to the squatters. Both de-stocking and the anticipated transformation of the squatter to a waged resident labourer spelt the same basic predicament for him, i.e. his elimination as an independent and prosperous producer-cum-labourer and reduction to an impoverished labourer. Even before this process was completed, the squatter community lost a considerable amount of their economic independence, a factor that was accompanied by widespread discontent. This dissatisfaction was most evident amongst Kikuyu squatters in the Nakuru, Naivasha, Ravine and Laikipia areas,[121] which had been the main strongholds of the squatter peasant option.

Squatter insecurity

The inter-war period was crucial for bringing into focus the temporary and precarious status of squatters in the White Highlands. As well as facing possible expulsion at the expiry of his contract, a squatter might suffer the added agony of having his grown-up sons prosecuted for trespass or unlawful residence if they were not paid employees of the farm on which they resided. Settlers insisted that all male youths above the age of sixteen should register on an individual basis or cease to reside on the farms. Since the farms were unable to absorb all the youth, by continuing to reside with their parents most of them were considered illegal squatters and liable to prosecution.[122]

Although many administrators and settlers were primarily concerned with livestock, the District Commissioner for Laikipia was more concerned about 'the ultimate position of the numbers of squatters' children who have grown up, or are growing up, and who are to all intents and purposes detribalised. They know no other homes beyond the farms where they were born'.[123] He foresaw an issue of great political significance rapidly arising where young men born or brought up on settler farms and who knew no other homes became unemployed and returned to their homes on the farms where they were not wanted as squatters. Often, they would reside illegally, commit minor offences or become vagrants, and then be repatriated to the Reserves where they had 'neither the desire nor the encouragement to stay'.[124] They would then return and eventually become criminals. The security of the squatter youth depended upon the benevolence of the settler, for 'if the farmer . . . [gave] him a permit to reside for a limited time all . . . [was] satisfactory, but the employer may not do so; neither can he give him employment and if the youth stays then he apparently is trespassing or unlawfully residing. But he knows no other home'.[125] As one District Commissioner observed, 'there is more trouble to be expected on the farms from squatter children than stock'.[126]

By 1935 the composition of the Kikuyu population in Laikipia was as shown in table 2.6.

TABLE 2.6

Wakikuyu	7,642
Squatter children who had reached manhood and were still in the district	372
Squatter children who had reached manhood and were working out of the district	120

Table 2.7 shows the criminal cases recorded in Laikipia between January 1934 and April 1935; 75 per cent of the offenders were Kikuyu.[127]

TABLE 2.7

Trespass	170
Illegal residence	116
Vagrancy	62

The nature of these crimes is an indication of the sorts of social controls the settlers tried to impose on their labourers. Compared with squatters from other ethnic groups, the Kikuyu squatters were 'more prone. . .to sever their connection with their reserve'[128] when they went out as squatters. In the White Highlands they established separate communities which were becoming increasingly threatened by the settler decision to reduce squatter population, cultivation and grazing. The observation by the Laikipia District Commissioner to the effect that 'the Kikuyu on farms appears to be a colonist and not a squatter'[129] overlooked the basic problem facing the squatter community in the shifting relationships within the squatter-settler enclave. For, although the squatters had lost their hold in Central Province, they had evolved a coherent community in the White Highlands which was subject to Kikuyu ethnic mores and cultural and social restraints. Even as far back as the early 1920s, the squatters had already evolved a lucrative socio-economic sub-system, which had given them a sense of belonging in the White Highlands.

But the growth of the settler economy and its entrenchment in the colonial hegemony had systematically eroded the squatter community by increasingly marginalising the squatters into wage-labourers, thus giving them only a temporary lease for working in the White Highlands. By the late 1920s, the squatters' world was crumbling beneath their feet and subjectively they no longer felt like colonists.

The assertion that the colonial administration had no squatter policy[130] was somewhat exaggerated. The government was overtly concerned with creating an adequate and cheap supply of labour, both for the settlers and for the public sectors, and introduced a host of financial and legislative laws to precipitate and control labour. Colonial interventions in the labour demands of the settlers were direct and intense, despite settler complaints to the contrary. That the provisions were sometimes inadequate and needed constant amendment and revision does not mean that there was no labour policy. On the contrary, the government's native policy was reinforced by a great amount of labour legislation. The settlers felt betrayed because the government did not always come to their rescue soon enough, but then so did the Africans.

The squatters in fact nursed bitter feelings of betrayal.[131] Since some of them had been lured to the Rift Valley with promises of unlimited land for cultivation and grazing, the settler assault had indeed flown in the face of prior promises. Although they never articulated their feelings formally (at least not in the period before 1939), squatters seethed with disappointment over the way the government had failed to come to their aid during the settler assault, when squatter and settler had become locked in an unequal economic relationship. But despite this, the squatters still managed to adopt various forms of resistance against the settlers who were closing in on them.

During the first half of 1937, the squatters refused to sign on again under the 1925 Ordinance.[132] Sometimes, the settlers overlooked the government's recommendation that on expiry of their contracts they should re-engage the squatters for a further period of one year. In such cases, the squatters usually resisted the settler's obstinacy by continuing to live on his farm illegally. Some of the squatters would leave the farms as soon as their crops were ready, much to the inconvenience of the settler farmers who had hoped that the squatters 'would help them to harvest their own crops'.[133] While settlers and squatters were awaiting the enactment of the new Ordinance, the settler felt confident that the new legislation would give him greater powers over squatters, whereas the squatter could only hope against hope that the measures of the act would not be too stringent. In the meantime, some of the discontented or evicted squatters continued to drift to the urban centres or to Central Province. Others left settler farms to settle in the Tinet Forest in the Mau area, where there was no settler supervision and official interference could be easily avoided.[134] When confronted with interrogation from the administration, these Kikuyu squatters could always claim to be members of the Dorobo community, which had been pushed into the forest by colonial land alienation.

Squatters and litigation

It was very difficult for a squatter to lodge a complaint against a settler because, if he did, he was aware that 'he would receive notice, and be ordered to leave the farm within six months, and lose not only his grazing for his cattle but, in many cases, his very home'.[135] In addition, once the settler had taken action against him, he could never count on any help from the judiciary or administration. Litigation was long and tedious and, more often than not, failed to alter the initial decision taken by the settlers. Such squatter vulnerability can be seen from the following case in which frustrated former squatters sought redress, first from the Labour Office, then from the court and then again from the administration, with very little success.

Kariuki Wainaina, Mwangi Githingi, Mwangi Mwathe, Njuguna Kuria, Nganga Mukuria, Muthema Mungatu and Gakirio Muchiri had been squatters at a Mr Haddinot's farm in Turi for a number of years. When Mr Rutherford bought the farm in February 1937, he also kept the squatter labourers who had been working for Mr Haddinot. After about three months, a disagreement developed between Mr Rutherford and his squatters and as a result he dismissed thirteen of them, including the above appellants. The squatters were upset that, although Mr Haddinot had given them permission to cultivate, Mr Rutherford had denied them any time to harvest their crops. Neither had they been compensated for what was obviously a considerable harvest. Apparently Mr Rutherford had dug up their European potatoes and sold them, which was why the squatters had taken the case to court in the first place, although to no avail.

As a last resort they tried to appeal to the administration to intervene in what they believed to be a flagrant violation of their rights through collusion between their employer and the Superintendent of Police. Their letter to the Chief Native Commissioner provides some insight into the squatters' attempts to comprehend and use to their advantage the labour laws that governed their relationships with the settlers. It also illustrates their frustration. Part of the letter said:

That your petitioners had reported this case (case No. 340/37-Nakuru Supreme Court) to the Supreme Court Nakuru and it was attended at rule, and it was against our will. Because we were told that we should not be paid our crops. That hitherto your petitioners have been squartters [sic] of Mr Rutherford feeling perhaps that they have been safeguarded by operation of some section regarding squartters [sic] Ordinance laws of Kenya and to violate the Royal Charter dated 3rd September 1888 granted to the Imperial British East African Company. That our 230 bags of potatoes have been sold by Mr Rutherford and our crops of maize are not on our authority. For that we trust that you will issue necessary direction to the matter and the final decision of our case is on your hands sir. Finally therefore, state that we have worked for Mr Rutherford just a period of two months and twenty eight days and we were unpaid by him which reads Section 55 (i) Chapter 139 laws of Kenya. Our kipande were signed by Superintendent of Police Nakuru at time of discharge. We were forcibly deprived by Rutherford and Superintendent. That we pray that his Majesty's government will restore our crops back to us.[136]

The Nakuru Labour Officer acknowledged that Mr Rutherford treated his labour badly and would cause further trouble. He was of the opinion that, although the squatters were 'morally entitled to compensation, legally they had no claim'.[137] Mr Rutherford refused even to consider paying them for the crops he had taken for his own use. Although the squatters had been under squatter contracts with the previous owner of the farm, they had no agreements with Mr Rutherford under the RNLO. It was for this reason that the Labour Officer was unable to compel Mr Rutherford to compensate them.

He did, however, advise the squatters that if they wanted further action they could open a civil case. This they had done and lost. Squatters could safeguard their crops on European farms through RNLO agreements, but, even under valid contracts, they could be discharged with no compensation paid for their crops. Squatters without contracts might 'endeavour to establish the right to reside by planting crops without being on agreement',[138] but this was not the case with these eight squatters. After visiting the farm, the Labour Officer was of the opinion that Mr Rutherford had granted them permission to plant, which gave them a moral right to their crops. But, 'on evidence before him, the Resident Magistrate found that this was not the case',[139] hence his judgement against the squatters' suit. While the magistrate, Mr Cresswell, hoped that the case would be settled through arbitrators, like the Labour Officer, he feared that if this proved successful other squatters would sue civilly, thus putting Mr

Rutherford to great expense. Mr Cresswell intended to advise Rutherford to let the Kikuyu reap their crops or receive compensation, but realised that there was no guarantee that Mr Rutherford would accept his advice.

There were several such cases of squatters trying to appeal to members of the administration, who were torn between upholding a stable and contented labour force on one hand, and coping with tenacious settler employers, who to a large extent were a law unto themselves, on the other. In the ensuing conflict, there was always a high probability that the settler would have his own way. Hence, for the squatter, there was no solace in litigation. In most cases the settler's decision was final. But this was only one of many ways in which squatters fell victim to the manipulations of the settlers.

For example, the settlers reduced squatters' salaries even lower than the previous years so that by 1935, the average wage for a squatter was 5 shillings per month with no ration.[140] Some of the labour contracts offered no cash payment at all, rations being the only form of remuneration.[141] The ration included skimmed milk (*mathace*), maize flour (*posho*) and occasional rations of beans, meat and salt.[142] Meanwhile there was a temporary but steady upward rise of wages for monthly labourers due to an increased demand for labour created by the squatter exodus.

The new RNLO would give the settlers the power to reduce the number of squatters on their farms, reduce the acreage of land under squatter cultivation and limit or eliminate squatter livestock. At some stage, it was anticipated that Kikuyu squatters who might be evicted when the Ordinance was put into effect could be settled in an area lying near the northern border of Trans-Nzoia, or in the nearby Pokot Reserve.

This government plan for a Kikuyu settlement in Pokot was motivated by two other objectives. Firstly, it was hoped that these Kikuyu squatters would provide a potential labour supply for the Trans-Nzoia District coffee farms. Secondly, administrative officials believed that a Pokot contact with the progressive agricultural Kikuyu would be beneficial to the government's attempts to prevent Pokot agriculturalists from becoming pastoralists.[143] (Outside Central Province and the Settled Areas, the government referred to the Kikuyu as a progressive agricultural group, whereas inside these areas it portrayed them as economically destructive people who destroyed any land they used.) None the less, despite profuse correspondence between the various administrative officials concerned, the whole issue remained nebulous and nothing came of it.[144] It was, however, indicative that the government was conscious of the problems that had already begun to surface as a result of the settler assault.

In the period between 1937, when the Ordinance was passed, and 1940, when it was put into effect, the squatters remained ignorant of its contents. During this interim period, squatters were expected to continue to attest on some temporary basis pending the adoption of the Ordinance. This ambiguous arrangement helped to intensify speculation among the squatters concerning the terms of the new Act. It also succeeded in precipitating an atmosphere tense with anxiety, exasperation and desperation. Ultimately, squatters reacted by open defiance. They not only refused to sign the contracts but also continued to squat illegally on the settler farms, sitting back, so to speak, buying time to await the outcome.

One major effect of this squatter response to the impending Ordinance was a massive disruption of labour. The government appealed to the African administrative bureaucracy, including Chiefs Waruhiu, Koinange and Njonjo, to persuade the squatters not to withdraw their labour. It was expected that the chiefs would explain the importance of labour to the squatters, while at the same time dispelling false rumours about the Ordinance. But the squatters were still very anxious about their precarious position. As Kimondo Muchemi put it, they:

> hated their temporary status in the area; they also hated the restrictions imposed on them, including small *shambas* for cultivation and the restrictions on livestock. But they had no way of airing their grievances against the *wazungu*; they feared being dismissed. This at times was done just before they harvested their crops.[145]

During the inter-war period, the squatters had waged an uphill battle to consolidate their economic and social presence in the Settled Areas. What the settlers and administrators had seen as a generation of footloose, detribalised and lazy idlers was really a community in search of a foothold in the Settled Areas. Constant Kikuyu squatter movement from one farm to the next had basically resulted from and was an expression of insecurity and discontent. Improvements in settler agriculture, which had been bolstered by state subsidies, encouraged settlers to expand further. In so doing, they had imposed more labour obligations on the squatters and demanded the reduction of independent squatter production. On their part, the squatters had been trying to maintain as much independence and dignity as they could salvage from a hostile colonial state. Both settlers and squatters had taken a keen interest in the 1937 RNLO. While the squatters had feared that it would seal their deteriorating status, the settlers had hoped it would provide the legislation they needed for dealing with the squatter 'menace'. When it did come, the Ordinance sanctioned past and future settler restrictions on squatter activities. The Ordinance transferred the control of squatters from the colonial administration to the settlers through the settler-controlled District Councils.

Despite the restrictions and the general deterioration of their plight, in various ways the squatters continued to try and make their stay in the White Highlands more bearable. It is with aspects of this 'self-help' strategy that the next chapter is concerned.

Notes

1. *East African Standard* (EAS), 2 November 1911, Ulu Settlers Association Resolution.
2. Buell, R. L., *The Native Problem in Africa*, Vol. I, London, Frank Cass, 1965 (first published 1928), p. 350.
3. KNA, PC RVP 6A/25/3, Ag. PC Ukamba, Mr Traill, Addressing Acting Chief Secretary, 7 May 1918, 'Native Cattle on European Farms'.
4. ibid.
5. ibid.
6. ibid.
7. Quoted in Ghai, Y.P. and McAuslan, J.P.W.B., *Public Law and Political Change in Kenya*, Nairobi, OUP, 1971, p. 83.
8. KNA, PC NZA 320/4/2, Chief Native Commissioner to Senior Commissioner, Nyanza, 17 March 1925.
9. Similar sentiments were expressed in the Legislative Council at a later stage. See for example Legislative Council (Leg. Co.) Debates, 24 May 1938, Vol. IV, pp. 58–64.
10. Ghai and McAuslan, *Public Law*, p. 83.
11. See Leg. Co. Debates, 28 July 1937, Vol. II, p. 130.
12. ibid.
13. There were several suggestions that previous convictions against Africans should be recorded on their *kipande*. After discussion it was decided that, since the men would have served their sentences already, it would be against the principle of British justice to make such records. See RH, MSS. Afr. S. 1506.2, Njoro Settlers Association General Meeting, 5 June 1929.
14. See Okoth-Ogendo, H.W.O., 'The Legal Organisation of Colonial Agriculture, 1900–1960: An Essay in the History of Dependency, Autonomy and Co-optation', Staff Seminar Papers No. 18, 1976/77, Department of History, University of Nairobi, p. 9.
15. KNA, Native Affairs Department, Annual Report, 1925, p. 2.
16. KNA, Naivasha District Annual Report, 1922, Special Report, p. 1.
17. ibid, p. 2.
18. KNA, Native Affairs Department, Annual Report, 1923, p. 1.
19. KNA, Naivasha District Annual Report, 1927, p. 1.
20. Ghai and McAuslan, *Public Law*, p. 95.
21. KNA, Nakuru-Naivasha Province Annual Report, 1926, p. 75.

22. See Van Zwanenberg, R.M.A., *Colonial Capitalism and Labour in Kenya: 1919–1939*, Nairobi, EALB, 1975, pp. 236–40; see also Tignor, R.C., *The Colonial Transformation of Kenya: The Kamba, Kikuyu and Maasai from 1900 to 1939*, Princeton, Princeton University Press, 1976, pp. 310–23.

23. Van Zwanenberg, *Colonial Capitalism*, pp. 241–52.

24. RH, Lord Francis Scott Papers, Microfilm Reel 15.

25. ibid.

26. Interview, Njoroge Gakuha, 18 September 1976, Njoro.

27. KNA, PC RVP 6A/25/3, DC Kapsabet to PC Eldoret, 4 November 1933. See also KNA, PC RVP 6A/25/3, 'A Note on the Squatters Problem' by V.M. Fisher, Principal Inspector of Labour, Nairobi, June 1932. See also KNA, NAD, AR 1937, p. 187, which stated, 'The Resident Native Labourer may be the mainstay of the farm, but he does not always prove an asset *except as providing a cheap source of labour* at the expense of the fertility of the land.' Emphasis is mine.

28. KNA, PC RVP 6A/25/3, DC Kapsabet to PC Eldoret, 4 November 1933.

29. KNA, PC RVP 6A/25/3, DC Nakuru to Ag. PC Rift Valley, 24 May 1931.

30. ibid.

31. KNA, Nakuru District Annual Report, 1932, p. 6.

32. As late as 1935 some settlers made no cash payments to their employees. In 1935 alone, this contravention of the Employment of Native Ordinance was evidenced by 1,581 notices served to European defaulters. See KNA Native Affairs Department, Annual Report, 1935, p. 191.

33. KNA, PC RVP 6A/33/2, Correspondence from Kenya Police Headquarters, Nairobi, to all Officers-in-Charge of Police Units in the Settled Areas, 22 December 1927.

34. Interview, Gachago Kagere, 28 October 1976, Nakuru.

35. ibid.

36. Interview, Mary Wangui Macharia, 16 September 1976, Njoro.

37. Interview, Kamau Wanyoko, 13 September 1976, Londiani.

38. Interview, Ngoci Ndegwa, 29 December 1976, Nakuru.

39. Interview, Riiyu Ngare, 30 December 1976, Nakuru.

40. Interview, Gachago Kagere, 28 October 1976, Nakuru.

41. Interview, Muchemi Kimondo, 8 October 1976, Subukia.

42. Interview, Bethuel Kamau, 8 October 1976, Subukia.

43. ibid.

44. ibid., and Ernest Kiberethi Kanyanja, 13 October 1976, Elburgon. Ernest was one among several squatters who transported their livestock to Central Province for safe-keeping and/or sale at better prices. Njuguna Muharu, 14 September 1976, Molo.

45. Interview, Mrs Kamau Wanyoko, 13 September 1976, Londiani.

46. ibid.

47. Interview, Nganga Kimani, 16 September 1976, Njoro.

48. Interview, Gitau Gathukia, 16 September 1976, Njoro.

49. Ngushu Kamara, 17 September 1976, Njoro. Nganga Karanja Koinange's father lost his job because the settler said he could not support a squatter with six wives (interview, 16 September 1976, Njoro).

50. Interview, Ernest Kiberethi Kanyanja, 13 October 1976, Elburgon. Mrs

Kamau Wanyoko emphasised that the settlers' claim (in the Londiani area) that they needed the squatters to de-stock so that they could plant pyrethrum was hypocrisy (*ungumania*), that the real reason was that the settlers did not want the squatters to accumulate livestock (interview, 13 September 1976, Londiani).

51. Interview, Gikunju Gakuo, 18 December 1976, Nakuru.
52. Rosberg, C. and Nottingham, J., *The Myth of Mau Mau: Nationalism in Kenya*, Nairobi, EAPH, 1966, p. 252.
53. KNA, Native Affairs Dept., Annual Report 1927, p. 61.
54. RH, MSS. Afr. S. 1506.2, Njoro Settlers Association Minute Books, General Meeting, 12 October 1928. See also KNA Nakuru District Annual Report, 1928, p. 5.
55. RH, MSS. Afr. S. 1506.2, Njoro Settlers Association, General Meeting, 23 April 1929.
56. KNA, Nakuru District Annual Report, 1928, p. 6.
57. Interview, Shuranga Wegunyi, 25 October 1976, Nakuru.
58. KNA, Native Affairs Department, Annual Report, 1929, p. 77.
59. KNA, Naivasha District Annual Report, 1929, p. 3.
60. ibid., p. 4.
61. ibid., p. 3.
62. ibid., p. 7.
63. RH, MSS. Afr. S. 1506.2, Njoro Settlers Association Minute Books, Executive Meeting, 27 June 1929.
64. ibid. See also General Meeting, 23 July 1929.
65. KNA, PC RVP 6A/33/2, DC Elgeyo Marakwet to PC, Nzoia Province, 14 April 1930, 'Re: Resident Native Labourers Ordinance, 1925'.
66. ibid.
67. KNA, PC RVP 6A/33/2, PC Nzoia to DC Elburgon, Kitale, Tambach and Nandi, 'Re: Resident Native Labourers Ordinance, 1925', 8 April 1930.
68. KNA, Nakuru District Annual Report, 1930, p. 2.
69. KNA, DC KBU 24, District Annual Report, 1931, pp. 9–10. See also KNA, PC RVP 6A/27/7, 'A Note on the Squatter Problem' by V.M. Fisher, Principal Inspector of Labour, Nairobi, June 1932.
70. Rosberg and Nottingham *Myth of Mau Mau*, p. 250. See also Kenya Land Commission Report, p. 467.
71. KNA, DC RVP2/1-/1, Nakuru District Annual Report, 1930, p. 2, emphasis added.
72. Van Zwanenberg, *Colonial Capitalism*, p. 216.
73. ibid.
74. KNA, PC RVP 6A/27/7, 'A Note on the Squatter Problem' by V.M. Fisher, Principal Inspector of Labour, Nairobi, June 1932.
75. KNA, Naivasha District Annual Report, 1932, p. 10. See also KNA, Nakuru District Annual Report, 1932, p. 4; Nakuru District Annual Report, 1933, pp. C, D; and Nakuru District Annual Report, 1934, p. C.
76. KNA, Nakuru District Annual Report, 1931, p. 4.
77. KNA, Nakuru District Annual Report, 1934, p. C.
78. A Mr Pardoe of Kekopey in Naivasha area sought to introduce a clause in his contract with new squatters allowing him to sell any excess squatter stock.

He would give the money to the squatter. He was informed that such a clause would not have any effect in court. See KNA, PC RVP 6A/25/3, DC Naivasha to PC RVP, 21 November 1932, and PC RVP to DC Naivasha, 2 December 1932.

79. See for example KNA, PC RVP 6A/25/3, PC Central Province to PC RVP, 25 May 1935, and PC RVP to PC Central Province, 30 March 1935.

80. Instances of such cases abound. For example, in June 1928, the Thompson's Falls District decided that all squatter-owned cattle should be returned to their reserves at the expiry of their owners' contracts. By mid 1933 the occupier of farm no. LO 2915 still had squatter cattle on his farm. The District Association sought the help of the PC for Rift Valley Province in the matter, to which he replied there was 'no legal prohibition against Mr Wace having native owned cattle under the provision of the Resident Native Labourers Ordinance' and that unless there was reason to believe that the law in this respect was being broken 'no action can be taken under present circumstances'. See KNA, PC RVP 6A/25/3, Hon. Sec. Thompson's Falls District Assoc. to PC Nakuru, 4 July 1932, and Ag. PC NKU to Hon. Sec. Thompson's Falls District Assoc., 12 July 1932.

81. KNA, PC RVP 6A/25/3, 'Squatters 1931–1938', Secretary Hoey's Bridge Farmers Association to DC Eldoret, received on 13 February 1936. See also KNA, PC RVP 6A/25/3, 'Notes with Regard to Squatters under the Native Labourers Ordinance No. 5 of 1925: Rules Approved by District Council, Eldoret, May 1934'.

82. KNA, Native Affairs Department, 1933, p. 109.

83. KNA, PC RVP 6A/25/3 'Squatters 1931–1938', 'Notes with Regard to Squatters under the Native Labourers Ordinance No. 5 of 1925: Rules Approved by District Council, Eldoret, May 1934'.

84. KNA, PC RVP 6A/25/7, PC RVP to Colonial Secretary, 21 December 1936.

85. KNA, PC RVP 6A/25/3, 'Squatters 1931–1938', PC Central Province to PC RVP, 26 March 1935: Resident Native Labourers.

86. KNA, PC RVP 6A/25/3, PC RVP to PC Central Province, 30 March 1935.

87. KNA, PC RVP 6A/25/7, Colonial Secretary to PC RVP, 16 November 1936.

88. KNA, PC RVP 6A/25/7, Colonial Secretary to PC RVP, 20 November 1936.

89. KNA, PC RVP 6A/25/7, Re 'Kikuyu Squatters', Assistant Superintendent of Police, Naivasha, to PC RVP, 26 November 1936.

90. KNA, PC RVP 6A/25/7, Lab 27/5/2, 'Re: Kikuyu Squatters in Naivasha District', DC Nakuru to PC RVP, 28 November 1936.

91. ibid.

92. ibid.

93. ibid.

94. KNA, PC RVP 6A/25/7, Ag. PC RVP to Colonial Secretary, 21 December 1936.

95. KNA, Native Affairs Department, Annual Report, 1936, p. 162.

96. KNA, PC RVP 6A/25/7, DC Laikipia to PC RVP, 4 December 1936. See Rosberg and Nottingham *Myth of Mau Mau*, pp. 96–100.

97. Interview, Kiiru Arphaxad Kuria, 21 September 1976, Elburgon.
98. ibid.
99. ibid.
100. KNA, Native Affairs Report, 1936, p. 45.
101. See Ghai and McAuslan, *Public Law*, p. 93.
102. KNA, Nakuru-Ravine-Naivasha District Annual Report, 1937, pp. 3–4.
103. Interview, Kiiru Arphaxad Kuria, 21 September 1976, Elburgon.
104. KNA, Native Affairs Annual Report, 1938, p. 88.
105. RH, MSS Afr. S. 753 14.r.24, Kenya Forest Department Annual Reports for 1935, 1937, 1938 and 1939.
106. KNA, Nakuru-Ravine-Naivasha District Annual Report, 1937, p. 16.
107. Major Cavendish Bentinck, Leg. Co. Debates 1934, Vol. 2, p. 559.
108. Report of the Kenya Land Commission, Nairobi, Government Printer, 1934, p. 11.
109. KNA, Native Affairs Department Annual Report, 1937, p. 187.
110. KNA, PC RVP 6A/27/7, 'A Note on the Squatters Problem' by V.M. Fisher, Principal Inspector of Labour, Nairobi, June 1932.
111. KNA, Native Affairs Department Annual Report, 1937, p. 187. See also p. 207, where it says that for the squatter the desire to get work and earn wages was not a principal desire. This author's emphasis.
112. Major Cavendish Bentinck, Leg. Co. Debates 1934, Vol. 2, p. 538.
113. Leg. Co. Debates, 'Resident Labourers Bill', 1937, Vol. 2, p. 163.
114. ibid.
115. ibid., p. 127.
116. KNA, Native Affairs Department Annual Report, 1938, p. 88.
117. Leg. Co. Debates, 'Resident Labourers Bill', 1937, Vol. 2, p. 162.
118. ibid., p. 347.
119. Mr Long, Leg. Co. Debates, Vol. 2, 1937, p. 163.
120. ibid.
121. KNA, Native Affairs Department Annual Report, 1936, p. 76.
122. KNA, Rift Valley Intelligence Report, March 1935.
123. KNA, Native Affairs Department Annual Report, 1935, p. 163.
124. KNA Rift Valley Intelligence Report, March 1935.
125. ibid.
126. KNA, PC RVP 6A/25/3 'Squatters 1931–1938', DC Laikipia to PC Nakuru, 'Squatter-born Natives in Farm Areas', 17 June 1935.
127. KNA, Rift Valley Province Intelligence Report, March 1935, DC Laikipia to PC Nakuru, 17 June 1935.
128. ibid.
129. KNA, Native Affairs Department Annual Report, 1935, p. 163.
130. Throup, D. W., 'The Governorship of Sir Phillip Mitchell in Kenya, 1944–1952', unpublished Ph.D. thesis, Sidney Sussex College, Cambridge, 1983, p. 154.
131. Interview, Wilson Mwangi Njau, 13 October 1976, Elbrgon, Mrs Kamau Wanyoko called the settler onslaught *ungumania* – hypocrisy (interview, 13 September 1976, Londiani).
132. KNA, Native Affairs Department Annual Report, 1937, p. 207.
133. ibid., p. 207.

134. Interview, Kamau Wanyoko, 13 September 1976, Londiani. See also KNA Lab 9/320, 'The Resident Labourers Ordinance: Aberdare District Council, 1944–51', Major L.B.L. Hughes to DC Naivasha, 16 March 1949 for a settler's view of life in a forest reserve.

135. KNA, Native Affairs Department Annual Report, 1935, p. 190.

136. KNA, PC RVP 6A/4/12, Mwangi Githingi and Kariuki Wainaina to Chief Native Commissioner, 'Case No. 340/37 Nakuru of Mr Rutherford and the following people, 2 November 1937', 4 November 1937.

137. KNA, PC RVP 6A/4/12, Labour Officer Nakuru to PC RVP, 9 November 1937.

138. ibid.

139. ibid.

140. KNA, Native Affairs Department Annual Report, 1935, p. 190.

141. ibid.

142. Interviews, Ndegwa Wambugu, 3 October 1976, Njoro, and Njoroge Mambo, 4 October 1976, Elburgon.

143. KNA, PC RVP 6A/25/7, DO Kitale Mr Hyde-Clarke to Izard, 2 April 1937.

144. KNA, PC RVP 6A/25/7, Commissioner for Local Government Lands and Settlement to PC RVP, 3 March 1937; Ag. PC RVP to DO Kitale, 5 March 1937; PC RVP to F.B. Baincroft of Elgon 31 March 1937; Officer-in-Charge Turkana District to DO Kitale Mr Hyde-Clarke, 18 March 1937; Hyde-Clarke to Izard, 2 April 1937; PC RVP to Commissioner for Local Government, Lands and Settlement, 3 March 1937; Secretary Trans-Nzoia District Association to DC Kitale, 24 March 1937, asking for assurance that the area to be given to such Kikuyu settlers does 'not cut into the White Highlands as area reserved for European settlement'; Ag PC RVP, SOV Hodge to DC Kitale informing the latter that, should the programme be implemented, Kikuyu settlement would be in West Suk Native Reserve, not in Trans-Nzoia District.

145. Interview, Muchemi Kimondo, 8 October 1976, Subukia.

Three

Social Organisation
among the Squatters

We must acknowledge that a skilled class of workmen who will keep
up the habit of daily work for a life-time – a most important factor in
the development of East Africa – is only to be obtained by
denationalisation.[1]

Having seen how the Kikuyu squatters concentrated most of their
energies on acquiring land for cultivation and grazing – a task which
became increasingly difficult after the mid-1920s – we shall now
examine some of the ways in which these people organised their lives
around various institutions in an attempt to turn the White Highlands
into a place in which they could feel 'at home'. One way in which they
did this was the wholesale transfer of cultural and political institutions
such as elders' councils (*ciama*), circumcision (*irua*) and marriage
ceremonies from the Central Province homeland. This meant that, in
many ways, life in the Settled Areas carried on much as it had done
before.

But unlike their Central Province homeland, the White Highlands
were a settler enclave where the rough edge of European domination
was most evident. The squatters had to cope with their positions as
workers in a colonial situation; for example, they had to find ways of
providing education for their children in the absence of any
government-sponsored educational programme for the White Highlands. They overcame many obstacles to develop self-help (*harambee*)
school systems, which they did by accepting what help they could get
from two organisations based in Central Province, the Kikuyu
Independent Schools Association (KISA) and the Kikuyu Karinga
Schools. As these systems evolved, both their socio-cultural and their
educational objectives changed, for the squatters were forced to make
organisational adjustments to meet the growing challenges from the
settler economy.

Elders' councils (*ciama*)

Ciama were established on all European farms that had Kikuyu squatters, and were run according to traditional Kikuyu cultural norms, values and practices. Membership of the *kiama* (singular) was restricted to elderly and respected squatters or ex-squatters still resident on settler farms.[2] If the farm overseer, or *nyapara* as he was called, was a young man, he was required to make a payment of a ram (*ngoima*) before he could join the *kiama*.[3] On some farms, settlers were also allowed to join the *kiama* on payment of an *ngoima* fee,[4] but had no more status or influence in the *kiama* than any other of its members. Since decisions had to be approved by the majority of the council's members, the settler was unable, on an individual basis, to affect the direction of the *kiama*'s deliberations.

The *kiama* dealt with all aspects of life, from settling disputes between squatters to circumcision, marriage and other traditional rituals. Incidences of unlawful pregnancy, in which the young man responsible refused to marry the woman in question, or cases of theft, rape or any other anti-social practices, were arbitrated by the *kiama* and sentences passed. If the culprit disagreed with the verdict, the *nyapara* would then refer the issue to the settler.[5] Inherent in the operation of the *kiama* was an attempt to safeguard the interests of the squatter community and to maintain a healthy social structure within the community.

If the members of one *kiama* felt that an issue was sufficiently important to warrant an inter-farm *kiama*, especially on disputes involving people from different farms, then such a group was convened. If the complainant or the accused disagreed with the decision of the joint *kiama*, the issue could be referred either to a township chief or to the District Commissioner's Office.[6]

Fines imposed by the *kiama* usually took the form of a ram (*ngoima*), which would be slaughtered and eaten by the elders of the council.[7] Sometimes, however, the fines would include compensation for whomever had won the litigation, in which case animals handed to the *kiama* would be passed on to the successful litigant. There seem to have been no fixed penalties for most crimes and both informants and officials complained that at times *ciama* imposed excessively heavy fines.[8] Perhaps this could be attributed to both the accused and the complainant each having to pay an *ngoima* fee, even where there was no case to answer, for having engaged the elders in the suit.[9] In any event, official discontent with the *ciama* eventually became so great that in 1924 they were proscribed.[10]

Official opposition to the kiama

While some administrative officials flatly denied that the squatters had any social control mechanisms at all, those who did acknowledge the existence of the *kiama* were highly critical of its deliberations and questioned its legitimacy. Farm *ciama* especially were regarded as wholly unconstitutional 'as . . . [were] their judgements',[11] but not, however, in the eyes of the squatters, 'the majority [of whom] expressed surprise when informed that such judgements were *ultra vires*.'[12] The administrative authorities opposed these *ciama* for two major reasons. In the first place, litigants' dissatisfaction with *ciama* decisions had resulted in administrative officers having to preside over a large number of civil suits. And secondly, *ciama* failed to address the aspects of squatter activity that caused most concern to settlers and colonial administrators alike. These included desertion, illegal squatting, uncontrolled cultivation and grazing, and the utilisation of forest reserves. Since the *ciama* made no attempt to curb these activities, the administration failed to see their utility.[13] They may also have felt the need to eliminate a rival hierarchy of authority in the Settled Areas.

In the place of *ciama*, the administration recommended the establishment of a travelling court made up of five respected Kikuyu from Kiambu, Muranga (Fort Hall) and Nyeri (the Kikuyu homelands) to operate in Nakuru, Naivasha and Rumuruti.[14] This officially-backed native tribal court, however, only materialised in the White Highlands in 1931. In the meanwhile, and even for a long time after the travelling courts were established, the *ciama* continued to operate to maintain peace and order amongst the Kikuyu. The officials of the new travelling court were empowered to deal with civil cases arising among the squatters and, apart from being set up on a formal basis, were very similar to the *ciama*.[15] They operated in rotation on the various farms in the Settled Areas, but in most cases, the local *ciama* continued to deal with the bulk of the disputes. Only if any of the people involved in the dispute disagreed with the *kiama*'s decision was the case filed with the nearest second class court or with one of these formal tribunals. In time they too became subject to official retribution, as more and more cases of bribery were brought against them.[16]

Had they been empowered to do so, the *ciama* might well have agreed to deal with administrative matters. In retrospect, however, it is just as well that they did not, especially since their success would have been measured against the extent to which they had helped the government to solve its problems with the squatters. Although government and *ciama* would inevitably have held conflicting views, from the government's point of view it would have made sense to have established a rapport with the *ciama* as a means of acquiring a better and more sympathetic understanding of the squatter phenomenon. That this was not allowed and that the *ciama* failed to develop into rallying centres for squatter grievances is one of the many historical contradictions of the squatter community. The government's suspicions about the efficiency of local *ciama* in the Settled Areas was therefore responsible for the formation of native tribunals in 1931.

Circumcision

Circumcision was another important Kikuyu custom that was transported wholesale to the Settled Areas. The practice, which marked the transition from childhood to adulthood, formed the basis of the Kikuyu age-grade system and was used to induct the initiates into the community's norms and mores.[17] In the Settled Areas, the surgery was usually performed on Sundays when the squatters were free from official duty. The majority of surgeons (known as *aruithia, muruithia* in the singular) were themselves contracted squatters, which meant that their presence in the Settled Areas was entirely legal. On 'retirement' from settler employment some of the older surgeons remained on settler farms with their relatives and continued to practise their profession.

On some farms it was necessary to receive written permission for the ceremony to take place[18] because a licence had to be obtained from the administrative officials for brewing traditional liquor. Once permission was granted by the settler, prospective initiates would be gathered from several neighbouring farms and assembled in a central homestead, where they would stay for eight days after circumcision. Several temporary huts (*iganda*) would be erected around the homestead to house the initiates, who might number anything between 30 and 80. Sometimes, the *iganda* were erected around the surgeon's homestead, if that was where the ceremony was to take place.[19]

Before squatter land became scarce, the prosperity of the community could be gauged from the amounts of foodstuff and traditional liquor that were prepared for the occasion, which was invariably much more lavish than its counterpart in Central Province. Likewise, the surgeon's fees were higher in the Settled Areas.[20] Two goats were paid for each initiate, one for the surgeon and one for the sponsor, and since the initiation was a vital part of the Kikuyu way of life, even in the Settled Areas, the job was highly lucrative.

In the previous chapter, we saw how the onset of the *kifagio* campaign resulted in an increase in bride-wealth as squatters sought to dispose of their livestock profitably. Because livestock were vital to most rites, rituals and transactions, these were disastrously undermined by the de-stocking campaign. As an ex-squatter explained, 'Kikuyu traditions began to die away with the extinction of the goats, because the traditions necessitated slaughtering [of livestock]. This was not possible in the absence of goats.'[21] By 1937, only one labourer per farm in Nakuru District was allowed to keep goats for selling to other squatters for various rituals and transactions.[22] Given the progressive impoverishment of the squatter community from the late 1920s, which became very much worse immediately after the Second World War, it was obvious that cultural activities among the squatters would be seriously affected. But, apart from cutting down on their festivities, the squatters had to make other adjustments to cope with their deteriorating economic strength. For example, the surgeon was increasingly paid in cash, partly because in this way he could avoid the burden of owning forbidden animals, but also because his clients possessed few or no livestock.

By continuing to perpetuate cultural practices reminiscent of life in Central Province, squatters brought a coherent structure to Kikuyu immigrant communities in the Settled Areas. Unlike other migrant labourers, the Kikuyu transported the whole socio-economic fabric of their indigenous society to the Settled Areas, where until the *kifagio* disturbances, they experienced no difficulty in carrying out their various rites and rituals. The ready availability of livestock, the central prerequisite for most of these ceremonies, meant that at some levels these cultural activities were even more extravagant than in Central Province.[23] The squatters adhered to a strict and elaborate socio-cultural framework originating from Central Province, which would seem to indicate that settler allegations of the Kikuyu in the Settled Areas being 'detribalised' and lawless people who knew no tribal restraints were based solely on colonial bias and ignorance.[24]

The struggle for education

Some pioneer squatters who moved to the White Highlands before 1918 had received at least minimal elementary education from missionary schools in Central Province.[25] In the Settled Areas, however, they encountered a situation in which for a long time neither missionaries, government, nor settlers had any plans for educating squatters. Ill-equipped and unprepared for the task, the squatters were forced to take it upon themselves to initiate an educational programme for their children. Although they were later on given some help by missionaries, this tended to be confined to supervision and evangelisation. The rest of this chapter will concentrate on how the squatters organised themselves to provide this education for their children. It will examine the problems they encountered from both the colonial administration and the settlers, how they coped with changing situations in the White Highlands, and how they sought to incorporate help from different bodies.

The racial structure of education in Kenya ensured that African education lagged behind that of the other races, namely the Europeans,

Asians and Arabs. Up to the mid-1930s, the various missionary groups that had established missions in Kenya were responsible for African education in the Reserves. The odds against which these missions had to operate, and the rudimentary nature of the education they offered, have already given rise to a fairly large body of writing.[26] But basically African education was neglected. The taxes collected from Africans were chanelled into the central government treasury, and the money was used to subsidise a transport, educational and social-services infrastructure which was being set up largely for the benefit of the white community. The government assumed that not only would the settlers develop a viable economy but for a long period they would also provide the country's ruling elite, for whom it was essential to provide the best education possible.

Where Africans were educated, it was with a view to producing a certain kind of manpower, such as junior clerks, clerical personnel, artisans and technicians, to service the colonial administration. Settlers needed semi-literate or semi-skilled Africans as clerks, farm overseers, carpenters, masons and fitters.[27] During the early colonial period, these jobs were filled by Asians, much to the displeasure of the settlers who argued that Asian labour was far too expensive. Advocating technical education for Africans was thus evoked by the need to obtain cheap labour, as well as to reduce the number of Asians in the country, who were posing a major threat to the European community by challenging its political and economic supremacy.

The African Reserves were comparatively better off because there, however rudimentary it may have been, education was at least introduced by the missions. But even here, the demand for education far outstripped what the missionaries could provide and once Local Native Councils were established in the Reserves in 1924, they too contributed money for educational purposes. Later the government also contributed to education in the African Reserves, but initially only in the form of grants. Until the mid-1930s, however, missionary bodies, including among others the Church of Scotland Mission, the Church Missionary Society and the White Fathers, had a monopoly over the provision of education. But this would soon change.[28]

KISA and Karinga schools

The Karinga school movement and the Kikuyu Independent Schools Association (KISA) grew up as a reaction against mission control over formal education in general, but especially against the missionaries' onslaught on Kikuyu traditions.[29] The centre of the controversy was over the issue of female circumcision (clitoridectomy), which the missionaries condemned and which they forbade their adherents, both church members and pupils, to undergo. Breakaway churches and movements like KISA and Karinga then set up their own independent schools, which were organised on a self-help basis. Between them, the two groups managed to establish several schools in Kikuyuland.[30]

Although both groups had political overtones, the Karinga movement, which was started in the more politically conscious Southern Kiambu, was more radical in its outlook, combining purely educational matters with political issues such as land alienation and population pressure in Southern Kiambu.[31] As Rosberg and Nottingham point out, the Karinga movement was widespread, extending its school network to 'the various colonies of the Kikuyu dispersion . . . in the forest villages in the Rift Valley farms, in Kisii and Kipsigis in the West, in Moshi and Arusha in Northern Tanganyika and at the Olenguruone Settlement'.[32] With its spiritual centre in Southern and Western Kiambu, the Karinga movement was able to make a complete break with the mission.[33]

KISA operated largely in Northern Kiambu, Fort Hall and Nyeri districts, where land grievances were less acute than in Southern Kiambu. Being more concerned with educational and religious matters,[34] KISA had tried to collaborate with the missions in the baptism and ordination of its followers, but in the absence of such support, affiliated to the South African based African Orthodox Church and proceeded to oversee the welfare of the various KISA schools.[35]

Neither KISA nor the Karinga movement evolved a formal or protracted strategy over the years to establish control over or to organise schools in the Settled Areas. Individuals conversant with the ideology of the groups within Central Province merely moved to the Settled Areas and injected the spirit into the squatters. Although some contact was maintained between the leaders of the Karinga schools in Central Province and people selling its ideas in the Settled Areas, there is, however, no evidence of any outright control of schools in the Settled Areas by Karinga school proponents from Central Province. Since the movement 'flourished among those who lived on the rough edge of Kenya's racial frontiers',[36] this perhaps explains the establishment and ready acceptance of an education strategy of self-reliance in the Rift Valley Settled Areas.

Over and above its administrative problems, the Karinga movement was also without any regular source of finance, so that its impact on the squatters was reduced to that of instilling in them the importance of self-reliance and diligence in establishing schools. Although their ideology was warmly received in the Settled Areas, it would be presumptuous to assert that the evolution of squatter schools was solely the product of the Kikuyu Karinga movement in the Settled Areas, for

KISA was also important in motivating the squatters. It should, moreover, be borne in mind that the squatters' involvement in providing schools for their children predated both the KISA and Karinga movements, which only really developed after the 1929 clitoridectomy crisis.

Self-help among squatters: the quest for education

The socio-economic milieu in which it had to operate was the single most crippling impediment to squatter education. Or, to put it more crudely, the question of educating squatter children revolved around the labour needs of the settlers. Where it appeared that the demand for education would in any way jeopardise the supply of child labour to the settler economy, education would have to take second place. Juvenile labour was particularly vulnerable in coffee, tea and pyrethrum growing areas where the peak harvest periods called for a lot of labour. At such times, the children provided an abundant and cheap supply, but at other times throughout the year they also performed all manner of odd jobs on settler farms as kitchen hands, herdsboys or just as *totos* (children) working alongside their parents.[37]

In some instances, having children of an employable age was a precondition for the squatter's own employment[38] and, on farms where child labour was vital, preference was definitely given to prospective squatters with 'employable' children, as opposed to those who were single or had very young families.[39] The extent to which child labour was utilised is borne out in the special District Labour Census of the Nakuru-Naivasha-Ravine District, which is reproduced in table 3.1.

TABLE 3.1: *Natives Employed in District*

Registered Natives	Watoto (children)	Resident Squatters	Working Squatters
33,206	8,932	11,473	9,392

Daily Paid Casuals		
Men	Women	Children
329	1,367	928

Source: KNA: Nakuru-Naivasha-Ravine District Annual Report, 1943, p. 10.

Earlier, the 1928 agricultural census gave the number of children employed on farms as 17,300, and their rate of pay as six to seven shillings per month.[40]

To ensure that their children went to school, some squatters sought employment on farms where the settler owners allowed them to run schools. In time, the settlers began to realise that the presence of a school on the farm was in itself an inducement to labourers.[41] As a result, even in areas where child labour was needed, some settlers struck a compromise by allowing schools to be established on their farms, provided they did not interfere with labour demands. School was therefore held either in the afternoons after the children had worked on the settler farms, or in the evenings after the squatters and their children had retired from work and had had a rest. On some farms, classes were held in the mornings or at weekends, when labour demands were minimal. But whatever the arrangements, they were never exactly conducive to learning.

Squatters had to have the European landowner's permission before they could build a school on a farm. In the early days, the settler more often than not refused to grant this permission on the grounds that the school would draw away necessary labour. Once permission was granted, the squatters would pool their resources to put up the school building, which was usually a mud and grass structure and always badly lit. Apart from putting up the school, the community self-help group (*muingi*) was also responsible for the teacher's salary.[42] But, if a settler was sympathetic, he would give financial and other aid to the school project[43] and, at times, might even go a step further and conduct some of the classes himself. His wife too might give formal or other instruction like child care, cookery or general hygiene.

Under normal circumstances, the squatters hired the services of an African teacher,[44] whose educational achievements mostly amounted to less than five years of formal education, usually in Central Province. What this meant then was that, at best, the pupils were given only a very bare introduction to the three Rs (reading, writing and arithmetic), beyond which the teachers were incapable of progressing. The act of charity on the part of the settlers in offering to teach in some of these schools is indicative of the haphazard nature of squatter education. In the absence of any centralised and clearly defined educational curriculum for African children, it is difficult to quantify, or even evaluate the quality of this settler teaching, other than to assume that, in so far as they came from a wide range of backgrounds, standards among settler teachers varied considerably. What is clear, however, is that the education of squatter children remained rudimentary for a very long time.[45]

Lord Francis Scott allowed his squatters to establish a school on his farm in Rongai, Deloraine Estate, where Mararo Ngendo was engaged on 20 March 1928, primarily as a clerk, but also to teach the squatter children in the evenings. His salary was 45 shillings per month, plus an additional five shillings per month for his teaching services. Lord Francis Scott was in no doubt about where his priorities lay: 'Mararo is engaged by me as a *karani* [clerk] . . . It is clearly understood that the teaching part is in no way to interfere with farm work.'[46] The school hours were stipulated as follows:

Wednesdays 4.30 p. m. to 5.30 p. m.
Saturdays   3.00 p. m. to 5.30 p. m.
Sundays   9.00 a.m. to 11.00 a.m.[47]

Clearly teaching was seen as a sideline in Mararo's job, especially since some of his pupils were employed as *toto* workers and could only attend classes when they were given time off from work.

In Nakuru District, most schools catering for squatter children were located in the Forest Reserves, where pupils were not required to work[48] and where the Forest authorities were better disposed towards squatter education. But in the Turi and Molo area, where the introduction of pyrethrum coincided with the *kifagio* campaign, the squatters perceived the elimination of their stock as an attempt to impoverish and subordinate them to settler capital and as a strategy for appropriating child labour. One of the respondents, Ernest Kiberethi Kanyanja, spoke of how 'Europeans began to count the animals [squatter livestock] because they had planted flowers [pyrethrum] and the children who were grazing [squatter stock] were expected to avail themselves for labour [to pick pyrethrum]'.[49] Similar sentiments were recalled by Karanja Kamau, who said that:

> Keringet people did not put up a school until 1938 when the European agreed [gave permission]. He had refused because the school would take away the workers [children] from him. So we took our children to Maigoya school in Molo Forest. Most of the schools were in the Forest [Reserves] because there was no pyrethrum there [for the children to pick].[50]

Keringet was a pyrethrum growing area and the demand for child labour there was high, especially during the picking season. Squatters who sent their children to Forest schools rather than have them work for the settlers did so at the risk of losing their jobs.[51] On some farms these juvenile workers were not even on the payroll, but merely 'went to help their parents'.[52] Where school hours clashed with working hours, settlers often allowed some of the children to attend classes while the rest worked on the farms.[53]

Because of the many problems they faced, squatter progress in the educational field was rather slow. The few schools that did exist did so unofficially and usually provided a largely inadequate education. This was reflected in the 1930 Native Affairs report, which noted that 'a few squatter farms have unofficial schools, the squatter children being taught by a native teacher, generally a squatter, who has been instructed by a mission'. But even more revealing was the observation by the Director of Education who, almost a decade later, stated *inter alia* that:

> Up to the present, practically nothing has been done for the education of natives in the White Highlands. There are a few isolated schools run by the church side of societies, but government neither gives nor provides schools. The whole question deserves serious consideration. The situation being as it is, it seems difficult to deprive natives of a chance of some education, more especially when schools are self-supporting, unless of course the schools are conducted in such a manner which is likely to be detrimental to the physical, mental or moral welfare of the pupils.[54]

Even the isolated mission schools referred to by the Director were financed and operated by the squatters themselves.

Kikuyu Private Schools Association

The spread of private schools among the squatters in the White Highlands has to be viewed within the context of education's subordination to the settler economy. In addition, the situation was compounded by a colonial administration that was unwilling to finance or develop squatter education while simultaneously demanding high standards as a prerequisite for the schools' operation. At the same time, the government was concerned to prevent the setting up of private schools from being combined with political activities, as had been the case in Central Province. The struggle for schools in the Settled Areas was made more difficult by the presence of missionaries who claimed control over schools in certain areas and who were used by the government to vet Kikuyu educational ventures. This intricate interplay of forces was evident in the struggle of the Kikuyu Private Schools Association (KPSA) to provide schools for squatter children in Nakuru District in the 1930s.

Richard Kamau Njuguna, who was the man behind KPSA, became locked in a fierce battle with the Department of Education as he sought authority to continue a number of schools he had established for squatter children on the settler farms and in the urban townships of Nakuru District. The government had ordered some of these schools to be closed down and those still in operation were also threatened with closure. The fairly detailed exposition of what followed is an attempt to provide some insight into further squatter struggles and the government's position *vis-avis* squatter education.

The major bone of contention was over the government's conviction that it would be futile to give the go-ahead to schools in any way connected with the KISA or Karinga movement, because the standard of education they offered was so abysmally low. The Director of Education had drawn up certain stipulations to increase the efficiency of these schools in Central Province, but since these requirements were being only 'tardily met' he was reluctant to allow any new schools in either the Settled Areas or Central Province until such time as he was satisfied with schools in Central Province.[55]

In 1937, Richard K. Njuguna eventually met the Director of Education and managed to convince him that the schools he was organising were in no way connected with either the KISA or the Karinga schools but were his own private venture. For his organisational services, Njuguna was paid 60 shillings per month by a squatters' educational committee, to which each member paid a 10 shilling subscription fee. The committee was composed of 56 members, the bulk of whom came from the Elburgon area, which worked out at an average of five members from each school.

While the Director argued that it would be easy to close any private schools sited on Crown Land, he expressed anxiety as to what would happen to schools situated on settler land and operated with settler consent. This revealed a major flaw in the administration's attitude towards squatter education. The government's insistence on certain standards as a basis for allowing schools to operate in the Settled Areas was anachronistic.

Since neither the government nor the missionaries offered squatter teaching personnel any supervisory or training facilities, it was ridiculous for the government to insist on teachers attaining a particular standard. Basically, the situation was that, although the government failed to provide schools for the squatters, it insisted that, unless the squatters could produce an efficient educational infrastructure of their own, the government would close down the schools they had established. But quite apart from the squatters' hunger for education, the schools had become integrated into the settler economy and even the Director of Education had to acknowledge that the provision of schools on farms attracted labour. He thought it 'would be unfortunate if the farmers concerned objected to the closure [of these schools] because an embarrassing situation would arise'.[56]

The schools in question were Ndothua, Chowa, Marioshoni, Kirangi and Visoi, all of which were in the vicinity of Elburgon. It was eventually decided that the registration of these schools would be dependent on the report of a government officer upon inspection. But in the event, the report came, not from a government officer, but from the Reverend R. G. M. Calderwood from the Church of Scotland Mission in Kikuyuland.

Calderwood made a tour of Western Nakuru District where his church was involved in educating Africans, or more specifically, Kikuyu squatters. Before examining his comments and recommendations, it is as well to remember that the missionaries were every bit as wary and conservative as the settlers and administrators about the wisdom of educating Africans. Most, if not all, missionary groups subscribed to the notion that formal education could be dangerous for Africans and that technical or industrial education provided a better and more practical alternative. It is hardly surprising, therefore, that Reverend R. G. M. Calderwood's report revealed an aggressive compulsion by the missions to control education in the country.

Calderwood reported that Njuguna probably only controlled the schools at Marioshoni and Chowa and had yet to gain control of the other schools. He then went on further to discredit Njuguna's endeavours by saying that he appeared to be on a money-making venture and that he (Calderwood) was extremely doubtful that Njuguna had anything 'to offer in the way of schools'. Calderwood also doubted that the owners on whose land the schools were erected had agreed to what was happening or to what was projected for the future. Calderwood considered the schools of such little significance that he recommended the hire of an African subinspector of schools to operate on a bicycle, 'as the time required and the distance to be travelled by a European in a car would be out of proportion to the matter under consideration'.[57]

Njuguna had purchased a plot (number 14) in Elburgon from an Asian and was hopeful that the administration would register this shop, which he considered suitable for a school. In the letter below, Njuguna was appealing on behalf of pupils who were being denied classes because their school in Elburgon had been closed down. There were between 50 and 53 children from the Forest Reserve, 73 from European farms, and 93 from the township, making a total of 213 pupils. In attempting to gain the Director of Education's support, in a rather pathetic plea, Njuguna stressed how his school upheld the government's commitment to creating loyal citizens:

> The schools to all nations is only to control them in good character and to grow in knowledge and health; *and to make them better to know how their masters wants them to do in good order, and to obey their masters too, especially to the government*, please excuse me for trouble.[58]

It is improbable that Njuguna envisaged an educational system that would produce subservient Africans, but possibly he adopted a seemingly collaborative stand to allay the administration's fears and consequent restrictions on African education. But the curt manner in which the District Commissioner replied to Njuguna's plea was hardly encouraging. He wrote, 'The P.C. has decided that your school at Elburgon Township shall not be registered' and that 'no question of transferring it to Njoro Township therefore arises. The school is definitely closed'.[59] The decision was also confirmed by the Acting Director of Education. As a final blow, Njuguna was warned that 'the question of educating African children in the Rift Valley Province- . . .[was] now under consideration'[60] and that in the meantime he was forbidden to open any schools in Njoro. This was in 1938, approximately 30 years after the Kikuyu squatters had first settled in the White Highlands, and the administration was obviously still totally unconcerned about the immediate needs of the pupils.

Among those entrusted with the new scheme for squatter education were the District Commissioner in Nakuru District, the Provincial Commissioner in the Rift Valley, and the Acting Director of Education. Under the guidance of the latter, it was decided that a report on African education would be submitted for scrutiny to the government which would, in turn, subsidise approved schools in the Forest Reserves and on European farms. The teachers for the schools would, in the first instance, be appointed by the Forest officer-in-charge or by the European settler on whose land the school was situated. In both cases, the teacher would have to be approved by the Education Department. It was the Director's firm decision that, pending the introduction of the above scheme, it would be unwise to register or approve any private schools for Africans in the Settled Areas. The government had thus failed to adopt a positive attitude toward squatter education. While its involvement in squatter education remained confined to imposing restrictive measures, it emerged more committed than ever to stifling even the most basic of squatter initiatives to provide education for their children.

The missions

The Church of Scotland Mission (CSM) was the only group to profess a positive interest in educating squatter children in the White Highlands, and it too had its own crippling limitations. For a start, the mission's impecuniosity restricted its involvement in squatter education to supervising and training teachers in Central Province and then encouraging them to go and teach in the Settled Areas.

When the mission first became involved in the Settled Areas in 1928, its missionaries were forbidden to use mission funds to subsidise education in the area, 'owing to the pressing needs of our educational work in the Reserve'.[61] The Rift Valley was therefore not only bypassed by the government, but also by the mission's budget. The CSM was 'in contact' with a number of schools in Elburgon, Molo, Lumbwa, Kericho, Kaptagat, Subukia Valley, Thompson's Falls, Rumuruti, Nanyuki, Naro Moru and Ngobit. In all these schools, the local people, i.e. the squatters, paid the teachers' salaries, although in a few cases the settler made a contribution as well.[62] But there were no cases of teachers' salaries being paid by the missions. The CSM's strongest asset was that, unlike other missions which used Swahili as their medium of instruction in the hope of appealing to people from all ethnic groups, CSM missionaries used the Kikuyu language (*Gigikuyu*) and concerned themselves only with Kikuyu people. An appreciable number of forest and farm clerks, and some farm overseers, were among former CSM boys who sought help, spiritual and otherwise, from the CSM.[63]

The CSM hoped to combine evangelical and educational work in the Settled Areas. Its church work in Nakuru was supported by the African church in Kikuyu, which financed and met the travelling expenses of two full-time workers (pastors). Its finances were also supplemented by church offerings collected in the Settled Areas. The CSM, whose operational headquarters were located in Tumu Tumu in Central Province, supervised various categories of schools, including sub-elementary, elementary and adult night-schools, which catered for forest squatters in the Forest Reserves and for labour at the timber concessions. The missions also supervised schools in townships and on privately owned land.

In the Nakuru region, where the greatest number of Kikuyu squatters lived, most of the schools were located in the Forest Reserves, especially in the Elburgon area. Although there were no specific school plots with definite boundaries, a typical school with a mission 'connection' had certain physical characteristics, including three houses, of which one was for two teachers to share, one was for a female evangelist and the other for an ordained pastor. One of the schools in Elburgon had 132 pupils on its roll and it was a sad testament to African education in the Settled Areas that the two teachers in this school were both unqualified. One had reached the educational level of 'Standard Six', while the other was a 'Standard Three' drop-out, and yet they were in charge of a 'class three' group of pupils ready for examination for entry into primary school. A pointer to the contradictions and disregard surrounding squatter education was that Calderwood expressed the opinion that the work being done by these teachers was of good quality.[64]

The KPSA (Njuguna's venture) and the CSM (represented by Calderwood) competed with one another for land, registration, teachers, and the general control of a given area. In 1937, a dispute arose over one of the two sub-elementary schools operating in the Elburgon area (in Gicagi and Ndothua respectively), with both the KPSA and the CSM claiming authority over the school in Ndothua. In a school at a Mr Hoddinott's timber mill in Elburgon, the headman of the mill expelled the teacher (possibly a mission adherent) and installed a KPSA man without informing the European manager 'of any change of religion'.[65] The inference here was that the two camps were equivalent to two mutually repellent religious and ideological poles. Twenty-five adherents of the CSM appealed for the return of their building, denouncing the KPSA's usurpation of the CSM school. Even in the Settled Areas, divisions created among Africans by the mission, both over doctrine and over the control of schools, were evident.

The mission had resident evangelists in most places, who superintended religious work both at schools and in the surrounding areas. The Kikuyu who were employed in small numbers as dressers and clerks on the Kericho Tea Estates did not set up schools of their own, as the African Inland Mission (AIM) and the Church Missionary Society (CMS) already provided them for the Kisii, Kipsigis and Luo labourers. While in the Forest Reserves the missions and squatters were tenants-at-will of the Forest Officer, on the farms the control of schools lay with the settler landowner.

Like the government, the missions were averse to the independent schools movement. Calderwood claimed that the KPSA was just a name adopted by Njuguna to allay the suspicions of European farmers. He alleged that in reality the followers of the KPSA were supporters of the Karinga schools. Whether the two movements were in any way connected is not evident, or even relevant. One thing that is clear, however, is that the KPSA does not seem to have had any overt political interests. It was mainly concerned with providing schools for squatter children and, in that it lacked the kind of 'arrogance' and outspokenness that characterised the Karinga schools, it never gave rise to any obvious political grievances. It is perhaps because of the apolitical context of its endeavours that Calderwood condemned the KPSA as a mediocre scheme where 'probably the main objective of the likes of R. Njuguna and the priests of the new churches is to earn a living', going on to say that 'running schools and churches on a Pan-African basis and boasting of no European interference proves quite a profitable business'.[66] Calderwood anticipated that the movement would provide a focus for stirring up trouble generally and locally, whenever an excuse offered itself, but there is no record of this ever happening.

The African Orthodox Independent Church was also active in the

Settled Areas, where it provided a combination of evangelisation and modest instruction. But the 'Protestant' nature of this breakaway Church, which had its main body of Kenyan support in Kiambu, worried administrators and missionaries alike, and gave rise to wild accusations about the harm that this church as well as the KPSA were likely to cause. The CSM was engaged in a battle to control education in the Settled Areas, as in Central Province, and openly sought to incriminate its rivals. Despite its quite considerable financial difficulties, the mission felt confident that the government would give it the virtual monopoly to run schools in the Settled Areas.

Dr Calderwood was, however, quick to castigate the racial bias in the government's educational 'policy' and, by citing the squatters' plight, emphasised that, as taxpayers, they had just as much entitlement to some help 'as the people in the Reserves'. Thus, in 1937, 'native' education was unsatisfactory in the Reserves and disastrous in the Settled Areas. Although the squatters were making genuine voluntary efforts and sacrifices to set up schools, the hostility they confronted in the Settled Areas ensured that their efforts were wasted. Reverend Calderwood therefore felt that the situation was wholly unsatisfactory and suggested several improvements.

Among these was the recommendation that grants-in-aid be introduced for elementary schools that, on inspection, showed satisfactory progress. He also recommended that the services of African subinspectors and teachers from Jeanes School be extended to schools in the Settled Areas.[67] In a climate of mission control, it is hardly surprising that Calderwood also thought it necessary for the KPSA schools to be scrutinised for the verification of their existence and legitimacy. To this end, he advocated lobbying any European landowners who employed Kikuyu squatters and provided schools, for he wanted them to be informed that 'it would be wise to affiliate their schools with some mission or other, and avoid the danger of the Independent Movement gaining a footing'. It appeared that Calderwood's mind had been made up – the KPSA was potentially dangerous politically and the sooner it was quashed the better.

Squatter education was so bleak that Calderwood felt it would take many years before standards of efficiency could be enforced. The immediate problem was to get the Department of Education involved in financing and administering the schools in the White Highlands. Calderwood argued that night-schools and adult classes should be considered as social services that could be left in the hands of missions and landowners. Work for children, however, did have a claim on the Department and on Central State revenues. On the question of manpower, Calderwood suggested that such elementary teacher training centres as Tumu Tumu might offer to train a few teachers while in-service courses of two to three weeks' duration would be arranged by the missions through the Education Department.

Nothing specific was said about what kind of education the Africans should acquire, but Calderwood did mention in passing that Forest Officers might be appealed to, not only to put up with the day schools, but to take an active interest in them and 'use them to try and inculcate into the young Kikuyu better ideas about forests and their value and to teach them the proper methods of farming and caring for trees'.[68] Although Calderwood mentioned that his views should in no way be taken as representing those of the CSM, he lobbied for the mission in such a way as to make it difficult to distinguish between his opinions and the mission's interests. He openly condemned the KPSA and recommended a mission takeover in its place. He then went even further and defined solutions to the educational crisis which the CSM, the Educational Department, the forest authorities and the white settlers were supposed to implement. Calderwood thus became the CSM's main representative.

After the Second World War, it became apparent that the need to provide educational facilities for African children in the white Settled Areas was high on the list of government priorities, but that a lack of qualified teachers held up progress in this direction.[69] At the same time, it was considered necessary for squatters in the Settled Areas to pay rates comparable to those that the Africans in the Reserves paid to the Local Native Councils, for the money thus raised could finance education for squatters' children.[70] It was argued that, since District Councils had no African representatives, it would be constitutionally wrong for them to levy taxes on Africans, or even to administer services financed mainly by Africans. Hence it was necessary for School Area Committees to be set up in the Settled Areas and towns, with government, local authority, missionary and African community representatives overseeing the provision of education for Africans. District Councils could help by advising on the licensing and control of schools and possibly by holding land on which schools serving a number of farms could be built. Otherwise, it was generally agreed, services offered for Africans in the White Highlands would fall far behind those that the Local Native Councils offered in the Reserves.[71]

Colonel Michael Blundell's observation that 'what is happening now is that any African with intelligence is sending his children to be educated in the Native Lands Unit'[72] was a modest summary of the situation. Blundell felt that the District Councils, together with the Central Government, should provide educational and other services for Africans in the White Highlands. He hoped that a challenge from the District Councils to the effect that the 'government should accept the responsibility which I think it has failed to accept'[73] would elicit positive action from the government.

Some settlers were opposed to the idea of having to pay rates for the benefit of Africans. But, in saying that 'what we should aim at is for District Councils to have control of Africans in the White Highlands by providing services for them',[74] Colonel Blundell, who had made the proposal, really had the settlers' political interests at heart. He entreated the Europeans in the White Highlands not to let the issue get obscured by racial issues because, as he put it, 'there is a political responsibility on yourselves to see that Africans do not grow prey to communism', which is more likely to happen to those living 'in a slum area' than to 'their fellow Africans in the Native Land Units'.[75] Blundell's concern appeared to have been to reinforce the subservient status of squatters through controlled social services, including an educational infrastructure.

The main purpose of this chapter has been to show how, through social organisation, Kikuyu squatters safeguarded the fabric of their community and endeavoured to provide education for their children. But, it should be remembered that, in both objectives, the squatters were consistently thwarted by both the settler community and the colonial government. The changing balance of the settler economy demanded extensive squatter de-stocking, which had adverse effects not only on the squatter economy but also on their social and cultural organisation. Their attempts to provide education for their children were variously criticised and vetoed by a government that gave them no financial help, yet wanted to ensure that their educational undertakings were politically neutral. They also faced opposition from the missions, but, despite all these drawbacks, the squatters were determined to make their stay in the White Highlands more bearable.

Notes

1. KNA, DC NVA 4/1, East Africa Protectorate Confidential Memorandum for PCs and DCs 'Native Policy Outside Native Reserves', EPC Girouard, Governor, 18 May 1910.
2. Interview, Karanja Kamau, 21 October 1976, Nakuru.
3. ibid.
4. Interview, Gitau Gathukia, 16 September 1976, Njoro.
5. Interview, Solomon Muchangi, 16 September 1976, Njoro.
6. ibid.
7. ibid. and Muta Njuhiga, 1 November 1976, Bahati.
8. Interview, Kihiko Mwega, 25 October 1976, Nakuru.
9. Interviews, Gachago Kagere, 28 October 1976, Nakuru, and Kishike Mugwega, 25 October 1976, Nakuru.

10. KNA, Naivasha District Annual Report, 1924, p. 3.
11. KNA, Naivasha District Annual Report, 1926, p. 4.
12. ibid., p. 5.
13. KNA, Naivasha District Annual Report, 1922, Special Report, p. 2.
14. KNA, Naivasha District Annual Report, 1924, p. 3.
15. Interview, Kihiko Mwega, 25 October 1976, Nakuru.
16. KNA, Naivasha District Annual Report, 1933, p. 5. See also Nakuru-Naivasha District Annual Report, 1935, p. 11.
17. See Kenyatta, J., *Facing Mount Kenya*, Nairobo, Heinemann Educational Books, 1971, p. 2.
18. Interview, Maria Wanjiku, 18 October 1976, Nakuru.
19. Interview, Karanja Kamau, 21 October 1976, Nakuru.
20. Interview, Kihiko Mwega, 25 October 1976, Nakuru, and Gacheru Manja, 4 October 1976, Elburgon.
21. Interview, Gachago Kagere, 28 October 1976, Nakuru.
22. KNA, Native Affairs Department, Annual Report, 1937, p. 208.
23. Interview, Shuranga Wegunyi, 25 October 1976, Nakuru.
24. See KNA, Native Affairs Department, Annual Report, 1926, p. 8.
25. Interview, Arphaxad Kiiru Kuria, 21 September 1976, Elburgon.
26. Anderson, J. *The Struggle for the School*, London, Longman, 1970. See also Sifuna, D. N., *Vocational Education in Schools: A Historical Survey of Kenya and Tanzania*, Nairobi, EALB, 1976; *Revolution in Primary Education: The New Approach in Kenya*, Nairobi, EALB, 1975; King, K. J., *Pan Africanism and Education in the Southern States of America and East Africa*, Oxford, Clarendon Press, 1971.
27. See Sifuna, D. N., 'European Settlers as a Factor Influencing Government Policy and Practice in African Education in Kenya 1900–1963', *Kenya Historical Review*, Vol. 4, No. 1, 1976, pp. 63–83.
28. See Rosberg, C. and Nottingham, J., *The Myth of Mau Mau: Nationalism in Kenya*, Nairobi: EAPH, 1966, p. 127.
29. ibid., pp. 125–6.
30. ibid., p. 126. See also Ndungu, J. B., 'Gituamba and Kikuyu Independency in Church and Schools' in McIntosh, B. G. (ed.), *Ngano*, Nairobi, EAPH, 1969, pp. 131–50.
31. Rosberg and Nottingham, *Myth of Mau Mau*, p. 131.
32. ibid., p. 126.
33. ibid.
34. ibid., p. 130.
35. While acknowledging the support of the African Orthodox Church, the KISA also formed its own church, the African Independent Pentecostal Church see Rosberg and Nottingham, *Myth of Mau Mau*, p. 130.
36. Rosberg and Nottingham, *Myth of Mau Mau*, p. 131.
37. Interview, Karanja Kamau, 21 October 1976, Nakuru.
38. Earlier references to child labour are to be found in the Native Labour Commission Report, 1912–1913.
39. Interview, Karanja Kamau, 21 October 1976, Nakuru.
40. KNA, Native Affairs Department, Annual Report, 1927, p. 100.
41. KNA, Nakuru-Naivasha-Ravine District Annual Report, 1938, p. 38.
42. Interviews, Mithanga Kanyumba, 14 September 1976, Molo, and Nganga Karanja Koinange, 16 September 1976, Njoro.

43. Interview Nganga Karanja Koinange, 16 September 1976, Njoro.

44. Interviews, Nganga Githiomi, 2 October 1976, Rongai, and Gacheru Manja, 4 October 1976, Elburgon.

45. A European inspector of farm schools visited the district and advised some farmers on the management of their schools. Where possible the Department of Education provided the syllabus, but the supply of qualified teachers was lamentably inadequate. See KNA, Nakuru-Naivasha-Ravine District Annual Report, 1938, p. 38.

46. RH, Lord Francis Scott Papers, Microfilm Reel 15, p. 335.

47. ibid.

48. Interview, Wilson Mwangi Njau, 13 October 1976, Elburgon.

49. Interview, Ernest Kiberethi Kanyanja, 13 October 1976, Elburgon.

50. Interview, Karanja Kamau, 21 October 1976, Nakuru.

51. Interview, Ngushu Kamara, 17 September 1976, Njoro.

52. Interview, Ernest Kiberethi Kanyanja, 13 October 1976, Elburgon.

53. Interview, Wilson Mwangi Njau, 13 October 1976, Elburgon. See also KNA, PC RVP 6A/12/11, 'Report on a visit by Reverend R. G. M. Calderwood to Schools above Nakuru which Maintain a Connection of Some Kind with the Church of Scotland Mission', 1–10 November 1937, which observed that 'the children who helped their parents picking pyrethrum get schooling in the afternoon'.

54. KNA, PC RVP 6A/12/11, Director of Education to PC, RVP, Nakuru, 'Kikuyu Private Schools', 19 October 1937.

55. See KNA, PC RVP 6A/12/11, Director of Education to PC, RVP, Nakuru, 'Kikuyu Private Schools', 19 October 1937. See also ibid., Head Education Department to PC RVP, 19 October 1937. Kikuyu Private Schools.

56. KNA, PC RVP 6A/12/11, Director of Education to PC RVP, Nakuru, 'Kikuyu Private Schools', 19 October 1937.

57. KNA, PC RVP 6A/12/11, 'Report on a Visit by Reverend R. G. M. Calderwood . . .', 1–10 November 1937.

58. KNA, PC RVP 6A/12/11, Richard K. Njuguna to PC RVP, 15 January 1938. Emphasis added.

59. KNA, PC RVP 6A/12/11, Director of Education to Richard K. Njuguna, 18 January 1938.

60. KNA, PC RVP 6A/12/11, Director of Education to Richard K. Njuguna, 2 February 1938.

61. KNA, PC RVP 6A/12/11, 'Report on a Visit by Reverend R. G. M. Calderwood . . .', 1–10 November 1937.

62. Interview, Karanja Kamau, 21 October 1976, Nakuru.

63. KNA, PC RVP 6A/12/11, 'Report on a Visit by Reverend R. G. M. Calderwood . . .', 1–10 November 1937.

64. ibid. One of the two teachers, the Standard Three one, was in effect no more educated than the Standard Three pupils in his school. He had only had elementary schooling and no primary school education.

65. ibid.

66. ibid.

67. For the origins and development of Jeanes School, see Anderson, *Struggle for the School*, pp. 20–1, 26, 39, 60, 126, 133, 135 and 142.

68. KNA, PC RVP 6A/12/11, 'Report on a Visit by Reverend R. G. M. Calderwood . . .', 1–10 November 1937.
69. KNA, Deposit 2/401, Local Government, District Councils 1948–1950.
70. ibid.
71. KNA, Deposit 2/401, Local Government, District Councils, 1948–1950, Report on District Council Development.
72. KNA, Deposit 2/401, Local Government, District Councils 1948–1950, 9th Annual Conference of District Council Representatives held in the Council Chamber of the New District Council Offices, 20 October 1948.
73. ibid.
74. ibid.
75. ibid.

Four

The Crisis:
Decline in Squatter Welfare
1938–48

The resident native labourer may be the mainstay of the farm, but he does not always prove an asset, except as providing a cheap source of labour at the expense of the fertility of the land.[1]

We have been sending several letters of similar kind to the government but this we hope will be the last one with the fullest confidence that it will save us from the slavery of the Rift Valley government. We do strongly oppose to remain under this slavery in the white Settled Areas. Counting from 1939 to 1946 we have been struggling sending our govert [sic.] the expression of our difficulties and asking to be released from them. We hope the government will put an end of it and change the present state of deep sorrow to exotic joy.[2]

By the late 1920s it had become clear that the active and autonomous role squatters played in the White Highlands was completely incompatible with the white settlers' economic and political interests. Consequently, the settlers had begun to implement various measures to restrain squatter cultivation and grazing. For the squatters, these measures brought insecurity, blackmail and economic degeneration. What had happened to them before the beginning of the Second World War was negligible compared to what was to come in the post-war period, when the settlers enforced stringent measures which totally destroyed any independence the squatters might previously have enjoyed in the White Highlands.

The period between 1938 and 1948 became the turning point for squatter welfare both inside and outside the White Highlands. Anti-squatter feelings, which raged high among European settlers, fuelled the introduction of ill-conceived and unimaginative measures, which were highly disruptive to the squatter community. Although vulnerable and unrepresented, the squatters grew in strength, especially in the period between 1939 and 1947, and refused to take the onslaught lying down.[3] This was borne out when the Department of Labour failed to force the squatters to sign the new labour contracts. Squatter resistance was embodied in the mass public defiance of regulations surrounding the white elephant of the era, the Olenguruone scheme. In the time between the enactment of the 1937 RNLO and 1952, the government had to contend with ever increasing acts of organised defiance, which took the form of labour strikes, labour withdrawal, violence and sabotage, and which culminated in the Mau Mau uprising. But before looking at these, let us first turn to the 1937 Act.

The 1937 Resident Native Labourers Ordinance: provisions and implications

In contrast to the somewhat haphazard measures of earlier Acts, the 1937 RNLO provided the legal basis for a much more rigorous and vicious form of squatter control by the settlers. With the administration of matters relating to the squatter community being passed from the central government to settler-controlled District Councils, the Ordinance gave the European settlers powers to limit the number of acres under squatter cultivation, to eliminate squatter stock and to increase the number of working days from 180 to 240 and then to 270 days per year.[4] It also emphasised that squatters were not tenants and that their right to remain in the White Highlands lasted only so long as they worked for a settler. District Councils were given the local option to deal with specific conditions in their areas. Further agreements could be made under the Ordinance, depending on the special conditions obtaining in a particular area, but even more important than this was that squatters could be evicted if they rejected the above conditions or if they were declared redundant.

The Secretary of State insisted that implementation of the Ordinance should be delayed until land was found for those who were going to be evicted. But despite this period of reprieve during which squatters continued to pursue the peasant option in the White Highlands, some settlers proceeded to impose drastic measures to restrict squatter cultivation and to reduce the squatters' stock.[5] The war, however, gave the squatters an additional period of grace during which they increased their agricultural production and took advantage of the better wartime prices, the settlers' energies being concentrated on the war effort. In the Naivasha area, which was predominantly a stock industry region, the settlers did not hesitate to implement immediate and exceedingly harsh regulations relating to the reduction of squatter livestock. But even here squatter incomes, which averaged between £40 and £140 per annum, compared favourably with the incomes of Kikuyu households in Central Province. These incomes were derived mainly from crop and livestock sales, with wages comprising only an insignificant proportion of their total income.[6]

The illusory wartime prosperity merely accentuated the severity of the settler campaign against the squatters. After 1945, conditions for squatters continued to deteriorate drastically as '. . .throughout the 1940's the settlers were engaged in what amounted to a crash-program to reduce the independence of the squatter both as a producer and a labourer in the White Highlands'.[7] Although the Department of Labour made some attempts to temper the harsher aspects of the settlers' demands, these were ineffective because of the District Councils' general power over the squatter community. The Department of Labour was mainly concerned about the speed at which settlers were reducing squatter land and cattle. It feared that stringent limitations of squatter livestock would result in an influx of livestock into Central Province, which, apart from the Reserve being unable to cope with an additional population, was itself overstocked. To forestall a crisis in the Reserve, the Department of Labour hoped to make the District Councils see sense in the need for a much more gradual de-stocking and de-squatterisation policy.

The Labour Department had failed to recognise that the 1937 RNLO not only legitimised the restrictions that the settlers imposed on the squatters, but also confirmed the settler community's co-optation into the colonial state machinery, which allowed the settlers to direct the course of labour affairs in the White Highlands. On the one hand the Ordinance entrenched settler domination by giving the settlers extensive control over squatter labour, livestock and cultivation, while on the other it resulted in widespread squatter discontent which culminated in the outbreak of the Mau Mau revolt. Thus, despite its initial restrictive effects on the squatters, the boomerang effects of the Ordinance went beyond the government's and the settlers' anticipation and proved to be the death-knell of both the settlers and the squatters as viable communities in the White Highlands.

Amidst the hue and cry raised against the squatter 'menace' in the post-war period, there was an initial brief period when even the mixed and plantation settlers, who were heavily dependent on squatter labour, supported implementing stringent measures against the squatters. The possibility of squatters forming a colonist category that might acquire rights to the lands they occupied was orchestrated beyond reality and temporarily succeeded in blinding settlers to their immediate labour needs as they supported draconian measures against squatters. The squatters refused to re-attest under such stiff regulations and also resorted to other acts of resistance, including strikes and sabotage. This soon persuaded the mixed and plantation farmers to abandon their extremist stand, for it threatened to ruin their production.[8]

By September 1944, however, all the District Councils' chairmen had agreed that squatter livestock should be eliminated from the White Highlands area immediately.[9] But since the various Settler Associations in the Nakuru District had already passed resolutions to reduce squatter stock as early as 1941, this can hardly be represented as the 'beginning of a new phase' in the reduction of squatter cattle.[10] The labour obligations imposed by the various Settler Associations and the number of livestock they agreed to allow their squatter labour to keep were stipulated as shown in table 4.1.[11]

TABLE 4.1

Area	Days' labour	Cattle	Goats	Sheep
Subukia (B+F)	240	none	none	none
Rongai (M)	240	none	none	15
Njoro (W+F)	270	none	none	15
Molo/Mau Summit (W)	—	none	none	none
Solai (W+M)	270	none	none	20
Ravine (F)	240	none	none	20
Elementeita	—	none	none	15

B = Beef   W = Wheat   M = Maize   D = Dairy   F = Forest

A resolution was passed that native labour hired under the 1937 Ordinance would be required to work for a minimum of 240 days and would not be allowed to keep cattle and goats and not more than 20 sheep. Cattle were to be allowed in the Ravine ward north of the Ravine-Kampi ya Moto road. A vote for no sheep at all in the Molo ward was carried 8 to 2. Hence by 1941 Nakuru District was unanimous about the need to eradicate squatter cattle and goats and to reduce drastically the number of sheep.

These farmers, like those in other areas, proceeded to reduce squatter livestock, the labourers' major source of income, without addressing the question of a compensatory increase in squatter wages.

The generally held view that the squatter was a cheap source of labour was a misconception, for, in comparison with other forms of labour, the squatter who averaged about 50 shillings per month was still relatively better off.

The colonial government had played into the settlers' hands by introducing an Ordinance that shifted responsibility for the squatter community from the central government's Department of Labour to the settler controlled District Councils. It was therefore hardly surprising that at a later stage the Labour Department found it difficult to elicit concessions from the settlers, who had no intention of surrendering their new-found strength.

The Labour Department obviously envisaged whole families going out to work for the settler in order to support themselves. The then current rates of eight shillings per thirty-day ticket for the squatters and six shillings per ticket for their dependents, women (*bibis*), children (*totos*) and helpers (*saidia*),[12] indicate that the new rates were no better than those that had been in operation previously. In fact the new terms, which were geared to a reduced squatter usage of settler land, would ensure a reduction in squatter income. This would particularly affect squatters in the dairy and stock areas, which offered very little employment for women and children. But what is even more extraordinary is that the Labour Department, the settlers and the Colonial Office were under no illusion about the imminent impoverishment of squatters resulting from the ongoing reconstitution of labour relations. The Commissioner for Labour, Wyn Harris, calculated that by November 1945 a squatter was making about 80 shillings per month, of which 50 came from the sale of stock and 30 from the sale of produce.[13] By eliminating stock and reducing land under squatter cultivation, a major source of squatter income would be removed. If settlers were to compensate squatters for this compulsory loss, they would have to increase their wages at least tenfold.

An examination of the incomes of 50 squatters in the wetter part of Naivasha District indicated that about 14 of them averaged an income of 1,224 shillings per annum, 19 an income of 1,030 shillings and the remaining 17 an income of 530 shillings each.[14] In the poorer drier areas, incomes were even lower since production was affected by the unfavourable climate. This discrepancy was evident in the amount of income derived from stock sales and from the sale of slaughtered animals. Thus, of a sample of 46 squatters, those in wetter areas averaged about 302 shillings from their stock, whereas those in poorer areas made an average of 127 shillings per annum.[15] In more lucrative areas, such as the Kinangop region, squatter household incomes averaged about 1,200 shillings,[16] while those in Nakuru District averaged 630 shillings (see table 4.2).

TABLE 4.2

Income from the sale of crops	Shs. 374
Income from the sale of livestock	Shs. 120
Income from squatter labour	Shs. 90
Income from labour of women and children	Shs. 46
TOTAL	Shs. 630

The already hamstrung Labour Department then tried to prescribe measures to minimise the dislocation that the Ordinance was about to cause.[17] Besides advocating a more gradual de-stocking policy, the Labour Department emphasised the need to increase squatter wages to counteract the loss of income heretofore gained from peasant farming, and also suggested that squatters should be given a salary of 10 shillings a month and a daily 2 lb. ration. It was anticipated that this would go a long way towards ensuring a properly remunerated squatter labour force without having any adverse effects on the settlers' profit margins. Table 4.3 shows the calculation that Wyn Harris made of an average squatter family's basic minimum annual income.[18]

TABLE 4.3

Squatter wages	Shs. 120 per annum
Wages for wife and children	Shs. 150 per annum
Income from sale of produce	Shs. 40 per annum
Rations equivalent	Shs. 120 per annum
TOTAL	Shs. 430

He felt that the increase in squatter wages could be offset by a higher level of settler production, but the settlers were totally opposed to increasing squatter wages and a conflict ensued. Wyn Harris then tried to bypass settler opposition by instructing the attesting officers to refuse to put into effect any contracts unless they offered a salary of 12 shillings plus rations.

Very little progress was made between 1945 and 1950, while the colonial government wrestled with the problem of creating an acceptable squatter policy. It became evident that there was no consensus on squatter policy among the various productive interests that the settlers represented. After 1950, each District Council was left to deal with its own squatters. Hence the proliferation of local options between the various districts.

Hyde-Clarke, who was the Labour Commissioner of the period, emphasised the need for a very gradual phasing out of the squatters' dependence on land, for at the time they were more dependent on income derived from land than from wages. He proposed that the balance be shifted, so that in the next stage, which might take a whole generation to consolidate, squatters could depend more on wage incomes and less on sales from the use of land. This would put them on the same footing as the Scottish crofters. In the next stage, they would be gently eased into being almost entirely dependent on wage incomes, relying only minimally on a small vegetable garden which offered no surplus for sale. This bore a close resemblance to the traditional British cottage labourers. The grand finale would come when the resident labourer no longer cultivated land in the White Highlands and relied entirely on wages.[19]

Although the District Councils never in fact adopted this strategy, they did continue to formulate policies to suit the needs of their own areas, but in all cases these were detrimental to squatter welfare. The Naivasha area, for example, waged an all out war against squatter livestock, even to the extent that when a Mr Colville asked permission to allow his squatters to keep goats, he was flatly refused. Such an uncompromising attitude was common in this particular district,[20] where local options never really took root. Here, as in the Aberdare and Nakuru Districts, the squatter community became seriously dislocated.

For some squatters, the Forest Reserves offered temporary refuge from the settler onslaught. Thus, 'if a man refused to sign on as a squatter on a farm he . . . [could] proceed to engage himself as a casual worker in the forest where he . . . [could] obtain practically the same facilities for cultivation as he . . . [could] on the farm'.[21] As a consequence, illegal squatting in the Forest Reserves was exacerbated. In areas with inadequate supervision, both legal and illegal squatters undertook extensive utilisation of forest land. The classic case of this was in Ol Arabel Forest Reserve in Laikipia where nine squatters cultivated about 84 acres of land between them. They had not entered into a contract and the law only eventually caught up with them in 1947.

The settlers had for a long time been expressing their displeasure at the Forest Department for allowing squatters such extensive cultivation and grazing. But extensive squatter cultivation was actually advantageous to the Department's programme of afforestation, depending as it did on a system of shifting cultivation,[22] which also proved popular among the squatters.

In a bid to resist the onslaught, the squatters who remained on the farms refused to renew their labour contracts and, in a pattern reminiscent of the late 1930s, either continued to reside illegally on settler farms or drifted to the Reserves and urban areas.[23] Farm labour strikes, arson, acts of sabotage and general despondency became rife, especially in areas where settlers had taken stringent measures against squatters. In the Trans-Nzoia area, a more amicable agreement was reached whereby de-stocking would be effected over a period of five years. Even this, however, did not go down well in the Nyanza and Nandi Reserves, which were the major recipients of outgoing stock and squatters.

So far, the settlers had managed to get their own way with the colonial government by ensuring that it imposed regulations which, within a short space of time, dislocated a community that had taken several decades to build. The extent of settler control over squatter affairs is evidenced by even the labour inspectors eventually becoming answerable to the District Councils.[24] This settler hold over squatter labour so frustrated the Labour Department's attempts to temper the speed of de-stocking and reducing land under squatter use that Mr Hyde-Clarke sought to transfer the squatter issue from his department to the Department of Agriculture. In exasperation and despair, Hyde-Clarke wrote to Cavendish Bentinck, from the Department of Agriculture, stating that the squatter issue was 'concerned to a much greater degree with the proper utilisation of land, which is your responsibility, rather than with the proper utilisation of manpower, which is perhaps mine'.[25] These two issues had never before been regarded as separate and Hyde-Clarke's statement was a reflection of both the tenacity of the settler group and the waning bargaining powers of the Department of Labour. Unable to withstand opposition from within the Colonial Office and the District Councils, the Department of Labour could be said to have abandoned the squatters to the settlers' schemes. By the late 1940s, most District Councils had adopted very drastic actions against squatters.[26]

Increasingly confronted through intensified settler oppression with the unvarnished truth about the temporary and precarious nature of their residence in the White Highlands, the squatters began to gain a sharper insight into the causes of their plight. After 1945 their resistance to colonial oppression became better articulated and organised. In the Nakuru, Naivasha and Aberdare districts, many squatters refused to re-attest, which completely dislocated the labour force in some areas and caused widespread concern in others. In Central Province, squatters continually lobbied for the support of local Kikuyu administrative officials. They also organised themselves into the Kikuyu Highlands Squatters Association,[27] which sought to articulate the squatters' land rights and to establish reasons why the colonial government should resettle evicted and other desperate squatters. Deputations to the governor, Sir Philip Mitchell, and to the Secretary of State demanded solutions to the squatter problem and categorically blamed the colonial government for the squatters' miserable plight. But here, as in the Olenguruone case, the government remained intransigent, with both the governor and the colonial administration as a whole believing that a sympathetic attitude might be interpreted as a sign of weakness. The government's intransigence was, however, ill-conceived and badly timed. A rising wave of discontent and despondency, both in the White Highlands and in the Reserves, created a fertile ground for the politicisation, oath taking and subversive activities that culminated in the Olenguruone defiance and in the outbreak of Mau Mau.

The settler onslaught on squatters was strongest in the three District Councils with the highest concentration of Kikuyu squatters, namely Aberdare, Nakuru and Naivasha. Here too were the most outspoken and determined of the settlers, whose economic strength and access to centres of political power provided them with an additional impetus in their arrogance in dealing with the squatters. Even in the Uasin Gishu area, where it had finally been agreed that squatter stock would be eliminated over a three-year period, anxiety and agitation still developed among squatters and settlers. For the squatters there was no guarantee that there would be adequate room for their stock in Nyanza and Nandi,[28] for the settlers the possibility of a disrupted labour force loomed, and here, as elsewhere, squatters resorted to acts of violence directed against settlers and their stock.

In their campaign to control squatter production, the settlers managed to force the Forest Department to conform by placing them under District Council jurisdiction.[29] As stated earlier, the settlers' campaign to reduce squatter cultivation in the Forest Reserves was contrary to the development of the afforestation programme. But in an attempt to meet the settlers half-way, the Forest Department eventually agreed to hand over the administration of squatters employed by forest contractors to the settler District Councils, for even the Forest Department had found difficulty in containing the activities of concessionaire contractors and their labourers.[30]

The Settler Associations and District Councils passed various resolutions and recommendations and issued warnings about the control of forest squatters. Then, at the end of November 1948, the Nakuru District Council resolved that Forest Reserves 'come entirely under the District Council regulations',[31] unless the conservation of forests appealed against this decision. Elsewhere, settlers advised foresters on what constituted acceptable squatter contracts, how long these should last and how much livestock should be allowed. But because the relationship between the Forest Department and the District Councils was never clearly articulated, conflict between the two continued. However, the Forest Department did impose a clamp-down on any of its employees who engaged in activities that were detrimental to the forests, including illegal grazing, honey collecting (which could result in disastrous fires) and the use of forest wood.

As settlers tightened their control over squatters on the farms, the latter increased their reprisals by maiming settler stock and setting fire to settler property. A spate of strikes by farm-labourers broke out at the height of the de-stocking campaign. These anti-European feelings and actions were further fuelled and sharpened by what became known as the Olenguruone crisis.

Olenguruone

By the end of the Second World War the settlers were determined to press the squatter relationship to the point of crisis.[32] In some areas squatters were barred from keeping any livestock at all, and where livestock were allowed they were restricted to an average of only 15 sheep. Although they were usually allowed to cultivate between one and a half and two acres of land, with increased labour demands (ranging from a minimum of 240 to 270 days) and no wage increases, it would appear that their subordination was virtually complete. But the settlers still continued to press for further restrictions. Nevertheless, despite having their economic activities drastically curtailed, the squatters' political resilience still grew from strength to strength.

The squatters' reaction was inspired by what they had witnessed of another battle, the Olenguruone crisis, in which a direct conflict had taken place between the government and the former squatters or colonists of Maasailand. The Olenguruone crisis had arisen out of a whole range of factors, all of which came within the experience of the squatters. These included the findings of the Kenya Land Commission, the effects of the 1937 RNLO, the post-war government's 'agricultural improvement' and soil conservation programmes for Africans, the need to protect the White Highlands, and the search among the Kikuyu for a leader in their increasingly militant politics.

The 1932–33 Kenya Land Commission established that the Kikuyu needed more land than they had access to and thus recommended that some land be made available to them.[33] More importantly, the Commission acknowledged that some *githaka* right-holders had lost their land through alienation. Some of these right-holders had become colonists in Maasailand, while others had moved to the White

Highlands as squatters. A number of these squatters were then, in turn, declared redundant under the 1937 RNLO and, along with the colonists in Maasailand, were settled in Olenguruone, where a prolonged anti-government campaign developed which lasted for about a decade. The Kikuyu squatters adopted the Olenguruone crisis as a point of reference in their resistance against the settler assault.

Olenguruone was caught in the thick of the official post-war obsession with agricultural improvement and soil conservation in the African Reserves. In their campaign against squatters, the settlers shrewdly played the soil conservation card by pointing at the badly eroded African Reserves and emphasising the need to take action against squatter cultivation and grazing before it was too late. This fitted in neatly with their concern for the sanctity of the White Highlands. Perceiving Olenguruone as a test case for agricultural improvement, the government then imposed a host of agricultural regulations, which were resented by, and brought about the extensive impoverishment of, the residents. In the ensuing conflict, Olenguruone residents organised mass defiance of the regulations and sought allies from the equally disgruntled squatters in the White Highlands and from the Kikuyu in Central Province, especially Southern Kiambu where most of the Olenguruone residents had come from.

This was also where the most savage Kikuyu land alienations had taken place, forcing many families into becoming squatters in the White Highlands. Demands for the return of their stolen lands had been smouldering for years as rising population and diminishing landholdings fuelled the flames of discontent. The Kikuyu Central Association (KCA), operating mainly in Central Province but also maintaining contact with the Kikuyu diaspora, especially in the White Highlands, kept the battle for lost lands alive through petitions, memoranda and public meetings. Although banned in 1940, the KCA continued to operate underground and after 1944 when its detained leaders were released, it was revitalised by a massive membership drive and the introduction of a 'loyalty oath' throughout Central Province and the White Highlands. KCA leaders in Central Province liaised with KCA cells on settler farms and in the Olenguruone settlement. In Central Province, the KCA spearheaded the opposition to terracing and other soil conservation measures. As the tempo of opposition to government measures increased in Central Province and in Olenguruone, squatters from both areas drew strength from their oaths of loyalty.

Olenguruone provided a rallying point for all disgruntled Kikuyu, whether squatters, former squatters or those in Central Province, for all were seeking ways and means of dealing with the various aspects of colonial oppression and, ultimately, colonial rule. In the wave of militant politics that swept over Olenguruone, squatters in the Settled Areas and in Central Province also began to feel the need for leadership in this new phase of their history. At this point, Olenguruone came to be regarded as the centre of Kikuyu politics and leadership, providing great inspiration in the struggle against the settler assault. Significantly, in 1946 the administration of Olenguruone was transferred from Maasai to Nakuru District, thus placing its residents under the same yoke as the squatters – 'the slavery of the white Settled Areas'.[34]

The Olenguruone scheme

Olenguruone was purchased by the government in 1939 to provide land for squatters who, because of the greater measure of control exercised under the 1937 RNLO, might have to leave European lands. These included squatters declared redundant, as well as those who might choose not to contract as squatters under the provisions of the new Ordinance, which they considered very restricting. Technically, the Olenguruone settlement area formed part of the Maasai land unit. In total, it contained some 52,000 acres including land in different regions of Maasailand, the largest of which, Olenguruone, comprised 34,700 acres to the south of the Mau Plateau, hence the name of the whole scheme. When the chosen area was surveyed, it was found to be larger than originally surmised; consequently, 'certain Kikuyu who were living as trespassers in the Maasai Native Land Unit were allowed to use the additional land together with some 50 families of Wandorobo from the Tinet Forest Areas'.[35]

Olenguruone was administered as a government-controlled settlement scheme whereby approved farmers would be allowed to reside under conditions agreed by the Native Land Trust Board. It was basically set up as a model scheme for the various agricultural regulations the government had tried without much success to implement in the Reserves, with the specific purpose of 'cut[ting] out the worst of the Kikuyu social and farming customs'.[36] This could not be done if the settlers were to hold the land freehold and inevitably meant that the Olenguruone Kikuyu would become tenants-at-will of the Crown. For the majority of Olenguruone settlers, this was seen as posing a serious threat to their position, which they now regarded as more precarious than that of *ahoi* in Central Province.

Since the settlers knew that they could be evicted from their plots overnight, they felt they had no more security in Olenguruone than they did in the White Highlands. The administration, however, was quick to point out that the status of Olenguruone Kikuyu was not analogous to their former status (as *ahoi*) and that no such comparison should be made.[37] Theirs was a new status in which they neither own the land nor worked on it as labourers, for its proprietorship and utilisation were governed by the colonial authority.

This ambiguous position resulted in a host of protracted conflicts between the Olenguruone settlers and the government, in which the government adopted an arrogant and uncompromising attitude over the whole issue. This in turn led to increased politicisation of the residents and the transformation of the oath into a tool for mass mobilisation. Among the Kikuyu, the use of an oath as a sign of allegiance was a secret institution administered only to a select minority of core members of a group, who were almost always men. But in Olenguruone, men, women and children all took the oath in a bid to create unity among the Olenguruone residents in their struggle against the government. Olenguruone became the last testing ground for the government's commitment to the settler cause before the outbreak of Mau Mau.

The government perceived the Olenguruone scheme as a genuine move towards solving the problems of the dispossessed and redundant ex-squatters. Most of the Olenguruone settlers were Kikuyu who had formerly been resident in various parts of the Maasai Reserve and, like other Kikuyu who had settled in different parts of the colony, aroused suspicion and dislike among their hosts. There was widespread fear of Kikuyu encroachment among the Embu, Meru, Kisii, Kamba and Maasai people, all of whom had pockets of Kikuyu settlement in their areas. The extensiveness of Kikuyu cultivation, coupled with the rapid growth of Kikuyu communities in the areas in which they settled, precipitated agitated appeals to the government in a bid to control Kikuyu infiltration. As the 1946–47 report on Native Affairs stated:

> The Kikuyu particularly has become notorious for such attempts [at infiltration]; Kikuyu immigrants having gained a footing in other tribes' domain by ingratiating subtlety and specious promises too often reassert their tribal character as soon as they feel they have numerical strength to form an independent unit and to flank the chiefs and the internal native authorities of their hosts in the small areas where they congregate.[38]

None the less, there was still an appreciable amount of social and economic intercourse between the Kikuyu and their hosts; intermarriage, adoption and the sale of labour by the Kikuyu to the Maasai were common.

Until about the early 1930s, all Maasai cultivation was carried out either by Kikuyu employees or by educated Maasai who had Kikuyu wives. Infiltration and interpenetration was an appealing option for Kikuyu from both Central Province and the White Highlands. The Kikuyu thus cultivated both for the Maasai and for themselves although the latter was the more common option.[39] By 1936, it was evident that only a few areas in the Maasai Reserve were suitable for agriculture, namely Loitokitok, Ngong, Rorian, Il Melili and Nairage Ngare, and that it was only 'with the greatest difficulty that the Akikuyu . . . [were] prevented from monopolising them'.[40] The Maasai Annual Report of 1937 noted that the Ngong area was being deforested and eroded by Akikuyu immigrants and that steps should be taken to prevent it. A scheme was then drawn up to replace the Kikuyu with Maasai mixed farmers who would be given guidance on stock keeping by the veterinary instructor at the Ngong veterinary depot.

With the increase in population and a growing awareness of the importance of land, groups in other areas also became conscious of the Kikuyu presence among them, especially since the Kikuyu always transported their whole culture to their adopted homes. The uneasiness that this created among their hosts is portrayed in a report on Kikuyu settlement in Kisii in which it was said that:

A Sunday border market in Nyaribari [Kisii] is like a scene from Kiambu, or more accurately all the ingredients of Kikuyu settlement in highland country are there – donkeys loaded with sacks of potatoes, lines of burdened women struggling in, . . .groups of young men. . .at the doors of numerous Kikuyu-owned tumbled-down hotels, above all, the clamour in Kikuyu language.[41]

The government was particularly uncompromising over the status of Olenguruone Kikuyu settlers who had formerly resided in the Maasai Reserve. It stated that 'the Kikuyu from Maasai were not settled at Olenguruone by virtue of any recommendation of the commission [the Kenya Land Commission], but were accommodated because they were landless'.[42] It was the government's opinion that these lands were given neither as compensation, nor as a result of any claims put forward by these Kikuyu, but rather as a government 'rescue mission', for which the settlers were expected to be grateful and co-operative.

Contrary to government expectations, the Olenguruone scheme became a hotbed of political protest and agitation against the colonial state. In the heat of the conflict that arose, controversial claims and counter-claims were made by the two sides involved in the area. One thing was clear: the colonial government and the Olenguruone settlers were on quite different wavelengths. For example, the Kikuyu Olenguruone settlers from Maasai argued that the government had removed them from 'their' lands at Il Miriri and consequently wanted the government to regard their plots at Olenguruone as compensation for the lands they had left at Il Miriri. As one spokesman for the settlers' case put it:

Going back since the time we dwelt in Miriri where we dwelt at the very beginning and shortly we were told to move by the government to where we are now . . . we were promised to be provided with lands in exchange and were asked to give evidence at Chura Court, before settling in Olenguruone.[43]

These Olenguruone settlers presumed that being asked to give evidence before the Chura court established that they were previous *githaka* holders in Kiambu who had lost their lands through alienation. Having been moved first to the White Highlands, later to the Maasai Reserve, and then on to Olenguruone, it was understandable that they would want to regard their new land as compensation for what they had lost previously. But their submission was rejected.

The point of reference among ex-Miriri settlers was that other Limuru people had been given land at Kereita and Lari.[44] The Miriri people therefore failed to see why they too could not receive their Olenguruone plots as compensation. Inherent in the argument presented by the ex-Miriri Kikuyu was the notion that after a continuous period of utilisation, they had come to look upon the land at Il-Miriri as their *githaka*. It was for this reason that they felt they had been disinherited twice over and hoped that Olenguruone was compensation for this.

These settlers claimed that they had lived in Il Miriri from 'the very beginning' and that they had only moved to Olenguruone at the government's request, whereas Kikuyu migration to Maasailand had taken place within living memory. The claim to having owned the Maasai land from 'the very beginning' posed a dilemma which was overlooked by the colonial government on the spot. Were these Kikuyu claims a myth that needed to be exploded before the settlers could accept the terms of settlement at Olenguruone? Or, alternatively, had the government misunderstood an ongoing process of Kikuyu expansion?

The government's view was that these Kikuyu settlers had been squatting on Maasai land and therefore had no legal claim to it. In all probability this Kikuyu settlement in Maasai was done amicably, but what is more important is that, whenever they moved, the Kikuyu settlers inevitably had to clear what was virtually virgin land. In the absence of open hostility from the Maasai, the Kikuyu communities would settle down to pursue patterns of life similar to those they enjoyed in Central Province. Some of these settlers had also either intermarried with or been adopted by Maasai families, and a few had done both, which might explain their feeling of belonging. The claim to a Kikuyu presence in Maasai land in 'the distant past' was obviously aimed to give credibility to their case in the ears of the administrators.

The colonial administration grouped its subjects on an ethnic basis, and whatever processes had been operating between the Maasai and the Kikuyu were overlooked in the search for a neat ethnic pattern. The Kikuyu were squatters in Maasai land and they could not possibly have any land rights there, or for that matter at Olenguruone. The difference between the ex-Miriri settlers' self-perception and the government's adamant stand on the issue remained unresolved.

One possible explanation for such strong Kikuyu resentment of the Olenguruone scheme is that these settlers had been subjected to intensive repression within the White Highlands and, once out of the area, were bent on acquiring some dignity and independence. This was borne out when the transfer of Olenguruone to Nakuru for adminis-trative purposes caused further protest from the Olenguruone settlers, who regarded it as a move to continue their suffering under white settlers. They detested the 'slavery of the White Highlands'[45] and saw no reason why the servile treatment they had suffered there should be continued in their new domain.

Amidst all the claims and counter-claims that were bandied about, it became difficult to establish exactly what had transpired between the Olenguruone settlers and the administration before the settlement was opened. The leader of the Olenguruone settlers, Samuel Koina Gitebi, stated that the officer-in-charge of Maasai had informed the settlers in the presence of Senior Chiefs Josiah Njonjo and Koinange that they would be given land in Olenguruone on *githaka* terms[46] in compens-ation for the land they had lost in Kiambu-through alienation for settler use, and that there were to be no regulations over how it was used. He also said that the Olenguruone Kikuyu had been scrutinised by the Kiambu Local Native Council in the person of Chief Josiah Njonjo to establish which of them had been *githaka* owners and therefore eligible for land in Olenguruone.[47] It was in the light of this background that the Olenguruone people resisted a scheme that relegated them to a status that was more precarious than that of historical *ahoi*.

The Kikuyu also clung to what they perceived as a major legal flaw in the administration of the scheme. They were moved to Olenguruone towards the end of 1941, yet the rules that governed the scheme were only introduced in 1942. They claimed that they had accepted the land unconditionally and had not anticipated government directives as to how the land was to be utilised. This was borne out by Gitebi's letter of complaint when the new agricultural rules were imposed early in 1942.[48] The government overlooked this discrepancy in the timing of the *modus operandi* of the scheme and insisted that, long before they moved into Olenguruone, the people had been informed about the terms on which land would be held. Failure to observe the rules laid down would, the government insisted, result in eviction.

The Olenguruone scheme was made more vulnerable to criticism because it included some Kikuyu who were original right-holders from Kiambu, but who could not be settled in Kiambu due to shortage of land. These, like the Miriri Kikuyu, compared themselves to some of their kinsmen who were settled at Kereita and Lari in compensation for lands lost to white settlers at Tigoni. This latter group of Kikuyu were not subjected to any agricultural regulations in the usage of their land. In other words, the Kereita and Lari lands were owned on the same freehold basis as lands in the Reserves. Olenguruone settlers thus found themselves caught in a situation without precedent. The claim by the ex-Miriri settlers for similar terms of occupation as those in Kereita and Lari received a monolithic answer from the government, namely that the settlers must have misunderstood the terms under which the land was granted.

The settlement rules imposed on Olenguruone settlers included an intricate set of exacerbating regulations. Of the eight acres of land granted to each settler, it was recommended that not more than two and a half be under cultivation at any one time. Neither was the land to be cultivated continuously for more than four years initially, after which it was to rest under planted grass for not more than three years at a time. The two and a half acres of land under cultivation were expected to be used for cash and food crops, with the remaining five and a half acres together with four acres of common grazing, being used for eight or nine high-grade cattle or the equivalent number of sheep, which would provide meat, milk and butterfat 'for home consumption and a surplus for sale'. All permanent grassland on both private and common land was to be divided into fenced paddocks and was to be grazed in rotation. The residents were advised to hold the pastureland of 50 to 100 families in one block. This would then be subdivided into four to five paddocks which would be grazed in rotation.[49] New crops including wheat and vegetables were to be grown in rotation, while maize, which had by then become the Kikuyu's staple crop, was forbidden. Because the area, which comprised four steep valleys, rendered the plots prone to soil erosion, terracing, cross-contour planting and intercropping were of utmost importance. In addition, the heavy downpours of rain and extremely cold climate made the area highly unsuitable for settlement and cultivation.[50]

In many ways the scheme demanded a complete reorganisation of the people's agricultural practices and social set up. Having abrogated the Kikuyu system of land ownership in Central Province, the administration then imposed a completely new system for inheriting the allocated plots in Olenguruone, which was wholly at variance with common Kikuyu practice. Although each plot would be held for succeeding generations, 'it would only be inherited by the eldest son of the wife on that plot and not according to Kikuyu custom'.[51] In practice, then, not only was the government's system of land tenure in Olenguruone totally alien and different from any practice known to the settlers in that it prohibited the subdivision of land among the sons of a homestead, but it also stipulated that land in Olenguruone could not be sold, rented, mortgaged or disposed of in any way.

The Olenguruone settlers saw the whole scheme as a major exercise in blackmail aimed at covering up the government's contribution to the events that had led to its inception.[52] While the settlers and their patrons in Kiambu insisted that the acreage granted to individual homesteads was inadequate, the administration argued that the land was considerably in excess of that available to many *ahoi* and other landowners in the Kikuyu Reserves. In this connection, the government was once again reluctant to admit to the findings of the Kenya Land Commission that landholdings in Central Province were woefully inadequate. In effect, to compare land acreages in the Olenguruone scheme with those in Central Province was to miss the point and overlook a major crisis, thus making a bad situation worse.

This is exactly what the government did. Initially, land grants at Olenguruone failed to take account of family size, since the government intended the plots for 'normal families' and had no intention of undertaking 'to support abnormal' polygamous or extended families. The government refused to double the acreage to 16, so that in practice a man with one wife was granted the same size of land as a man who had two or more wives. The newly married sons of plot owners at Olenguruone were sent away from the scheme. Like their fathers before them, these young men were landless and it was only logical that they should follow their parents to their new domains. The government stated categorically that the Olenguruone people would have to find ways and means of supplementing what they got from the scheme. Although the government aimed to combat soil erosion and ensure the proper use of land at Olenguruone, the large sizes of the families already resident on the Olenguruone plots were to make this an impossible quest.

The government had laid too much emphasis on proper methods of land utilisation at the expense of the social and political stability of the Olenguruone Kikuyu. Olenguruone residents were concerned about the various agricultural regulations only to the extent that they confirmed that the land was not granted on *githaka* terms.[53] They refused to address themselves to the finer details of the scheme such as whether or not to terrace their land, plant vegetables or wheat, practise crop rotation or paddocking. Towards the end of the conflict, the issue at hand had changed into that of the very legitimacy of the government's appropriation of land in the country.[54] The majority of

Olenguruone settlers were virtually landless. Some of those who had come from Southern Kiambu were among the first victims of land alienation, while others, for a number of reasons, had moved to the Rift Valley and left their holdings to various members of their families. Since over time this land had reverted to the ownership of their *mbari* kinsmen, it had become difficult for former squatters to re-claim it and, in any case, a sizeable number of ex-squatters had been *ahoi* before they went out to the Rift Valley.

Within this framework, it was not unreasonable for the government to assume that these Olenguruone settlers would, within limits, appreciate its effort to provide them with land. This official outlook did not, however, take into account the rapid politicisation of the squatter community, which had occurred largely as a result of settler oppression. The official view that 'unwarranted importance [was being] attached to the political aspect not considering the economic aspect of it all'[55] failed to recognise the residents' concern for a more permanent solution to the problem of landlessness and their inherent vulnerability under a very unsatisfactory government-sponsored scheme.

The government failed to appreciate that the cumulative effect of squatter subjection produced people who no longer fell for piecemeal offers and who detested government schemes that reduced them to tenants-at-will of the state. In practice, this was the status of all Africans in the country, so, in rejecting the Olenguruone settlement offer, the settlers went a step beyond Central Province politics. Like other African Reserves in which the colonial government was battling against increasing population and diminishing landholdings, Central Province was also subjected to various agricultural measures and restrictions, which the residents bitterly resented, and which the agents of the administration continued to enforce. People in Central Province were also plagued with land shortages. In fact, the majority of Kikuyu peasants suffered great hardships under the impact of land shortages, unpopular agricultural measures and the various financial liabilities that the colonial administration imposed.

Paradoxically, the people in Central Province did not react in as overt a manner as the Olenguruone settlers. In their own way, then, the Olenguruone settlers established a brand of resistance that was unique in the 1940s and new within the context of Central Province and Rift Valley politics. Their opposition to the Olenguruone scheme, and therefore to the government's land policy, was tantamount to a quest to reverse the whole colonial structure, especially the racial stratification of the country's economy and politics, on which the alienation and sanctity of the White Highlands rested. The Olenguruone crisis really boiled down to a single issue, namely total opposition to any form of colonialism, including its land grants and progressive agricultural measures. The conflict lasted for ten long years. By the mid-1940s, Olenguruone residents had won the sympathies of other squatters, especially in the surrounding Naivasha and Nakuru Districts, and had also established close liaisons with supporters in Central Province, including the Kikuyu Highlands Squatters Association centred at Limuru. It was only a matter of time before the Olenguruone crisis would snowball into what was to become the uncontrollable Mau Mau movement.

Resistance at Olenguruone

Defiance at Olenguruone was instant and continued to escalate once the government had made its stand on the issue clear. Like the Kikuyu squatters on the surrounding settler farms, the inhabitants of Olenguruone, some of whom were ex-squatters, refused to sign the permits that authorised them to stay in the area. More importantly, they disregarded all the agricultural rules concerning cultivation and livestock keeping and proceeded to utilise the land as they pleased. The Olenguruone Kikuyu refused to work on projects in the scheme involving survey work, bamboo cutting and road-works. This necessitated the hiring of labour from Kisii country.[56]

By 1945 it seemed as if the Olenguruone Kikuyu were winning the psychological battle, for government threats of possible eviction were being met with stronger defiance. But they were definitely losing the economic battle. The area was unsuitable for cultivation and by 1945 the settlement was unable to grow sufficient food.[57]

Additional agricultural regulations to counter soil erosion, which were introduced by Colin Maher,[58] did little to improve the situation. Even his idea of adding an extra four acres, making a total of twelve acres, which he projected would give each family an income of 340 shillings per annum, provided little additional advantage,[59] especially for people who had pursued a lucrative peasant option in both the White Highlands and the Maasai Reserve. In fact it failed even to match Wyn Harris's recommended squatter income of at least 430 shillings per annum, suggested for post-war efforts to turn the squatters into contented wage-labourers. Wyn Harris calculated that, while the bulk of squatter income would come from wages (120 shillings from the squatter's wage and 150 shillings from his wife's and children's pay), rations equivalent to at least 120 shillings could also be obtained, as well as an extra 40 shillings from the sale of surplus agricultural produce.

By contrast, the Olenguruone settlers' incomes were derived totally and solely from the land. Thus, while a squatter's income of 430 shillings per annum excluded the value of subsistence foodcrops consumed by the squatter's family, the Olenguruone figure of 340 shillings was all inclusive. From the two and a half acres that an Olenguruone settler was allowed to cultivate, he could expect to plant one and a half acres with wheat, which would yield 12 bags to be sold at 20 shillings each, fetching a total of 240 shillings. On the remaining one acre, half would be planted with potatoes yielding about 20 bags, which at 3 shillings per bag would fetch 60 shillings. The remaining half would be planted with maize and beans, which would yield two bags worth 40 shillings, making a total of 340 shillings per annum.[60] Because Olenguruone was an isolated settlement, there were no job prospects there and this limited the settler's income even further. Employment on the scheme's community projects was unpopular, for these were seen as part and parcel of the whole oppressive apparatus.

Under what the government considered better terms of settlement, additional wives and the grown up sons of Olenguruone residents were each given their own five-acre plot. The original occupiers' increase to twelve acres of holding was, however, seen as merely a token gesture, which was what it was, especially since the families were still restricted to cultivating only two and a half acres of land at any given time. This, like earlier restrictions, generated further discontent among the residents.

The Olenguruone oath

The Olenguruone residents had revived the use of the oath as a tool of unity as early as 1943–44.[61] Under the threat of imminent eviction, the Olenguruone crisis radicalised the use of the oath as a means of eliciting mass unity against colonial oppression, as in a widespread and non-selective approach thousands of men, women (both young and old) and children took the oath. Olenguruone residents then spread the oath to the surrounding settler farms and to Central Province, especially Southern Kiambu.

As District Councils concentrated on ways and means of further restricting their squatter labour, the squatters became even more antagonised and therefore easy prey for the radical politics developing in Olenguruone. Squatter politicisation then focused on the Olenguruone case and, with the help of KCA militants, the oath spread rapidly amongst Kikuyu squatters throughout the Settled Areas.[62] KCA activists helped the squatters organise massive labour strikes aimed at wringing concessions from the settlers and which, along with various sabotage,[63] to some extent succeeded in destabilising labour in half of the White Highlands. The oath was especially Naivasha and Nakuru districts where the settlers had been particularly harsh on the squatters. Here the squatters refused to re-attest under the terms of the 1937 RNLO.[64] At the height of this squatter-Olenguruone collusion, a massive meeting was organised by the Olenguruone residents which took place in the latter half of 1946. The meeting, which was held in Naivasha and attended by several hundred squatter representatives sympathetic to the Olenguruone cause,[65] adopted Olenguruone as the squatters' rallying cry against settler oppression[66] and imbued them with renewed determination to defy 'the slavery of the White Highlands'.

The administration identified Olenguruone and Naivasha as the launching-pads for a destabilising political influence amongst squatters in the Nakuru, Naivasha and Ravine Districts

> Taking full advantage of the oath-swearing many hundreds of squatters were induced not to re-attest in the hope that either farming would be paralysed or the District Council's Resident Labour Legislation would be jettisoned. [However] with the whole heartfelt co-operation of the Labour Department and the great majority of settlers neither objective was achieved, but not before it was necessary to imprison ninety seven men from one farm for a deliberate flouting of the law of the land and this on the day of the arrival in the District of the Under-Secretary of State for the Colonies; the organisers thought their demonstration well-timed. It did in fact enable Mr. Creech Jones to obtain another view of the frame of mind of the African today and of the farmer's problem in relation to his labour.[67]

While by the beginning of 1947 squatter agitation had subsided in most places and re-attestation been resumed, the situation in Olenguruone had become even more tense. Earlier, in 1946, the reiteration by the District Commissioner for Nakuru, Major F.W. Carpenter, that the Olenguruone residents were *ahoi* and not *githaka* owners resulted in a resurgence of protest in Olenguruone.[68] By the middle of the year the majority of Olenguruone residents had taken the oath. On 22 March 1947 the Provincial Commissioner gave the residents two weeks notice either to comply with the rules of the settlement or to leave.[69] Similar warnings without definite deadlines had been served before but not effected, and neither was the above.

Subsequent attempts to evict defaulters were halted for about a year by legal complications arising over the nature of the eviction orders. Although no drastic action was taken initially, the government did confiscate livestock belonging to four leading defaulters, but even this did not stifle the indomitable spirit of the Olenguruone residents. It merely hardened their opposition. The 50 residents whose cases were due for hearing on 5 April began to feel confident that their defence would succeed and that the government would provide land for them elsewhere. It was clear that 'after the initial shock and surprise' of government action against the four defaulters, 'the defiant attitude [had] reasserted itself very quickly'.[70] Some administrators expressed concern that it had taken the government a whole year to evict four residents. They felt that unless the government took determined action and evicted all recalcitrant residents, the Kikuyu would 'have succeeded in imposing their will on the government against the better judgement of all who are informed on the situation'.[71] They felt that the government had dragged its feet on the issue for too long and that it was necessary to deal with all the remaining residents *en masse*. Cases, they felt, should not be left to drag on beyond the end of June.

Interestingly, however, the government did not immediately resort to direct evictions. Instead it decided to destroy the Olenguruone Kikuyu's property, shelter and food supplies in the expectation that residents would be sufficiently antagonised to leave the settlement of their own accord. Some residents did indeed seek temporary refuge with squatter friends on surrounding farms and for a while there was peace on the settlement. But this was the lull before the storm.

On 20 February 1949 the Court of Appeal for Eastern Africa ruled against the Olenguruone Kikuyu's application. Thus armed the government then undertook to evict all residents without settlement permits. Their huts and crops were to be destroyed and their livestock confiscated. Action was delayed until the end of September and then, within a week between 28 September and 3 October 1949, everyone in defiance of the law, which comprised the majority of Olenguruone residents, were to have their huts burnt, their livestock seized and their maize crops cut down. But despite this ravaging attack, a recalcitrant 2,200 residents remained behind, hiding in holes in the ground. By this time the people had become highly politicised and fearless in the face of vicious government attacks.[72] Subsequent government action at the beginning of 1950 comprised trials of all residents still on the scheme without valid permits. When the first batch refused to pay their 100 shilling fines, they were transported to the dry and inhospitable Bl Yatta area in Kambaland, which the Kenya Land Commission had recommended for the Kikuyu overspill.

Judging from the harsh tones of the following note found nailed to the door of Njoroge Waweru's hut during the initial July-August government assault, preparations to oust the colonial government were already underway in 1948:

> If you just think since you came to Kenya you have never seen an African with a gun. I am the one to inform you that the Africans have more power than you have with guns. Just wait until the year 1949 you will have to be sorry for the rules which you are giving us now and when it will be my turn to order you in the same way.[73]

Almost a decade of what had virtually amounted to a tug of war between the government and the Olenguruone people had produced an insecure, bitter and disinherited community. Mass defiance of government regulations elicited harsh reactions and by early 1949 the government had given up trying to force the people to adopt their agricultural regulations and instead resorted to imposing 'summary eviction, possibly together with the forfeiture of property, the demolition of houses and the impounding of cattle'.[74] While some of the residents moved to Southern Kiambu and others threatened to squat on European farms in Kiambu until such time as the government remedied the situation,[75] most of them continued to reside illegally in Olenguruone until they were forcibly evicted to Yatta.

One reason why the government remained so inflexible over the Olenguruone crisis was because it was convinced that if it allowed Olenguruone to be regarded as compensation for lands lost to European settlers many years ago, this would lead to 'a gaining of political ends and further pressure of Kikuyu needs'.[76] In other words, the Olenguruone Kikuyu would emerge as victors over the vital question of land. With this in mind, the government chose to remain firm in its dealings with the Olenguruone settlers. The belief that Olenguruone was being 'made a political pawn on the chess board of Kikuyu land aspirations generally'[77] further strengthened the government's uncompromising stand, which it clung to tenaciously as a matter of principle. It was afraid that, if it went back on any of its land policy decisions or gave any concessions in this case, not only would a whole host of other land claims be made, but by revealing the unjust and racial basis of its former land policy, the government would be shown up in a poor light.

In the end, the government only partially solved the settler problem by getting rid of unwanted squatters and their cattle. Having rejected the government's plan for them, the former squatters were still unsettled. The Kiambu Reserve, into which these people then flowed, already contained thousands more than it could comfortably accommodate. The situation was bound to generate further discontent and agitation, especially since Kiambu was rife with grievances against the colonial government. Those who drifted into the urban areas encountered an equally hostile situation.

Despite the magnitude of the Olenguruone defiance, it could be argued that until 1950 their action was largely defeatist. By rejecting the government-sponsored scheme, the Olenguruone settlers had scored a major psychological victory against the government, but in terms of positive concrete results for themselves they seemed to have achieved nothing. The significance of their defiance lay mainly in its pivotal role as a rallying point for Kikuyu unity against the colonial government and the Olenguruone crisis was largely important in strengthening the people's commitment to the single goal of dislodging the colonial government.

Prosecuting settlers caught by the government disobeying settlement rules failed to break the people's united front. In a report to the Chief Native Commissioner following the prosecution of four Olenguruone settlers on 18 March 1948, the Provincial Commissioner mentioned that 'the recent prosecutions instead of shaking the settlers have increased their morale and an extremely united front [of non-compliance] is being presented to the government'.[78] When residents travelled to other areas, they were received as heroes and lauded for having bravely withstood government incarceration. The Olenguruone crisis had thus played the important role of injecting militancy into both squatter and Central Province politics. It brought Rift Valley activists into closer union with their counterparts in Olenguruone and Central Province, which was a very significant development on the eve of the Mau Mau rebellion. The seeds of the violent protest that characterised the next phase of Kenya's history had been sown in Olenguruone before being transplanted to the Settled Areas and Central Province, for it was in Olenguruone that the ideology that questioned the legitimacy of colonial rule in the White Highlands in particular, and in the country as a whole, was first born.

The full impact of the Olenguruone spirit of protest really came to the fore in the subsequent armed struggle between recalcitrant squatters, ex-squatters, Kikuyu peasants, impoverished urban lumpen-proletariat and the colonial government. Until this period the colonial government had always acted as the settler community's agent, evidenced in its sanctioning of the 1937 RNLO, which merely escalated the squatters' insecurity and impoverishment. It also created Olenguruone. But, wherever they lived, in the following years the discontentment of squatters was to reach hitherto unknown levels. It was, then, only a matter of time before the whole situation erupted.

Notes

1. KNA, Native Affairs Department, 1937, p. 187.

2. KNA, PC RVP 6A/1/17, Letter sent to Senior Chief Koinange and copied to Chiefs Josiah Njonjo, Waruhiu Kungu, Munuhe Gatheca, Councillor Mbira Githehu, PC Nakuru and DC Kiambu, signed by Lazaro K. Gaitho on behalf of the Olenguruone people, 16 October 1946.

3. Furedi, F., 'The Social Composition of the Mau Mau Movement in the White Highlands', *Journal of Peasant Studies*, Vol. 1, No. 4, July 1974, pp. 491–2.

4. See Leys, N., *The Colour Bar in East Africa*, Negro University Press, New York, Reprint 1970, pp. 41–8.
5. KNA, PC RVP Lab 27/15, No. 5.
6. See CO, 533/549/38232/15 (1946–47), 'European Settlement: Squatters', P. Wyn Harris, 'A Discussion of the Problem of the Squatter', 21 February 1946; J.H. Martin, 'The Problem of the Squatter: Economic Survey of Resident Labour in Kenya', 24 February 1947.
7. See Kanogo, T. M. J., 'Rift Valley Squatters and Mau Mau', *Kenya Historical Review*, Vol. 5, No. 2, 1977, p. 244.
8. KNA, Lab 9/326 'Resident Labour: Trans Nzoia, 1945–51'; Lab 9/598, 'Resident Labour'.
9. KNA, Lab 9/97, District Councils Conference on 12–13 September 1944.
10. Throup, D. W., 'The Governorship of Sir Phillip Mitchell in Kenya, 1944–1952', unpublished Ph.D. thesis, Sidney Sussex College, Cambridge, 1983, p. 148.
11. RH, MSS Afr. S. 1506 Box 2 – File 3, Njoro Settlers Association 1941, Nakuru District Council to Subukia, Rongai Valley and Njoro Settlers Associations, and Molo and Mau Summit, Solai and Ravine Farmers Associations, 15/1/41.
12. RH, Lord Francis Scott Papers, Deloraine Estate Reel 16, Muster Rolls, Wage Records and Labour Allocations, 1941–43.
13. CO, 533/549/38232/15, Wyn Harris, 'Discussion of the Problem of the Squatter', February 1946.
14. KNA, Lab 5/36, 'Economic Survey of Resident Labour in Kenya, 1946–7'.
15. ibid.
16. ibid. See also CO, 533/549/38232/15, Wyn Harris, 'Discussion of the Problem of the Squatter', February 1946.
17. CO, 533/549/38232/15, Wyn Harris, 'Discussion of the Problem of the Squatter', February 1946.
18. KNA, Lab 9/1071, 'Resident Labourers Ordinance: The Problem of the Squatter: Ad Hoc Committee, 1946–48', 5 March 1947.
19. KNA, MAA 8/124, 'Central Coordinating Committee for Resident Labour'.
20. KNA, Deposit 2/599, Naivasha District Council meetings, Agenda, Minutes, 93rd Meeting, 20 February 1947.
21. KNA, Lab 9/10, Wyn Harris to the Conservator of Forests, 7 February 1945.
22. KNA, Lab 9/10, J.H. Ingham, Member for Agriculture and Natural Resources to Conservator of Forests, 25 September 1948.
23. KNA, DC NKU 1/5, 'Nakuru-Naivasha-Ravine District Annual Report', 1946, pp. 7–8; ibid, 1947, pp. 25–6. See also Furedi, F., 'Social Composition of Mau Mau Movement', pp. 492–7.
24. KNA, Lab 9/310, 'Resident Labourers General Ordinance Committee, 1949–1950', 9 August 1950.
25. KNA, Lab 9/309, 'Resident Labour General Report of Ad Hoc Committee 1945–50', Labour Department to Cavendish-Bentinck, 3 March 1947, quoted in Throup 'Governorship of Sir Phillip Mitchell', p. 172.
26. See KNA, Lab 9/316, 'Resident Labour: Naivasha County Council,

1941–1959'; Lab 9/320, 'Resident Labourers Ordinance: Aberdare District Council, 1944–51'; Lab 9/317, 'Resident Labour: Nakuru, 1945–1953'; Lab 9/10, 'Labour: Squatters in Forest Areas, 1944–50'.

27. CO, 533/543/38086/38 (1946–47).

28. KNA, Lab 9/1071, 'Resident Labourers Ordinance: The Problem of the Squatter: Ad Hoc Committee 1946–48'; Lab 9/325, 'Reduction of Resident Labour Stock, 1950–57'.

29. See KNA, Lab 9/10. Minutes of a Meeting re: Resident Labourers in Forest Reserves, Nakuru, 29 November 1948. See also KNA, Lab 9/10, Molo, Mau Summit, Turi Settlers Association, 13 September 1948.

30. KNA, Lab 9/10, G. Simpson, Labour Liaison Officer, Report, 15 May 1945.

31. KNA, Lab 9/10, Minutes of a Meeting re: Resident Labourers in Forest Reserves, Nakuru, 29 November 1948.

32. This was particularly evident in Naivasha District. See KNA, Lab 9/316, 'Resident Labour', Naivasha County Council, 1941–59.

33. A total of 21,000 acres and a sum of £2,000 were awarded as compensation for losses suffered by the Kikuyu. See Kenya Land Commissioner's Report, pp. 71–7, 112–14 and 129–33.

34. KNA, PC RVP 6A/1/17, Lazaro K. Gaitho to Senior Chief Koinange . . . 16 October 1946.

35. KNA, PC RVP 6A/1/17/1, 'Olenguruone Settlement'. For a detailed chronology of events at Olenguruone, see Throup, D. W., 'Olenguruone 1940–1950', paper presented to Sidney Sussex College, Cambridge.

36. KNA, PC RVP 6A/1/17, Olenguruone, 'Minutes of a Baraza held at Olenguruone', 16 October 1946.

37. KNA, PC RVP 6A/1/17/1, DC Nakuru to DC Kiambu, 29 October 1946.

38. KNA, NAD 1946–47, p. 35. See also KNA, PC SP 2/2/1, Handing-over Report 1947–53, 'Kikuyu Infiltration and Interpenetration in Maasai Land', which mentions that the Governor of Kenya in his speech to the Narok African District Council on the sanctity of the Maasai land as laid down in the 1911 agreement stressed that the observation of the above agreement depended on Maasai utilisation of their land so that 'it became clear to all that there was no room for others to enter and farm'.

39. KNA, PC SP 2/2/1, Handing-over Report 1947–51, 'Kikuyu Infiltration and Interpenetration in Maasai Land'.

40. KNA, PC SP 1/2/2 Vol. 2, Maasai Annual Report, 1936. See also Annual Reports for 1914/1915, 1920/1921, 1922/1923, 1925/1926, 1928/1929, 1930/1931 which abound with references to Maasai-Kikuyu farming arrangements.

41. KNA, K.961.144, Report on Native Affairs, 1940–47, p. 35.

42. KNA, PC RVP 6A/1/17/1, 'Olenguruone Settlement', Land, 30/80/2/III.

43. KNA, PC RVP 6A/1/17/1, Lazaro K. Gaitho to Chief Koinange, 15 October 1946.

44. See Rosberg, C. and Nottingham, J., *The Myth of Mau Mau: Nationalism in Kenya*', Nairobi, EAPH, 1966, pp. 243–4, 248–59 and 263 ff. on the Olenguruone issue.

45. KNA, PC RVP 6A/1/17/1, Lazaro K. Gaitho to Chief Koinange, 15 October 1946.

46. KNA, PC RVP 6A/1/17/1, 'Minutes of a Baraza'.
47. KNA, DC KBU 4/9, 'Olenguruone Settlement 1940–1944', PC Central to DC Narok, 23 July 1940.
48. KNA, PC RVP 6A/1/17/1, 'Minutes of a Baraza'.
49. KNA, PC RVP 6A/1/17/1, 'Olenguruone 1948–1950', Maher's Report, 22 January 1946.
50. See KNA, PC RVP 6A/1/17/2, 'Olenguruone 1948–1950', J. F. D. Buttery, 'Report on the Olenguruone Settlement', December 1948.
51. KNA, PC RVP 6A/1/17/1, 'Minutes of a Baraza'.
52. KNA, PC RVP 6A/1/17/1, Samuel Koina to Chief Native Commissioner, 8 April 1947.
53. KNA, PC RVP 6A/1/17/2, 'Olenguruone 1948–1950', S. K. Gitebi to HM King George VI, 19 December 1949.
54. KNA, PC RVP 6A/1/17/1, Officer, Department of Agriculture Njoro, to Officer-in-Charge Soil Conservation, Olenguruone, 25 November 1946.
55. ibid.
56. KNA, PC RVP 6A/1/17/1, 'Report on Olenguruone' by DO Olenguruone, 1948.
57. KNA, PC RVP 6A/1/17/2, 'Olenguruone 1948–1950', J. F. D. Buttery, 'Report on Olenguruone', December 1948.
58. Colin Maher was a keen developmentalist from the soil conservation unit of the Government. Agricultural and livestock keeping regulations at Olenguruone were based on his report. Although in itself sound, the report was most unsuitable for the climatic and geographical conditions in Olenguruone. Basically, the land was too steep and the climate too cold for cultivation. The report also overlooked important social land utilisation patterns among the Kikuyu. See KNA, PC RVP 6A/1/17/1, 'Olenguruone 1948–1950', Maher's Report.
59. ibid.
60. ibid.
61. Spencer, J., 'KAU and Mau Mau: Some Connections' in Ochieng, W. R. and Janmohamed, K. K. (eds.), 'Some Perspectives on the Mau Mau Movement', *Kenya Historical Review*, Vol. 5, No. 2, 1977, p. 206. See also Rosberg and Nottingham, *Myth of Mau Mau*, pp. 253–4.
62. There was an overlapping of the Olenguruone 'Unity' oath and the KCA 'Loyalty' oath which gathered momentum in the 1947–48 period, see Spencer, 'KAU and Mau Mau', pp. 204–5.
63. See KNA, DC NKU 1/5, Nakuru-Naivasha-Ravine Annual Report, 1946, pp. 2 and 6.
64. ibid. See also KNA, Lab 5/35 94.
65. KNA, Lab Dept. 3/41 39A.
66. KNA, 9/601, 'Resident Labour General 1942–45', Hyde Clarke to Mitchell, June 1946. Interview, Ernest Kiberethi Kanyanja, 13 October 1976, Elburgon.
67. KNA, Nakuru-Naivasha-Ravine District Annual Report, 1946, p. 6.
68. KNA, PC RVP 6A/1/17/1, 'Olenguruone, 1946–1948', 'Minutes of a Baraza'. Olenguruone was transferred from Maasai to Nakuru District in 1946.
69. KNA, DC NKU 6/2, 'Olenguruone, 1947–1950'; Wyn Harris to Olenguruone Kikuyu, 25 March 1947.

70. KNA, PC RVP 6A/1/17/1, PC Morgan (RVP) to P. Wyn-Harris, 8 May 1948.
71. ibid.
72. KNA, DC NKU 6/2, 'Olenguruone, 1947–1950', DC Nakuru, 3 December 1949.
73. KNA, DC NKU 6/2, 'Olenguruone, 1947–1950', D.F.D. Buttery, DO Olenguruone to R.F.D. Ryland, DC Nakuru, 3 August 1948.
74. Rosberg and Nottingham, *Myth of Mau Mau*, pp. 256–7.
75. KNA, PC RVP 6A/1/17/1, Ag. DC, 'Report on Visit to Olenguruone', 17 December 1946.
76. KNA, PC RVP 6A/1/17/1, Njoro Plant Breeding Station to Senior Agricultural Officer, 4 December 1946.
77. KNA, PC RVP 6A/1/17/1, Carpenter, F .W. to PC RVP, 10 December 1946. See also Acting Chief Native Commissioner to PC RVP, Nakuru, 17 March 1947.
78. KNA, PC RVP 6A/1/17/1, PC RVP to Chief Native Commissioner, 8 May 1948.

Five

Politics of Protest:
Mau Mau

The squatters were perhaps the most suppressed, dispossessed and insecure social group in Kenya, especially in the post-war years.[1]

People [Kikuyu squatters] in the Rift Valley fully supported the Mau Mau Movement. They hated the Europeans. They had lived next to them for a long time and had seen their mistakes.[2]

The Kikuyu [squatters] in the Rift Valley were fighting for land in that area. The other *nduriri* [non-Kikuyu especially from Western Kenya] did not know how to fight for land. People like the Maasai did not know how to fight for land. They had given in [to the colonial administration] and had been moved to several places to make room for Europeans. So the Kikuyu had to fight and later claim any area.[3]

Post-war political mobilisation

During the years following the declaration of the Second World War, the political activities of the KCA (then proscribed and its leaders detained) were reduced to a few intermittent local meetings. These were to prevent the party from dying altogether and to raise funds for the detained leaders and for Kenyatta, who was still abroad.

The release of the detainees in 1943 and 1944 gave the reconstituted party a new lease of life. In Kiambu, KCA leaders were generally recruited from two sources, from the General Council of the KCA, which was originally established in the mid-1930s, and from the *mbari* committee. This was initially made up of clan (*mbari*) leaders who had represented the Kikuyu Land Board Association when it gave evidence on Kiambu Kikuyu land claims to the Kenya Land Commission of 1932–33.[4] To ensure the former detainees' loyalty to the party's political struggle in Kiambu, it was decided that they should be required to take an oath. But, unlike the earlier KCA oath, which used the Bible and the soil as its symbols, in place of the Bible this one used goat meat.[5] This oath, sometimes referred to as the *mbari* oath, was a radical departure from past practices and symbolised the changing political style towards militancy. Although the oath was initially designed expressly for the detainees, by 1945 all the KCA leaders in Kiambu had taken it.[6] And then, after 1947, it spread to Muranga and Nyeri.[7] After this, the oath was selectively but widely administered to trustworthy KCA members, both men and women, throughout Central Province.

Earlier on, in 1944, an elitist multi-tribal group, the Kenya African Union (KAU) had been formed to support Eliud Mathu, the newly appointed African representative to the Legislative Council. Under government pressure, the group was then renamed the Kenya African Students Union (KASU) but none the less continued to concern itself with the Africans' major political and economic grievances. In 1946 it reverted to its original name, KAU.

Being composed of younger and more educated Africans than themselves, the older KCA leaders were at first suspicious of KAU. This, however, all changed in June 1946 when Kenyatta arrived, took the KCA loyalty oath, joined KAU and then, in June 1947, became its president, thus giving the party legitimacy among KCA members.[8] From then on, KCA leaders participated in KAU membership drives as Kenyatta sought to establish KAU branches throughout the country.

There was a period when the membership drives of the two parties overlapped and many people joined both. This was especially true between 1947 and 1950 when the drive to take the KCA loyalty oath was at its height and when local control of the KAU party machinery was in the hands of KCA leaders. After 1950, KAU gained ascendancy, as did mobilisation for the use of violent action.[9]

But where did the squatters fit in all these political developments? In the Rift Valley, worsening conditions for squatters on settler farms and the escalating conflict between Olenguruone settlers and the government 'gave added impetus to KCA'.[10] Most evicted squatters joined the KCA which, by 1940, had become well established throughout the major part of the Rift Valley.[11] In 1944, a KCA Provincial Committee was set up to help Olenguruone people threatened with eviction.[12] But although local KCA committees in the Rift Valley kept in touch with leaders in Central Province, the squatters took it upon themselves to organise local politics in the White Highlands.

By 1945, there were 202,760 registered squatters in the White Highlands, of which 122,181 were Kikuyu. In Nakuru District, there were 36,492 and in Naivasha 22,682, of which 22,136 were Kikuyu. The Forest Reserves in the White Highlands contained a total of 21,143 Kikuyu squatters.[13] Kikuyu squatters thus comprised more than half the registered 'resident native' labourers. Tamarkin's remark that 'the squatters were perhaps the most suppressed, dispossessed and insecure social group in Kenya, especially in the post-war years'[14] was an accurate observation of the state of affairs in the country.

Statistics taken from the 1948 census gave the population densities as 770; 515; and 537 people per square mile in Kiambu, Fort Hall (Muranga) and Nyeri respectively. In themselves, these figures spelt extreme hardship among the peasants and land litigations were numerous.[15] In the White Highlands, the alienation and enclosure of squatters within a hostile enclave enhanced their suffering and bitterness.

The Olenguruone crisis increased the gathering storm of desperation among Kikuyu squatters, ex-squatters and peasants in the Reserves. In the White Highlands, the Olenguruone oath of unity was administered wherever Kikuyu squatters could be found. In the Reserves, the oath was administered by local activists who had taken the oath in Olenguruone before returning to Central Province, along with several Olenguruone residents who had come to help them spread the oath. James Beauttah, who had been a veteran politician in Central Province since the mid-1920s, remembered Samuel Koina, the leader of the Olenguruone people,[16] introducing the Olenguruone oath to the people of Kiambaa and Githunguri. This oath was then said to have been combined with the KCA loyalty oath to become the oath of unity.[17] Ernest Kiberethi, who had been a squatter in Nakuru District and who had taken the Olenguruone oath, confirmed that 'the oath was for all Kikuyu, Embu and Meru, not for Olenguruone people only. Everybody was annoyed'.[18]

An offshoot of the Olenguruone oath was that politics of protest became publicised in Central Province, and even more so in the Settled Areas. For a while the secrecy and extreme caution that had hitherto characterised politics on the European farms were partially discarded as squatters rallied behind their distressed comrades and kinsmen in Olenguruone, so that by 1949, after massive squatter oath-taking in the Rift Valley, '*siasa* [politics] had become public'.[19] Morale was high among the Olenguruone residents, despite the government's decision to evict them.

As they travelled to the Yatta area in Eastern Kenya where the government had decided to resettle them, they were confident of winning their struggle. They believed they were 'heading for a great victory...demanding our land and freedom'.[20] This demand for land and freedom was central to Mau Mau ideology.

KCA and KAU mobilisation

Although initially launched on a small and selective basis, by the middle of 1947 the KCA oath had turned into a widespread campaign, which was increasingly conducted in conjunction with the newly-formed KAU. Under tight security, the KCA continued to steer the oath-taking campaign up to the end of 1949, but 'from 1950 onwards, KCA became less, not more significant in the Kikuyu heartland'.[21]

The same was true of the situation in the White Highlands. Here, especially in the southern half of the region, which had the highest concentration of Kikuyu squatters who were also highly politicised, the loyalty oath was initially a joint venture by Central Province KCA and Olenguruone or local KCA leaders. For example, in 1947 Kenyatta held a massive KCA rally at Njoro in Nakuru District where the loyalty oath was administered. This Njoro 'tea party' then led to an increase in oath-taking.[22] While liaison between KCA Rift Valley and Central Province leaders had been sporadic in the pre-war period, between 1945 and 1950 it was intensified as leaders sought to bring stronger pressure on the colonial government. After 1950, however, it became difficult to coordinate or even to monitor the activities of the various KCA cells in the White Highlands.[23] As the pace of oath-taking increased and younger KCA activists became disillusioned by the gradualist constitutional political position of the older KCA members, militancy became apparent.

The oath administrators then cast their net wider to include not only men whom the KCA had vetted but all 'trustworthy' Kikuyu, both men and women. In Nairobi, trade union leaders were employed to spread the oath. Because Nairobi was a smaller unit than the Rift Valley or Central Province and because the Africans there were concentrated in locations, during the period up to 1950 it was probably relatively easy to co-ordinate the oath-taking ceremonies. But since it was impossible to impose sufficient surveillance to prevent information leaks in Central Province and the White Highlands, oath-taking in those areas was more decentralised, for both security and geographical reasons. But everywhere the oath administrators had to recognise that the Kikuyu community represented different interest groups, some of which were opposed to the oath and therefore posed real dangers to the movement. This was especially true in the White Highlands, where squatters lived in such close proximity with their arch enemies, the settlers. Since the aim of the oath was 'secretly to unite, discipline and foster political consciousness among the Kikuyu'[24] with the ultimate aim of obtaining land and freedom, it is hardly surprising that violence and intimidation were used to bring recalcitrant persons into line.

Militant politics among the squatters

The Olenguruone crisis had radicalised the use of the oath as a tool of unity everywhere and an intelligence report in 1948 recorded that squatters were taking the oath in the Njoro and Elburgon areas of Nakuru District.[25] On the farms, settlers continued to wage their battle to reduce squatter stock and the number of acres under squatter cultivation.[26] Desperate, dispossessed and impoverished squatters, who joined former Olenguruone residents to swell the ranks of the unemployed poor in the urban centres and rural sectors of the White Highlands, offered 'a fertile ground for the development of political militancy and agitation'.[27]

Those squatters who remained on settler farms had to contend with real economic hardship. While for a long time prepared to overlook low wages in the interests of having sufficient land to cultivate, by the late 1940s, every penny of the squatter's salary was important. With less land available to them and with a reduction in their livestock, squatter frustrations reached a new high as they began to resent being inadequately remunerated for the long hours they worked. As one former squatter put it, 'a person would be allowed to keep 15 goats only, yet the work one was doing was very exhausting, so one realised it was not worth it to work for fifteen goats. This is what annoyed us.'[28] The squatters saw their economic deprivation as linked to their political subordination and it was these two problems that they hoped to eradicate when they took the oath and swore to support the Mau Mau movement. When asked why he took the oath, the same former squatter replied:

> . . .because I had been suppressed so severely. I took the oath so that my children would not be enslaved in the [same] way I had been. So that they would not have privations as I had been subjected to in the form of 8 shillings monthly salary despite the fact that I had a large family so that the 8 shillings could not support them. . . After I had taken the oath, I was shown the necessary action for getting rid of the European. . . I believed they were necessary and I realised I ought to go to the forest.[29]

The next section will look at what this political mobilisation actually meant to the squatter community.

The social basis of Mau Mau in the White Highlands

Hundreds of highly politicised squatters were awaiting the inevitable confrontation between the Kikuyu and the government. But who had organised such militancy among the squatters and what was the social basis of Mau Mau in the Settled Areas? Frank Furedi, who carried out research among Kikuyu squatters in Nakuru District, argued that it was the squatter elite and petty traders who had been responsible for the development of Mau Mau in the Settled Areas.

Furedi maintained that because the squatters lived in a small face-to-face community which could exert pressure on individuals and in this way minimise dissent,[30] socio-economic differences within the community had no affect on how squatters responded to increasing militancy. He argued that it was the settler-created elite, including foremen and clerks, and the wealthier petty traders and teachers, who had already proven themselves in their occupations, who emerged from among the squatters as the natural leaders of Mau Mau.

I, on the other hand, have argued that the Mau Mau leadership among the squatters developed from the grassroots of the community. More recent research reveals that squatters adopted a heterogeneous response to Mau Mau and that socio-economic differences in the squatter community were clearly relevant in the development of and response to Mau Mau. The squatter elite, who owed their privileged position to the settlers and were in constant contact with them, were on the whole viewed with suspicion by rank and file squatters, who feared they might betray the struggle by revealing its secrets to the settlers. The disruptive, demanding aspects of Mau Mau posed a real threat to property and business, which would seem to suggest that the wealthy petty traders would be excluded from its ranks. But some of them did participate in Mau Mau activities, though in more marginal positions than suggested by Furedi. How squatters responded to Mau Mau must have been affected by the knowledge that, even before the movement was catapulted into its forest phase, it was claiming victims who were opposed to it. In Nakuru, the development of militancy was initiated by a younger generation which resented the gradualist and reformist style of the older politicians.[31]

The close co-ordination of Mau Mau activities between the town of Nakuru and its rural hinterland in the White Highlands[32] suggests that there were probably similar developments in other parts of the Settled Areas. The rapid recruitment of younger people into the KCA corresponded with the emergence of an impatient and militant wing in the party. Weary of the slow and unrewarding strategy that the KCA and KAU had adopted in their nationalist struggle, these younger members advocated the use of violence, mostly for the purposes of rapid recruitment of party supporters, but also possibly as a result of the Batuni oath.[33] The groundwork for an armed confrontation with the colonial powers was in progress. In the course of its evolution, not only in its oath-taking ceremonies but also in its active forest phase, Mau Mau adopted tight security procedures which anticipated the presence of traitors. This was clearly evident among the Kikuyu squatters in the White Highlands.

Contrary to Furedi's findings, there was a high inverse correlation between socio-economic status and response to Mau Mau among the squatters. In general, the higher the position they held within the settler-created stratification system, the less likely they were to support the movement, for, as mentioned earlier, the rank and file of the squatter community were suspicious of these 'labour aristocrats' and slow to entrust them with the movement's secrets. It was rare for this category of people to hold key positions in the movement's organisation on settler farms.[34]

Furedi's main reason for believing that Mau Mau leaders among the squatters were recruited from the ranks of the farm clerks (*karanis*), skilled artisans, overseers (*nyaparas*) or wealthy traders rests on the assumption that these people had already proved their worth by holding dominant positions on the farm and were therefore looked upon, and indeed became, the driving force behind grassroots participation in Mau Mau.[35] Plausible as the argument may sound, it defies the historical reality with which the squatters had to grapple. This is revealed through examining the conical stratification structure of the squatter community and through looking at how this became translated into Mau Mau, especially in its early stages.

The foreman or overseer, the *nyapara* as he was popularly or unpopularly known, stood at the head of any squatter community. He was basically responsible for maintaining law and order among the squatters, especially in matters relating to work, but above all was entrusted with the task of ensuring good working relations between the settler and his workers. He was also expected to ensure that the labourers carried out the tasks relegated to them. The *nyapara* was looked upon, both by the squatters and by the settler, as the European farm owner's 'eyes and ears'. In other words, in the absence of the settler, the *nyapara* took over as the *mzungu* (the white man). In practice, however, the *nyapara* worked through a number of sub-foremen with whom he maintained close contact and only intervened if there were disputes or cases of continual disobedience. The *nyapara* always kept in close touch with the settler, who was usually the only person to whom he was answerable, except in cases where there were strong Kikuyu arbitrating *ciama*. Whether the *nyapara* was hand-picked by the settler or chosen unanimously by the labourers made no difference to the closeness of his contact with the settler.

In terms of both cash and other forms of remuneration, the *nyapara* was better rewarded than the rank and file of the squatter community and was entitled to additional privileges. For example, his *shamba* was usually larger than that of an ordinary squatter. Also, since he was in charge of allocating land to the squatters,[36] he could determine how much land he himself cultivated. It has also been asserted that, in allocating plots, most *nyaparas* 'always wanted to be bribed in order to give a large piece of *shamba* to the squatters',[37] which obviously reduced their popularity even further.

The *nyapara* would receive full-cream milk every day, while on many farms the rest of the squatters were given skimmed milk (known as *mathace*). His salary was also much higher than that of the ordinary squatter. By about 1950, *nyaparas* in Nakuru District received between 30 and 45 shillings per month as compared to an average of 10 to 15 shillings earned by the other squatters. In addition, the *nyapara* had easy access to the *mzungu*'s house. He was the settler's confidant and sometimes had his house near the *mzungu*'s, away from the ordinary squatter. In some cases his *shamba* was also next to the *mzungu*'s.[38]

Other highly placed individuals within the squatter labour community included farm clerks (*karanis*), house servants, cooks and drivers. Their tasks were much lighter than those of field squatters and they also enjoyed higher salaries than the ordinary squatter as well as other privileges. Within the socio-economic structure of the White Highlands, these squatters formed a privileged group that was 'doing well'. The very nature of their jobs dictated that they were closer to the settler, both socially and geographically.[39] At a time when squatter conditions were deteriorating and the squatters, in turn, were engaged in a bitter struggle to redress their circumstances, it is unlikely that they would have entrusted their cause to those closest to the very institution the squatters were trying to fight. But, given their position of privileged access, this group could be used to elicit vital information from the settlers and, although risky, there were occasions when the squatters did indeed seize just such an opportunity.[40] It was, however, wiser and more usual for the squatters to conceal their political activities from this group.[41] To assume that the squatters would automatically choose the leaders of their political struggle from the above group is to distort historical reality and to project the importance accorded to these people by the settler on to the squatters. In other words, because the settlers held the *nyapara-karani* group in high esteem, it did not necessarily follow that the other squatters would do likewise.[42] The possibility of betrayal by these individuals was in itself a sufficient deterrent.

It is also misleading to assume that teachers, skilled artisans, farm clerks (*karanis*) and *nyaparas* were generally the first to take the oath because they were the most respected men on the farms.[43] Although it is true that educated people, prominent politicians and prosperous businessmen were traditionally recognised as leaders in Kikuyu communities, and that *karanis*, *nyaparas*, teachers and skilled artisans comprised the social and economic elite on settler farms, it has to be recognised that, like their counterparts in other Kikuyu communities, with the onset of militant politics, these squatter aristocrats had 'lost their position and had to watch the turn of events, which they regarded as disastrous, without being able to oppose it.'[44] A widespread distrust of the literate group[45] had developed, and the teachers in the Settled Areas were no exception, while the *nyaparas* were seen as the settlers' representatives and therefore liable to report any suspicious activities to them. Recent evidence supports the view that on most farms the first group of people to take the oath would be comprised of a select few which largely excluded the above.[46] Former leadership patterns had become inappropriate as new loyalties began to threaten both the political and economic basis of the previous leadership. The form and pace of militant politics called for a total commitment to the cause with no visible or immediate gain. It called for adherents to place their possessions, wealth and family, totally at the movement's disposal.[47] For a group that valued financial liquidity and political moderation, the movement's demands were therefore likely to be seen as extremist.

On the farms, at least during the period shortly before and immediately after the State of Emergency was declared, administration of the oath followed a security-oriented procedure,[48] which was vital in view of the alien and hostile environment in which the squatters operated. The few who were first selected to take the oath were chosen for their political insight, respectability, and 'wisdom from God',[49] the last trait being acquired independently of any formal education or special training and therefore not necessarily present in the skilled artisans whom Furedi regards as natural Mau Mau leaders.[50] Again, those selected were usually older people who had been members of the elders' councils, the *ciama*. They invariably had the interests of the squatters at heart and represented a different system of authority operative among the squatters from that vested in the *nyapara*, who was really the *mzungu's* representative.

It is now widely believed that the *nyaparas* were definitely not among the first to take the oath and in some instances 'all other squatters would be oathed while the *nyapara* who was an enemy (*thu*) would be left [unoathed]'.[51] The *nyapara* would 'only be touched [given the oath] after all the other people [on the farm] were united through oathing'.[52] Security considerations apart, it would appear that the main objective in this strategy was to isolate the *nyapara* and, in so doing, create in him the psychological need for identity with, or acceptance by, the rank and file of the squatter community. Once this was established, it was easy to co-opt him into the movement. At other times, 'the good *nyapara* were oathed' while 'bad ones were left uninformed'.[53] Squatters' responses to *nyaparas* were to a large extent dependent upon their relationships with them, but if *nyaparas* were given the oath with the first group it was usually as a precautionary measure rather than as a mark of respect. It was to ensure that the most immediate link with authority on the farm was within control.[54] Once they knew on which side he was, the *nyapara* was dealt with immediately. He was either 'killed or used to mobilise the other [squatters]'.[55] Occasionally, therefore, the *nyapara* was given the oath along with the first group of Mau Mau supporters, so that once his loyalty was established, he could be 'used' to spread the oath.

A number of different methods were used for luring or forcing *nyaparas* into taking the oath, all of which reflected the suspicion with which they were regarded, with the squatters eventually evolving a system whereby *nyaparas* were 'broken in to' the oath rites and Mau Mau. As one of the informants, Muchemi, explained:

> A wise man would be sent to the *nyapara* to invite him to drink [intoxicating drinks] at a certain house. The *nyapara* would be waylaid, and taken to a different house where he would be beaten up before being told the story [of oath-taking and Mau Mau] at a later stage. He would then be told the reason [for his arrest] and given the oath in complete darkness so that he would not identify anybody [present during the ritual].[56]

This method of administering the oath to *nyaparas* in the Settled Areas appears to have been fairly widespread. Muchemi said that:

> The *nyapara* would be seized, beaten first even if he had not refused to take the oath and then he would be given the oath by force and challenged to go and report. If the *shamba* was [later] raided by the authorities, the *nyapara* would be killed, even by people from another *shamba*. At times the *nyapara* would be given the oath by people from other *shamba* sent by those from the *nyapara*'s *shamba*.[57]

Another informant, Kinuthia, observed that 'the *nyapara* and the cook were in the same group and were forced into oathing and threatened with death if they reported those who had taken the oath'.[58] It is clear that although *nyaparas* were basically on the squatters' side in the racially stratified squatter-settler enclave, they were treated with great suspicion by the squatter community. They became even more mistrusted in the period immediately before the State of Emergency was declared and it was thought necessary to take extra precautions when admitting these 'settler representatives' into a political organisation that set out to destroy the settlers and the colonial government.

While it was common practice to warn all participants that they would be severely punished if they disclosed the oath, an even tougher line was taken with the *nyapara-karani* group, for their constant contact with settlers constituted a high security risk for the movement. It was hoped that, by instilling fear into them, they would be deterred from informing the *mzungu* about the oath. Hard-core oath-resisters among the squatters were taken to other *shambas* for the ceremony. It was, however, usual to try to persuade the *nyapara* before resorting to the use of force, for it was believed 'that since he was Kikuyu he would understand'.[59] In other words, the squatters believed that, despite his alignment with the settler, the *nyapara* would appreciate the cause the squatters were fighting for and therefore refrain from betraying the struggle to either the settlers or the colonial government.

Some of the *nyaparas* who managed to retain their jobs by professing their loyalty to the government were really active as 'contacts' for the movement, as were some house servants, who proved useful in conspiracies against the settlers because they were able to acquire so much information about the Europeans.[60] Njuguna Kiorogo was one such *nyapara* who, on being interrogated, tried to protect his colleagues by saying that he had been given the oath by people who came from faraway Nyeri and, being a *nyapara*, was spared the unpleasant horrors of repatriation.[61] This kindly and selective treatment of *nyaparas* was seen earlier in relation to the *kifagio* conflict, when a *nyapara* would be given time to dispose of his stock, whereas other squatters would have theirs confiscated or killed immediately. The settlers and administration obviously regarded the *nyaparas* as potential allies.

Among the squatters, retired or unemployed kinsmen made the most suitable Mau Mau leaders as they could devote all their time to the movement's affairs. Self-employed traders living among the squatters were useful for running errands while on business trips, but obviously could not take on a more central role in the movement without jeopardising their businesses.

There must, however, even among the squatters, have been people who opposed Mau Mau. Christians, for example, or people appalled at the use of violence and by the unorthodox methods adopted by Mau Mau, especially the sexual aspects of the oaths, must, either openly or secretly, have criticised the movement. Surely here, as in Central Province, Nairobi and elsewhere, there must have been people who, if they had had the choice, would have refused to join Mau Mau as it existed. The social structure of the squatter community has been looked at here, not so much to identify the pertinent divisions within the community as to show how a squatter's perception of these divisions affected his or her attitude towards the movement, especially in its formative years, for there was clearly a correlation between socio-economic status and the resultant pattern of response to Mau Mau.[62]

The way in which vast estates were expropriated and then largely underutilised sharpened the squatters' awareness of the injustices of the establishment, especially since open intimidation, physical floggings neral ill-treatment were part and parcel of their day-to-day lives on the farms. Squatters constantly experienced the indignities of colonialism at the indiscriminate hand of the immediate colonial agent, the settler. Despite several decades of apparent acquiescence, punctuated by the occasional isolated act when labour was withdrawn or settler livestock maimed, the level of discontent among squatters was rising. The gathering storm of the 1940s was heralded not only by an increase of KCA activity in the White Highlands,[63] but also, and more strategically, by the desperate conditions suffered by squatters on the farms and in Nakuru Town, and by the massive rise in oath-taking among both urban dwellers and squatters following the radicalisation of the KCA oath, when goat meat, instead of the Bible, became the central symbol. The militancy and widespread nature of the oath bore a hitherto unprecedented urgency and enhanced political consciousness, unity and commitment.

The rise of violence

To some extent, Mau Mau must be seen as a new squatter response to a new and more oppressive *kifagio*. During the second half of the 1940s, settlers waged an all out campaign to eliminate the squatter peasant option which was seen to undermine capitalist farming. The settlers continued to clamp down on the squatters and to reduce their stock and cultivation and this, in turn, fuelled squatter political mobilisation and violence. Political consciousness, bolstered by intensive repression and suffering in both the rural White Highlands and urban Kenya created a taut situation. Mau Mau was 'largely the response of the landless in Kenya Reserves, the disinherited squatters in the White Highlands, and the Kikuyu urban lumpenproletariat.'[64] In the Settled Areas, 'Mau Mau was [also] the outcome of a prolonged agrarian struggle between Kikuyu squatters and European settlers'.[65]

In the Rift Valley, the emergency was preceded by acts of violence which emanated from the political mobilisation. In 1950, the official proscription of the unidentified Mau Mau Association followed the trial and conviction of Kikuyu charged with illegally taking the oath in the Njoro area. In August of the same year, the colonial administration posted a police officer to Nakuru 'for special duties in connection with Mau Mau activities'[66] and mobile unit cinemas and *barazas* were organised in an attempt to stamp it out.[67] In the Naivasha area the number of unprovoked attacks by Africans on Europeans became 'a disturbing feature',[68] while in Nakuru District an increase in offences against property was attributed to the low wages and high cost of living.[69] In November 1951 a white man, Mr Robert Hall of Ol Kalau, was killed and two people arrested for interrogation.[70] Violence in the Nakuru, Naivasha and Laikipia districts was on the increase.[71] These were the districts with the highest concentration of Kikuyu squatters. And increasingly people began to associate oaths and acts of violence with Mau Mau, even though at the time these were KCA-directed. At the beginning of the year the administration had noted with alarm the spread of Mau Mau out of Nakuru District into the high country around Timboroa, Ainabkoi, Kipkabus and Moiben, 'where there are a lot of Kikuyu among the farm and forest labour'.[72] Although there were no reports of sabotage on farms in this area, no one doubted that there was underground activity.

Early in 1952 political activists in various parts of the Rift Valley went on an all out attack to recruit any Kikuyu in the province who had not taken the oath. Dissatisfied with progress so far, they resorted to the use of force and intimidation to get everyone on to their side. Some Kikuyu who strongly opposed such measures became informers for the administration, with the result that there was a new wave of convictions. In the light of increasing reports of forced oath-taking and intimidation, the government called upon KAU to temper the violence. KAU leaders consequently visited many areas, including Nakuru, Gilgil and Naivasha, where meetings at which Kenyatta and other KAU leaders addressed the people were held. The largest of these rallies took place at Ol Joro Orok and Thompson's Falls on 29 June 1952.

Even before the State of Emergency was declared, the Nakuru, Naivasha and Laikipia Districts were singled out as special districts 'and enhanced powers were given to the administrative officers in charge'.[73] By August, conditions in Laikipia had deteriorated enough to warrant the declaration of a curfew in the area. But the oath continued to be taken in all these areas, and with even greater intensity in Naivasha. The murder of Chief Waruhiu, who for two weeks had been persuading loyal Kikuyu to join the government in stamping out terrorist activities, was the last straw. At this point the colonial government became convinced that drastic measures would have to be taken to contain the situation.

The security risk associated with arbitrary mass oath-taking has already been noted. By September 1952, shortly after the introduction of the Batuni oath, 412 people had already been imprisoned on charges of being members of the Mau Mau movement. Several hundreds more awaited trial on similar charges. Cases of squatters assaulting Europeans during this period became more frequent and a number of squatters were repatriated for just such attacks. 'A *mzungu* called Mickley John was killed by Mau Mau. As a result people from the eight surrounding *shambas* were repatriated on that one day.'[74] Subsequent arrests doubtless aroused great anger and wrath against suspected traitors of the movement. With the increase in violence and its attendant publicity, the settlers of Kenya felt most threatened. Out on their farms, they were surrounded by embittered Africans and were cut off from the security the colonial forces offered to their urban kinsmen. It became apparent that the African was no longer a protégé in need of protection but a dangerous foe. In turn, the settlers pressurised the government for more deterrent action against Mau Mau 'criminals'. They also proceeded to arm themselves. To a large extent, this settler panic was responsible for the declaration of the State of Emergency. The extent of settler distrust and fear of the bulk of their mostly squatter Kikuyu, Embu and Meru labour force was evidenced by the brutalities they inflicted after the Emergency was declared. These included blatant cases of arbitrary killing of Kikuyu labour, confiscation of their stock, forced confession, beating, and other forms of open intimidation. Squatters were perceived as a major security risk and a subversive group.

At the same time, increasing incidents of reported oath-taking, violent brutalities and general agitation in Central and Rift Valley Provinces, and in the urban areas, caused considerable apprehension in government circles. In its zeal to contain the situation, the government declared a State of Emergency on 20 October 1952 and, by so doing, unleashed events which had far-reaching consequences. The colonial government found it necessary to reorganise and rejuvenate its administrative and military structures in readiness for the imminent combat with the 'subversive forces'.[75] Central Province and Nairobi were the major targets of this combat. In the White Highlands, frightened European farmers began to expel their mostly squatter Kikuyu labourers, a process further accelerated by the introduction of a screening mechanism, which reinforced a new pass system applicable to all Kikuyu, Embu and Meru.[76] It was argued that Mau Mau violence was frightening off other sources of labour in the Settled Areas and that the only way of securing labour was to evict all Kikuyu. But even before the government took action, Mau Mau leaders had started to pressurise squatters into abandoning the farms.[77] Some of these early deserters went to Central Province, although others presumably went straight to the forest.

In all, approximately 100,000 Kikuyu squatters were repatriated to the Reserve.[78] For a period this resulted in a temporary disruption of labour in the White Highlands, although this did not take long to remedy. Labourers from other ethnic groups, especially the Luyia, Luo and Kamba, moved in to fill the vacuum left by the Kikuyu.

While the repatriation exercise was meant to contain and restrict the destructive activities of the Kikuyu, in the long run it served to strengthen the number of revolutionaries. Greater surveillance by the reinforced colonial forces, which included Kikuyu loyalists, increased the security risk of underground activities. In Central Province, the government undertook massive exercises to comb the area in search of culprits. The exercise entailed forced confessions, collective punishments, being confined to certain villages and forced labour, all of which produced fear, anxiety and the need to hit back against the constituted authority. These frustrations drove several thousand committed freedom fighters into the neighbouring Aberdare and Mt Kenya forests where strategies for reprisals were soon evolved.

Some of the squatter repatriates were driven to the forests as much through hunger as anything else. Most were landless and many lost what little stock they had owned through confiscation by European farmers or government personnel.[79] Herded into hastily-erected government transit camps, their only real choices were starvation, petty crime or life in the forests. Colonial oppression was regarded as a worse alternative than trying to eke out a livelihood in the forest and hundreds of ex-squatters poured into the forests either directly from the Rift Valley Province or after a short spell in the overcrowded and unwelcoming Reserves. The Reserves could barely support their own indigenous populations and additional arrivals from the Rift Valley merely made a bad situation desperate. It was little wonder then that hundreds of people chose to fend for themselves and to continue their anti-colonialist struggle in the forest.

The arrest shortly after the declaration of the State of Emergency of the elite African leaders of KAU and of the trade union movement failed to disrupt Mau Mau activities in Nakuru.[80] Although the administration had initially believed that some good would come to the country by removing the national leaders,[81] it is now obvious that, at least in Nakuru, operational structures had evolved that were largely independent of the elite national leadership. In any case, a large number of educated people pulled out of the movement when it began to adopt a violent course. Kenyatta publicly denounced Mau Mau as early as February 1951,[82] and continued to do so right up until 'the great denial' at his trial. In Nakuru, 'even those educated leaders who were forced to take the Batuni oath had no access to the movement's secrets and had little knowledge of its leadership, organisation and activities'.[83] The emerging pattern of politics in both urban and rural Nakuru showed that formally constituted political organisations were largely and regularly patronised by educated and semi-educated Kikuyu, but that in parts of the White Highlands inadequate educational facilities diminished their numbers and meant that Mau Mau became a largely grass-roots movement.

A loose and disjointed pattern had come to characterise the

movement as early as the middle of 1950. District and locational committees tried to oversee oath-taking and the collection of funds and ammunition, but none the less there were still many unsanctioned acts of intimidation, especially in Central Province and Nairobi, which increasingly endangered the movement's security.

While the major political activities of the KCA and KAU were monitored to keep track of the trend of events, the squatters were content with occasional representation at important meetings in Kiambu and Nairobi, which kept them 'in touch with the headquarters'.[84] Although the squatters did liaise with Kiambu and Nairobi whenever necessary, they did not await directives from these places before acting, but proceeded to organise themselves, initially in the preparatory 'unity' and military 'Batuni' oaths and later in the forest struggle. Once in the forest, they were in closer contact with comrades from Central Province, Nairobi and other areas.

New labour regulations, which insisted on all Kikuyu being photographed in preparation for the introduction of new labour records, were met with open defiance. Squatter protest leaders capitalised on speculation that those who were photographed would lose their land in the Reserves, be forced to work in the Settled Areas for life, and probably face death from Mau Mau. Compliance with the legislation was seen as collaboration with government forces. All the squatters in the Wanjohi and Kipipiri areas, for example, refused to be photographed and were consequently repatriated, though some had moved away voluntarily at an earlier period.

Freedom fighters operating from the Aberdares, Mau Hills and within Naivasha and Nakuru Districts were active in the Rift Valley. On 27 March 1953 'a large and well organised terrorist gang overran Naivasha Police Station and Divisional Headquarters, killing two constables and got away with ammunition'.[85] The raid was led by Mbaria Kaniu.[86] Within Nakuru and Naivasha Districts acts of terrorism against settlers and their property increased. Settler livestock and foodcrops became major targets as forest guerrillas sought to replenish other dwindling food supplies. The odd settler also sometimes fell victim to Mau Mau, either in a prearranged attack or in a chance encounter.

Whatever the circumstances, settler casualties invariably elicited demands for the repatriation of all Kikuyu squatters. Because of the atrocities of the period, settlers found it difficult to trust or retain even those of their employees whom they thought innocent. Infighting and mud-slinging broke out within the settler community as individuals accused their neighbours of harbouring Mau Mau supporters by not exposing their suspect labour, or by protecting them from incessant interrogation.[87] Europeans referred to those among them who hindered anti-Mau Mau operations as the white Mau Mau.[88] The Kikuyu as an entity were seen as guilty. Even the innocent were blamed for the crime of omission since they could have prevented 'the Mau Mau monstrosity from coming to birth if they had had the desire, the courage, or the will to do so'.[89] For their default they had to bear the penalty of repatriation. Furthermore, the brutality of the murders and the sexual aspects of the oath convinced the Europeans that they were dealing with 'primitive beasts and not ordinary humans'.[90]

In the Njoro area, settlers were quite militant in their demand for government action against Mau Mau atrocities. They were determined not to sit back and watch their area become another Thompson's Falls.[91] After a murder had been committed in the Ndothua area between Njoro and Elburgon, the Njoro Settlers Association asked for immediate action against the people in the vicinity of the crime. While the settlers had hoped for the confiscation of all livestock and the repatriation of the people in the area and had the support of the Rift Valley Provincial Commissioner, action was halted on higher authority. This so irritated the settlers that in an urgent meeting their President called for the resignation of all special magistrates and Kenya Police Reserve officers so that they, the settlers, could be 'free to take action on our own'.[92]

In a subsequent meeting, they resolved that Mau Mau was treason and that 'everyone caught at ceremonies or concerned with outrages be hanged quickly, possibly publicly and at any rate the bodies hung up on view'.[93] Any Kikuyu found in the area of a crime were to be removed and sent to public labour camps for ten years, where they would engage in afforestation, 'de-bushing' and generally working in the Tana 'fly' area with neither pay nor fancy rations. The meeting also recommended that the Kikuyu should be warned that a tract of tribal land would be confiscated for every outrage after 1 January 1953 and given over to reafforestation. More importantly, the Njoro Settlers Association decided that there should be no more Kikuyu squatters 'until Mau Mau was dead'. As if to underline the dangers of employing large numbers of Kikuyu squatters, the Association resolved that in future only a specified percentage of Kikuyu would be allowed to each employer (about 25 or 30 per cent of his total labour force) and that they were to be housed in compact villages. It was to be considered a privilege for the Kikuyu to be allowed to leave their Reserves and if they were convicted of any crime they were to be sent back to the Reserve and the privilege not to be renewed 'ever'.[94] And this included the Forest Department.

This reaction to the Mau Mau atrocities by the Njoro Settlers Association was not unique to the Nakuru area. In Naivasha and Laikipia, where Mau Mau was very active, drastic measures were taken to rid the regions of Kikuyu, Embu and Meru squatters. This forced repatriation from the White Highlands and District Townships continued up to 1954. It culminated in almost total mass deportation of the Kikuyu, Embu and Meru people. Between 1952 and 1954, repatriated ex-squatters experienced great hardship in the crowded Reserves. The whole experience was absolutely horrendous for them. One Kikuyu, who was worried about the return of Kikuyu labour to the Rift Valley, felt that the settlers could not possibly be aware of the implications of their actions:

> When I often read in the paper what Europeans are thinking of Kikuyu I am always with knowledge how they don't know the trouble which the Kikuyus have hard [*sic*] during the emergency which would not put a Kikuyu in the Mau Mau line unless he or she is mad. Some of you have not visited the villages and if they have they have seen only the houses without knowing what is going on inside the village. Many Kikuyus have not seen money for many months and they are living on beging [*sic*] food.[95]

The agonies of repatriation were even more severe if the repatriation had been occasioned by an atrocity in the immediate area. Any Kikuyu against whom there was sufficient evidence regarding his or her sympathy for and/or dealings with Mau Mau was immediately punished by detention, imprisonment, repatriation, or all three. And even in cases where 'information . . .[was] not sufficiently definite to form the basis of a criminal charge',[96] it was thought necessary to repatriate the persons concerned. It was fairly common for swoops to cover large areas surrounding the scene of a crime. For example, when a Mr Barker's house was burnt down in Njoro in February 1954, all Kikuyu within a ten-mile radius of the area were rounded up, totalling about 3,000 people.[97] In areas like Thompson's Falls, attacks against settlers resulted in the wholesale removal of all Kikuyu labour. Elsewhere settlers sought to reduce the percentage of Kikuyu labour in their employ to ensure that should the situation deteriorate further, the need to remove all Kikuyu labour would not cripple their economy.[98]

The squatters would be brought from the farms to a central point at the nearest administrative centre. If they were lucky they did not have to wait long at these transit camps before they were on their way to their areas of origin. Government transport was provided, usually in the form of open lorries. One of the squatters was Kirugumi, who remembered how 'when we got to Nyeri we would be sorted out, [Chief] Muhoya's people or people from other areas. . . then we would be sent to the camp where we would be interrogated. To be interrogated meant to be beaten. It wasn't just to be asked questions. It was to be beaten..'.[99] It was usual to 'interrogate' squatters at the initial collection points in the White Highlands, not only to establish where their home area was, but to find out what Mau Mau activities and connections they had forged in the White Highlands.

The hostile reception with which they were greeted in Central Province was made worse by the shortage of land.

Even if it was available, land in Central Province was far from sufficient for the squatters from the White Highlands[100] and at first relatives were faced with the burden of feeding and housing the new arrivals. Although not all were warmly received, some former squatters said that sympathetic kinsmen had rallied to help the repatriated families. One of these, Wanjugu, was luckier than most. As she said, 'I came to friends and brothers who gave me a plot from which I got crops to help me get by'.[101] Other families, however, lived on the verge of starvation for want of adequate land or job openings.

Mau Mau food supplies: the women's war

The settlers worried not only about squatter men and their violence, but also about squatter women and the way in which they supported their men in the Mau Mau struggle. Not only did they act as go-betweens and carriers of food and firearms, but they also 'generally provided a brazen system of intelligence which [was] hard to keep eliminated'.[102] The government considered that if it could 'weaken the morale and resistance of gangs by a complete denial of food',[103] then a major battle against the freedom fighters would have been won. To this end, the government initiated measures to ensure that all stock in the Settled Areas was kept in well-fenced *bomas* (pens) which were inspected regularly and were well guarded at night. At no time was the stock to be left unattended. In addition, all harvested food was to be guarded and suitably stored. Rations to labour were to be 'issued frequently in limited quantities and not in bulk'.[104] Finally, all Kikuyu, Embu and Meru labour was to be concentrated in labour camps which were to be inspected regularly for checks on strangers.

But, despite these precautions, pro Mau Mau squatters continued to act as the civil wing, the lifeline, without which the forest freedom fighters would no longer have been able to exist. For example, women took the opportunity of gathering firewood to pass on vital information and supplies to freedom fighters, especially in the areas bordering the forests. Once this tactic became known to the authorities, farmers were urged to ensure that firewood was only collected on certain days 'when farm guards . . . [could] accompany the wood gatherers and keep them under observation'.[105]

Collecting food for freedom fighters was an important task that required centralised organisation. For a long time, one of Wanjiru

Nyamarutu's responsibilities was to organise the collection, preparation and dispatch of food to freedom fighters in the Ndothua, Nessuit, Gichobo and Menangai Hill forests in the Njoro and Nakuru areas. She was accorded the rank of General-in-Charge of Food (*Genero Wa Rigu*) and had her own subordinate staff, who carried out her orders.

Wanjiru was the daughter of an ex-squatter in the Njoro Nessuit Forest area. Her political career, which predated Mau Mau, went back to the Olenguruone crisis. She had a brother-in-law whose son lived in Olenguruone and she herself had acquired a piece of land from this man. She cultivated the land to supplement the produce of her Njoro *shamba*. She had been active in KAU politics and was KAU treasurer in her area. She collected money which she sent on to the Central KAU office in Githunguri in Central Province. Wanjiru had taken the 1948/49 Olenguruone oath of defiance and was also divisional leader for Njoro during the Olenguruone crisis.[106] As a recognised leader among the Olenguruone people, she had overseen the administration of the Mau Mau oaths both in Nakuru and Njoro. She was also an early associate of the late Mzee Kenyatta, and as such could be said to have been in the mainstream of political developments in the period immediately before and during the Mau Mau rebellion.

Wanjiru belonged to the more militant category of freedom fighters. In the Nakuru and Njoro areas, taking the oath meant discarding 'western clothes' for unstitched pieces of cloth (*mashuka*) wrapped around the body in traditional Kikuyu style. The young and newly married oath-takers also had their upper ear lobes pierced (*gukaywo nyori*) as a sign of being pure Kikuyu (*Kikuyu karinga*). Although this ritual and traditional dress were optional, while they lasted they became 'the thing to do' among the movement's staunch adherents in the two areas, who also shaved their heads clean after the oath 'initiation'.

Wanjiru would gather information from her field workers about the food and other needs of freedom fighters in her area of jurisdiction. She would then relay the information to her subordinates who, under her direction, would mobilise the 'initiated' daughters and wives of squatters into gathering the necessary food for dispatch. Only those who had taken the oath were qualified to carry out this task. The others 'did not even know that this was taking place'.[107] Once gathered, the food was prepared independently, and put into Kikuyu baskets (*ciondo*) or waterpots to be dispatched to prearranged places by carefully selected young women.[108] While the various Mau Mau tasks called for the use of money, a woman who had taken the oath could not accept money for Mau Mau tasks from an unoathed friend or husband. Such money was considered unclean and the person an enemy.[109] The strictest discipline was necessary, even for members of Mau Mau's civil wing.

Together with other members of the movement, the girls chosen to run Mau Mau errands, such as delivering food, were made to understand, through the strictest threats, that being a Mau Mau woman was a serious and dangerous business and entailed extreme self-restraint in all sorts of ways. For example, it was impressed upon women who had taken the oath that they were not to get involved with non-Kikuyu men (*nduriri*),[110] the obvious implication being that a non-Kikuyu man would not belong to Mau Mau and was therefore an enemy. Even among the Kikuyu, women who had taken the oath did not have sexual relations with 'enemies', i.e. unoathed Kikuyu. Men were warned against marrying the daughters of unoathed Kikuyu men. Mau Mau women were barred from prostitution and the men from dealing with prostitutes, although the women were allowed to flirt with 'enemies' for the purposes of gathering vital information. At other levels too, members of Mau Mau were not supposed to maintain associations with unoathed friends except for the purposes of obtaining information.[111]

Wanjiru continued to raise money on a provincial basis. With the help of other movement members, both men and women, clothes, medicine, scrap metal for making rifles, bottles for making ammunition, etc., were bought and passed on to needy freedom fighters. Coats, rifles and ammunition were solicited from sympathetic soldiers, while medical aid and supplies were obtained, mainly from auxiliary staff at the District Hospital in Nakuru.

While delivering consignments, the women also passed important logistical data to the freedom fighters on the movement of troops, official raids, or possible informers. All this helped the freedom fighters to map out their next moves. These women obviously risked their lives to undertake these tasks and one should not underestimate their contribution. Wanjiru's initiatives, which succeeded only because of the teamwork of dedicated men and women, must have been duplicated all over the Rift Valley as men, women and children pooled their resources to keep the forest guerrillas going. The various roles played by women to help the movement are of enormous interest.

Although women comprised only about five per cent of the total guerrilla army, there was a larger 'civilian army' of dedicated women who, along with everyone else, had to reorganise their lives to fit in with the demands of Mau Mau. For women who held positions of authority, the deliberations were very time consuming and under normal circumstances would probably have put enormous strain on the domestic front. But times were not normal. The Mau Mau movement obviously brought cold war to families where only one of the spouses had taken the oath. Ideally, if a husband was the first to take the oath, he did not proceed to discuss the happening with his wife (or wives). She would have to await her turn to take the oath and vice versa. Hence, where a wife was the initiated party in a marriage, she continued to carry out Mau Mau tasks, such as contributing money, food, running errands, etc., without informing or consulting her husband. In fact, as far as the movement was concerned, an unoathed partner was an enemy – a prospective informer.[112]

Where a woman had risen to a position of authority in the movement and this in any way interfered with her domestic duties, her husband would have to go along with the new set-up or risk being regarded as an enemy of the movement and therefore a possible candidate for elimination.[113] Other women in the movement would stand in for their female colleagues as much as possible to help with vital domestic chores, but beyond this the husband had to cope as best as he could.

While a husband could not openly oppose a wife's decision to go to the forest, a Mau Mau Committee might relieve a woman of her duties if she had young children at home. Women who were still breast-feeding a child were not allowed into the forest. Likewise a pregnant woman would be released into civil life. Wives did not generally go into the forest – most of the forest women were single or widowed. Since security risks occasionally militated against the release of pregnant women, it was not unusual to have a mature woman to attend to the expectant mothers in the forest. Gakonyo Ndungi was one such forest 'doctor' during her two and a half years' stay in the forest.[114]

Some women fled to the forest for no other reason than to run away from the harassment of the Home Guards, but others went to avoid being arrested for previous Mau Mau activities. Guerrillas forced some women into the forest, where they performed whatever duties were allotted to them. In the Embu area, where Gakonyo lived prior to the outbreak of Mau Mau, many Kikuyu men and women went to the forest to escape attacks by the Ndia people, who objected to the presence of Kikuyu in their area. There were also women who had joined the male forest guerrillas because they wanted to participate in the combat.

At first, the presence of women among forest gangs was more often than not seen as a hindrance because of the general belief that women could not withstand the harsh forest environment and that they would distract the male guerrillas. For this reason, Gakenia and her 25 colleagues (this excluded four who had lured loyalist troops and then taken their rifles from them) were sent to a number of different neighbouring squatter homesteads after they had been in the forest for only three weeks, although later, and with better organisation, the 26 women were again co-opted into the forest forces.

Before a woman could be elected as a leader and co-opted into the Inner Secret Council (*Ndundu Ya Hitho*), she had to have taken the third oath, at which point it was held that she could not possibly turn against the movement. As far as positions of leadership went, once people had proved themselves trustworthy through acts of bravery, secrecy or dedication, then 'there was no man or woman leader',[115] for gender was immaterial. Merit was more important and 'Mau Mau would not oppose what a woman leader said'. The Mau Mau movement is credited with having created joint male-female councils where women's voices could be heard.[116] This particular development seems to have bolstered the women's confidence, and informants were quick to point out that, in the forest, 'a brave woman would have a rifle and fight like the men. If . . . [she] became pregnant, then . . . [she] lost the rifle'.[117]

It was considered bad discipline for a woman to fall pregnant while in the forest and, while she lost her honour, her male partner was subjected to punitive chores. A woman falling pregnant in such circumstances would sometimes be escorted to the nearest government post, which would allow her to give birth under government security and avoid being arrested by chance and possibly tortured.

Wanjiru did not stay long in Njoro after the State of Emergency was declared. She had been too active in the politics of the area and once she found out that the government was after her, she managed to get a pass to Nakuru on the pretext that her children were sick and needed to be taken to the District Hospital there. In Nakuru, where a particular house was set apart for nursing the wounded guerrillas, she teamed up with other Mau Mau supporters and continued her various tasks. These included overseeing the administration of the oath, helping to dispatch new recruits, and collecting money, both for fares for various Mau Mau errands and, especially, for buying supplies for local and other Mau Mau gangs. Although all these activities were the result of team efforts, the informants agreed that Wanjiru was the moving spirit behind most of them.

At this point, the mothers who also contributed the services of their children should be mentioned, for these children acted as members of vigilante committees, errand boys and girls and 'informers'. Children were given the oath from the age of about eight and, for the most part unwittingly, would gather and pass on information which was vital to the safety of freedom fighters and their supporters. One of the informants, Gakonyo Ndungi, showed pride in her son when she said, 'If you saw my young son Hinga on the road with his toy-wheel (*mubara*) you'd think he was playing. But he was really on duty. Small boys were oathed and they knew what to do.'[118] Young children were sealed with the sign of a cross and dedicated to Mau Mau work and sometimes even killed in the struggle, which was exceedingly painful for their mothers. Gakonyo remembers the mockery with which loyalist soldiers would break the news to these women: 'Come and see your child who has independence in the *shamba*'.[119] This would be in reference to a corpse that needed to be identified. At the height of the struggle, it became dangerous for Mau Mau members to identify their dead and Gakonyo reported that no one would confess any knowledge of the victim. That, she said, was the sort of commitment and self-discipline that the oath bound one to. Gakonyo stayed in the forest for two and a half years before being shot and arrested in a forest encounter with loyalist troops. She remained silent throughout her trial in Embu and served a prison sentence of three years and four months.

Among her various other positions, Wanjiru also held the title of Judge in Nakuru's Mau Mau Court, which allowed her to join the other court members in passing sentences for various anti-Mau Mau crimes, some of which carried the death sentence. Although under Mau Mau rule 19 women were forbidden to know about any killings on the grounds that they 'could not keep secrets',[120] Wanjiru's position in the movement obviously shows that in time these attitudes changed and that early reservations about the ability of women to withstand the brutal and secretive aspects of the struggle were amended. There was even a group of hardy women who, alongside the men, carried out the executions of offenders after sentence had been passed. Wambui X, who was one of these, was known as 'the killer' (*kamuirigo*). After her husband, himself a freedom fighter, had been killed in the forest, Wambui refused to remarry and dedicated herself to Mau Mau work. She is seen as representative of the kind of woman who, having undergone the worst of the hair-raising ordeals of Mau Mau, could not revert to domestic subjection because 'she could not be ruled, she knew everything. [Her] hands had become light, [she] could easily kill a useless husband'.[121]

The authorities eventually caught up with Wanjiru in Nakuru, where she was arrested and placed in Nakuru and Naivasha transit camps before being repatriated to Muguga, her parents' original home. Here her indomitable spirit remained unquenched and she soon teamed up with other ex-Rift Valley people who had been repatriated and, together with local supporters, they continued their Mau Mau operations, which were mainly to dispatch new recruits to the Ndeiya forest.

At the end of the Emergency, Wanjiru returned to Nakuru, and this time took a new oath, the Kenya Land Freedom Army (KLFA) oath. The KLFA was a vigilante organisation of Mau Mau diehards who swore to revive the forest struggle should the decolonisation process go against Mau Mau ideals. The KLFA continued to conduct selective oath taking and to accumulate more rifles and ammunition. Wanjiru was in charge of the safe-keeping of some of these weapons, but once again, just before Kenyatta was released,. the long arm of the law caught up with her and this time she was detained in Lamu. But whether in or out of the forests, female Mau Mau adherents remained gallant supporters of the struggle. This pro-Mau Mau pattern among Rift Valley women was reproduced wherever Mau Mau was operative.

In the Kinangop area, where the Kikuyu squatters continued to supply the forest forces with potatoes as late as June 1955, the settlers were forced to 'impose greater restrictions on the growing of this crop'.[122] Here, as elsewhere, 'a close watch was kept on Kikuyu labour, which was concentrated in labour camps to make surveillance easier and contact with freedom fighters more difficult. With time many farm squatters found it difficult to supply Mau Mau gangs, although forest squatters found the operation slightly easier.[123]

Mau Mau and the control of the Rift Valley

The alienation of land in the Rift Valley created three groups of people, each with a stake in the area, namely the Kalenjin/Maasai, the Kikuyu squatters, and the white settlers. Although the battle over land was predominantly between the Kikuyu squatters and the European settlers, the Maasai and Kalenjin also lost vast tracts of land through alienation. As a result, a considerable number of Kipsigis[124] and Nandi (subgroups of the Kalenjin ethnic group) were forced to work on settler farms in exchange for grazing rights for their cattle.

Although very little has been written on how ethnic groups other than the Kikuyu, Embu and Meru responded to land alienation, the apathy of the Kalenjin towards the movement that aimed to regain their lost lands is well known. Paul Pavlis's article on the 'Maasai and the Mau Mau Movement'[125] is essentially a statement of avenues of research into the Maasai's role in the Mau Mau revolt and basically therefore raises more questions than it answers. It does, however, establish that the Maasai were not indifferent to Mau Mau and that there were pockets of Mau Mau activity in Maasailand, although these have been attributed to people who were half Kikuyu and half Maasai. Pavlis concludes that Eurocentric interpretations of Mau Mau are inadequate, for Mau Mau's apparently 'tribalist' composition is really the result of former British tactics of instilling tribal divisions and suspicions into the Africans. One could explain the absence of mass support for Mau Mau among the Maasai by arguing that, although they suffered huge losses, the Maasai were still left with sizeable tracts of land in their southern Reserve which were accessible to their large herds. Their experience of land shortage was therefore very much less severe than that of the Kikuyu and the lack of any immediate and significant grievance among the Maasai must have dampened their enthusiasm for political agitation.

By 1952, the Mau Mau movement had begun to spread, especially in Nairobi,[126] to groups such as the Kipsigis, Kamba, Luo and Luyia. Anti-Kikuyu propaganda was to some extent responsible for the hostile attitude adopted towards Mau Mau by other ethnic groups, but even more destructive was the unanticipated violence that was so characteristic of the movement and that obviously led to it being resented, even among the Kikuyu.

The squatters' state of landlessness was the major and single most important source of their discontentment and, like their kinsmen in Central Province, they quite understandably directed their bitterness towards the European estates. As Barnett says, 'The vast European Highlands were both a source and symbol of their poverty and the owners of these estates were viewed as an obstacle to every form of Kenya African progress.'[127] About 0.7 per cent of Kenya's population held 20 per cent of the best land in Kenya, a disparity which was certainly more evident to the squatters than to any other group of Africans.

The Kikuyu responded to the apparent apathy of the other ethnic groups in the colony by adopting a dual 'custodial and expansionist' approach to the loss of their lands. In their custodial role they were essentially colonists and trustees, a role they regarded as specifically Kikuyu. This is heavily emphasised in the various Mau Mau songs and prayer forms, which stress that Kikuyu claims to the lost lands date back to antiquity, having originally been bequeathed to them by God (*Ngai*, also variously known as *Murungu* and *Mwene Nyaga*) through their ancestors Mumbi and Gikuyu. For example:

> *Ngai* gave us this country a long time ago
> When he was dividing the earth among all nations.
> And he said we should never give it up,
> But we were robbed of it
> By those colonial hordes that invaded our countries.
> *Ngai* we shall get back our land.[128]

Or, as in another song:

> Gikuyu was told by *Murungu*
> 'Do you see all this land?
> I want you and your children's
> children to dwell in it forever.'
> Even if you oppress us
> This country belongs to us
> We were given it by *Murungu*

And we shall never abandon it.
Mwene Nyaga in the millions of us
We will drive the foreigners out of the country
And we, the African people,
Will remain triumphant
Since this is our country.[129]

The centrality of land to the Mau Mau struggle became generalised in the minds of the Kikuyu who, through their myths, came to look upon all alienated lands, most of which were non-Kikuyu, as their own. And, to this extent, it is possible to detect expansionist tendencies (or motives) within the Mau Mau movement.

A 'custodial' explanation was, however, always given to explain why the Kikuyu were fighting not only for the land they themselves had lost, but for the whole of the White Highlands. In this custodial role, the Kikuyu adopted a paternalistic attitude in which they championed the land grievances of other ethnic groups that were portrayed as incapable of asserting themselves. As one of the informants put it:

> The Kikuyu in the Rift Valley were fighting for land in that area. The other tribes (*nduriri*) did not know how to fight for the land. People like the Maasai did not know how to fight for land. They had given in [to the colonial administration] and had been moved to several places to make room for the Europeans. So the Kikuyu had to fight and later claim any area.[130]

It is difficult to correlate the Kikuyu custodial and expansionist approaches to the land problem, but it would appear that as Mau Mau ideology crystallised,[131] a number of Kikuyu developed expansionist aspirations. Their attempts to provide a historical basis for Kikuyu claims to lost lands (outside the Kikuyu homelands) by reference to their mythical ancestors (Gikuyu and Mumbi) was perhaps a way of trying to legitimise their ambitions:

> Even if land [in the Rift Valley] had been taken from the Maasai, that did not mean that the area did not belong to the Kikuyu. If anything, the two people were related. They had close dealings with each other including inter-marriage and adoption (*guciarwo*).[132]

The text is self-explanatory. The Kikuyu hoped to acquire this land at the end of the struggle. Even when the forest fighters were still in the forest, they argued over the eventual disposal of the 'liberated land'. Educated forest fighters anticipated distributing the land to the landless Africans on the attainment of independence. But, as Barnett argues, the leaders of the illiterate forest fighters in the 'Kenya Parliament' questioned the 'legitimacy of the educated leaders' dominance of the 'Kenya Parliament' and held that the revolt, being fought by the illiterate should have uneducated leadership [and] that the White Highlands should be turned over to ex-Rift Valley squatters'.[133] In this respect, the squatters formed part of the expansionist lobby within the wider Kikuyu group and seem to have been well represented both in the forest forces and in the administrative and planning section of the forest combat, the Kenya Parliament. They were engaged in a relentless war which they believed would change their lives for the better:

> In 1950, people became very tough in the oathing business. We wanted to deal with the Europeans once and for all. The Europeans did not carry soil and pour it out here, why should they benefit so much from this place? We took the oath for land.[134]

The return of Kikuyu squatters to the White Highlands

Despite the prejudices that had been expressed against prospective Kikuyu labourers, by 1954 settlers were clamouring to get hold of Kikuyu labour in preference to that from other ethnic groups. This, they argued, was because not only did the substitute labour demand higher wages but it had also proved less efficient. In the Olkalau area, non-Kikuyu labourers were referred to as 'difficult in taking orders from their employers'. In addition, their work output was extremely low and what was done was of a 'low order'.[135] Kamba, Luo, Luyia and other non-Kikuyu, Embu and Meru labourers responded to the repatriation of Kikuyu labour by adopting an easygoing, uninterested approach to their work.

The South Kinangop Farmers Association was the first to ask outright for the return of Kikuyu labour. Other districts expressed mixed feelings on the issue, but none the less engaged in discussions on how best to implement it.[136] The first batch of 31 Kikuyu families was brought on a pilot scheme to work in the South Kinangop area for a salary of 40 shillings a month. When North Kinangop and Kedong Valley eventually received their Kikuyu labourers, the settlers agreed to start them off at 30 shillings a month. But the *shambas* given to these new employees were particularly small and consequently unable to yield sufficient food for the labourers' needs. While some farmers tried to help their labourers out by giving them extra food or higher wages, others did not,[137] and many Kikuyu merely ran away from the farms to report back to the labour offices. The official view was that these deserters gave futile reasons for their actions 'thinking they can run off and remain in the camp for a week and then get some easy job in the Township'.[138] The Kikuyu were said to be taking advantage of the relaxation of Emergency restrictions by engaging in free movement.

However, some of the Kikuyu who took up jobs on farms were mainly interested in acquiring their half-acre plots, as they were 'more worried about their food supply than their wage rates'.[139]

The gradual return of Kikuyu labour to the Settled Areas was achieved through a screening process, in which initial groups of declared loyalists were dispatched from Central Province to work on settler farms. The repatriation scheme had revealed the importance of the Kikuyu labour force. Later, with the provision of a 'nominated persons scheme', more Kikuyu returned to the Rift Valley and at first worked under monthly contracts. In 1956, when the squatter contract was reintroduced, many more former squatters trekked back to the Settled Areas after excruciating experiences in a series of transit labour camps. It is difficult to establish exactly how many of these returning ex-squatters registered as squatters on settler farms, but in 1955 the Labour Department recorded that there was a total of 44,970 people (together with their dependants) on squatter contracts. In 1961, the figure had dropped to 24,260, by which time the squatter system had started to give way to a system of monthly labourers.[140]

Labour conditions remained bad, or perhaps became even worse, for Kikuyu squatters who returned to the Rift Valley after 1954. However, the settlers had learnt to appreciate that squatter labour was practically indispensable to their economy. In Kinangop, as in other areas, settlers had come to realize that the Kikuyu were 'the only stable labour to work in that area'.[141] As a pyrethrum growing area, Kinangop was more than usually dependent on family labour, especially that of women and children and, as the settlers complained, only Kikuyu women were prepared to engage in wage labour.

After the extreme hardships of the Mau Mau period, the squatters were in no position to pick and choose their jobs. The settlers were quick to exploit the vulnerability of their new recruits by offering them exceedingly low salaries. The colonial government had dealt the Kikuyu a heavy blow and many officials had quite justifiably feared that the new 'docile' squatter would become easy prey to settler exploitation. This fear was not unwarranted.

With the help of labour inspectors, the Settler District Councils continued to harass squatters about their new herds of stock and about the amount of land they cultivated. In this respect at least, the squatter had returned to an area that was still openly hostile to the peasant option. Even during the Emergency, settlers continued to wage a relentless battle on squatter livestock. In the Njoro, Turi, Molo and Mau Summit wards, squatters were given until 28 February 1953 to dispose of all their stock.[142] In the Njoro ward, however, they would be allowed to own two sheep, which they had to keep in a pen.[143] But the problem of how to dispose of the stock without creating a disgruntled squatter community still loomed. As the Reserves were still over-crowded and the local markets would be flooded, thus making it impossible for the butchers to buy all the excess stock, Mr Purves, a settler in Njoro, urged the District Commissioner to initiate discussions with the District Council to allow the squatters until the end of 1953 to get rid of their stock.[144]

Elsewhere in the district, as a condition for residential employment squatters were allowed to keep no more than five head of sheep after 28 May 1953. In the Molo, Mau Summit and Turi areas it was required that 'one shall not cultivate otherwise [than] for the benefit of his employer an area of the farm exceeding one and a half acres,'[145] Under some circumstances, the council might give a squatter written consent to cultivate two acres, but at least in Londiani, under no circumstances was a squatter allowed to exceed two acres.

For a while, the Mau Mau crisis interrupted the work of the County Council Labour Committee, which was appointed in 1953 to discuss transition from squatter to cottage labour, but at the beginning of 1954 the Council became convinced that the time had come to act for, as they put it, 'should the previous system resume, it will be too late for a solution'.[146] The re-engagement of Kikuyu resident labour was seen to offer the ideal opportunity for introducing the cottage system which, they believed, should be seized, 'otherwise the problem might in a few years' time become insoluble'.[147] In the post-Mau Mau period, as on the eve of the Mau Mau uprising, settlers were unable to agree on a single pattern of action. None the less, quite stiff measures were imposed in Nakuru District, which continued to limit squatter cultivation. Elsewhere too, settlers implemented restrictive measures which the squatters found difficult, but since the reserve was unable to offer a viable alternative, they had no option but to acquiesce.

By the end of 1956, Mau Mau as an organised forest combat force against the colonial government was a thing of the past. The forest guerrillas had been defeated; thousands had died; others languished in detention camps and prisons. The freedom fighters, like the squatters, returned, not as heroes and heroines, but as defeated warriors. Their intense agricultural and socio-economic grievances remained unsolved. The squatter participation in Mau Mau had been in anticipation of a change in the socio-economic structure of the White Highlands. By 1955–56, it looked as if the settlers had won – or had they?

Notes

1. Tamarkin, M., 'Social and Political Change in a Twentieth Century African Community in Kenya', unpublished Ph.D. thesis, London University, 1973, p. 234.
2. Interview, Muchemi Kimondo, 8 October 1976, Subukia.
3. Interview, Gachago Kagere, 28 October 1976, Nakuru.
4. Rosberg, C. and Nottingham, J., *The Myth of Mau Mau: Nationalism in Kenya*, Nairobi, EAPH, 1966, p. 263. For some time, both the *mbari* committee and the General Council continued to function separately the former based at Banana Hill and the latter at Githunguri, (see ibid.).
5. ibid., p. 246.
6. Spencer, J. 'KAU and Mau Mau: Some Connections', *Kenya Historical Review*, Vol. 5, No. 2, 1977, p. 201.
7. ibid., p. 202.
8. Rosberg and Nottingham, *Myth of Mau Mau*, p. 214.
9. ibid., p. 215.
10. Spencer, 'KAU and Mau Mau', p. 228.
11. Rosberg and Nottingham, *Myth of Mau Mau*, p. 251.
12. Spencer, 'KAU and Mau Mau', p. 228.
13. The figures are computed from Van Zwanenberg, R. M. A., *Colonial Capitalism and Labour in Kenya: 1919–1939*, Nairobi, EALB, 1975, p. 219.
14. Tamarkin, M., 'Mau Mau in Nakuru', *Kenya Historical Review*, Vol. 5, No. 2, 1977, p. 234.
15. Sorrenson, M. P. K., *Land Reform in Kikuyu Country*, Nairobi, OUP, 1967, p. 79. See also Omusule, M., 'An Assessment of the Role of the Kenya Land Commission Report in the Mau Mau Outbreak', Paper presented at the Historical Association of Kenya Conference, Nairobi, August 1981.
16. Spencer, 'KAU and Mau Mau', p. 206.
17. ibid.
18. Interview, Ernest Kiberethi Kanyanja, 13 October 1976, Elburgon.
19. ibid., and Muchemi Kimondo, 8 October 1976, Subukia.
20. Maina wa Kinyatti (ed.), *Thunder from the Mountains: Mau Mau Patriotic Songs*, London, Zed Press, 1980, p. 56.
21. Spencer, 'KAU and Mau Mau', p. 203.
22. ibid., p. 204.
23. ibid.
24. RH, MSS Afr. S. 424, 'Mau Mau Ceremonies as described by participants', p. 345.
25. Corfield, F.D., *The Origins and Growth of Mau Mau: an Historical Survey*, Nairobi, Government Printer, 1960, p. 77.
26. Despite the rising storm, by 1952 some District Councils were still demanding total eradication of squatter cattle. See KNA, Labour Department Annual Report, 1952, p. 11.
27. Tamarkin, 'Mau Mau in Nakuru', p. 228.
28. Interview, Kirugumi Kagunda, November 1984, Nyeri, Granada Television Copyright.
29. ibid.

30. Furedi, F., 'The Social Composition of the Mau Mau Movement in the White Highlands', *Journal of Peasant Studies*, Vol. 1, No. 4, July 1974, pp. 501–2.

31. Tamarkin,, 'Mau Mau in Nakuru', pp. 230–1.

32. ibid., pp. 225–39.

33. This oath has been variously accredited to Kikuyu squatters in the Rift Valley and the Nairobi militants. See Rosberg and Nottingham, *Myth of Mau Mau*, p. 248; and Tamarkin, 'Mau Mau in Nakuru', p. 235.

34. Interviews, Nganga Githiomi, 2 October 1976, Rongai, and Karanja Kamau, 21 October 1976, Nakuru.

35. Furedi, 'Social Composition', p. 500.

36. Interview, Njuguna Kiorogo, 12 October 1976, Nakuru.

37. ibid. The informant was himself a *nyapara* and cited cash and liquor among the bribes given by other squatters. This refers to the post-World War One period.

38. Interview, Munge Mbuthia, 8 October 1976, Subukia. This was taken to mean friendliness between the two.

39. This included the *nyapara*, cook, farm clerks (*karanis*) and house servants. To a certain extent, the tractor drivers, milkmen and sub-foremen also belonged to a higher socio-economic category in comparison with the ordinary squatters who were field hands. Interview, Karanja Kamau, 21 October 1976, Nakuru.

40. Interview, Nganga Githiomi, 2 October 1976, Rongai. Nganga recalled that in the event of a conspiracy against the settler, the houseboy was considered strategic since 'he knew all about the European [settler]'.

41. Interview, Riiyu Ngare, 30 December 1976, Nakuru.

42. This should not be taken to mean that the squatters disregarded the *nyapara*'s authority but rather that, because of their jobs, the *nyapara* and his retainers were viewed as close allies of the settlers and therefore a danger to the ordinary squatters. Also grouped with the *nyaparas* were the milk clerks and *madaraka* (affluent) people, who were 'kept in the dark' about the oath (interview, Riiyu Ngare, 30 December 1976, Nakuru). It is necessary to note that the implied affluence of the *nyapara-karani* group, except in terms of wages, was more apparent than real. What really alienated them from the other squatters was their close contact with the settler. This, as pointed out earlier, was largely due to the nature of their jobs, but also to the position of trust delegated to them by the settler.

43. Furedi, 'Social Composition', p. 501.

44. Tamarkin, 'Mau Mau in Nakuru', p. 236.

45. Interview, Riiyu Ngare, 30 November 1976, Nakuru. Christians were also perceived as being anti Mau Mau and were therefore kept in the dark about Mau Mau plans. Interview, Reverend James Gakunju Gathigi, November 1984, Granada Television Copyright.

46. Interview, Riiyu Ngare, 30 November 1976, Nakuru.

47. See RH, MSS Afr. S. 424 'Mau Mau Oaths And Ceremonies As Described by Participants, 1954', pp. 345–9 for the various oaths and what they committed the people to. See also RH, MSS Afr. S. 1676 Mau Mau Miscellaneous Reports 'Translation of the Kiama Kia Wiyathi (KKW), Directive to District Committees, 21 March 1953', ibid., pp. 14–165 and 'The Rules for Mau Mau District and Locational Committees' found on 10 April 1953, ibid., pp. 17–20.

48. As in other areas, squatters on settler farms took precautionary measures to insulate the movement from traitors. Literature on loyalists in the Mau Mau revolt is still very scarce. See, for example, Ogot, B. A., 'Revolt of the Elders' in Ogot, B. A. (ed.), *Hadith 4: Politics and Nationalism in Colonial Kenya*, Nairobi, EALB, 1972, pp. 134–49, and Mukaru Nganga, D., 'Mau Mau, Loyalists and Politics in Muranga' in *Kenya Historical Review*, Vol. 5, No. 2, 1977, pp. 365–84.

49. Interview, Wanjiru Nyamarutu, 18 December 1976, Nakuru.

50. Furedi, 'Social Composition', p. 500. Wanjiru Nyamarutu noted that the artisans never knew the 'inside story about Mau Mau or the oath. They were not at the core of the movement', (interview, 18 December 1976, Nakuru). Gatutu wa Kamathengani, 29 December 1976, Nakuru.

51. Interview, Muya Ngari, 6 October 1976, Njoro. Riiyu Ngare, 30 December 1976, Nakuru.

52. Interview, Muya Ngari, 6 October 1976, Njoro. Wanjiru Nyamarutu, 18 December 1976, Nakuru. Several informants stated that the *nyapara* was regarded as *thu* – enemy.

53. Interview, Karanja Kamau, 21 October 1976, Nakuru.

54. Interview, Nganga Githiomi, 2 October 1976, Rongai.

55. ibid.

56. Interview, Muchemi Kimondo, 8 October 1976, Subukia.

57. ibid.

58. Interview, Kinuthia Muya, 14 October 1976, Nakuru. As well as threatening the *nyapara* with possible death should he tell on the squatters' participation in the oath, further steps were taken to ensure that he kept the secret. Njau adds that '. . .certain people would also befriend the *nyapara* to make sure that he did not report'. Interview, Wilson Mwangi Njau, 13 October 1976, Elburgon.

59. Interview, Kihiko Wa Mwega, 28 October 1976, Nakuru.

60. Interview, Nganga Githiomi, 2 October 1976, Rongai.

61. Interview, Njuguna Kiorogo, 12 October 1976, Nakuru.

62. Another writer who portrayed Mau Mau as a socio-economic struggle is Odinga, O., *Not Yet Uhuru*, London, Heinemann, 1968.

63. KCA appears to have commanded the squatters' respect but only captured their massive support once oaths began to be administered on a large scale in the post-World War Two period. In other words, KCA in the pre-war years remained the monopoly of a few people. Earlier, KCA was more of a *siri* (secret) than *siasa* (politics), interview, Wanjiru Nyamarutu, 18 December.

64. Tamarkin,, 'Mau Mau in Nakuru', p. 226.

65. Furedi, 'Social Composition', p. 486.

66. Tamarkin, 'Mau Mau in Nakuru', p. 230. See also Corfield, *Origins and Growth of Mau Mau*, p. 93.

67. KNA, African Affairs Department (AAD), Report on Native Affairs, 1951, p. 78.

68. ibid., p. 83.

69. ibid.

70. ibid.

71. The administration observed that oath taking and acts of violence were more difficult to uncover in Naivasha and Nakuru Districts than in Laikipia.

This was put down to the fact that the former districts were occupied by Kikuyu from the more politically conscious Kiambu and Muranga districts while squatters in Laikipia largely came from Nyeri. The former were said to be more indoctrinated with Mau Mau propaganda. See KNA, AAD, Report on Native Affairs – Annual Report, 1952, p. 62.

72. KNA, AAD, Report on Native Affairs, 1951, p. 99.

73. KNA, AAD, Report on Native Affairs – RVP Annual Report, 1952, p. 65.

74. Interview, Muchemi Kimondo, 8 October 1976, Subukia. See also KNA, Naivasha Annual Report, Crime and Judicial Matters, 1951, which states that 'a disturbing feature shows itself in the number of unprovoked assaults by Africans on Europeans'.

75. Britain's response to the forest fighters, especially in its military operations verged on a formally declared war. See Padmore, G., *Pan-Africanism or Communism*, London, 1953, p. 255. See also Clayton, A., *Counter-Insurgency in Kenya, 1952–1960*, Nairobi, Transafrica Publishers, 1976, for a discussion of British military activities in the combat.

76. Clayton, A. and Savage, D. C., *Government and Labour in Kenya: 1895–1963*, London, Frank Cass, 1974, pp. 348–9.

77. KNA, Naivasha District Annual Report, 1952, p. 3.

78. Rawcliffe, D. H., *The Struggle for Kenya*, London, Gollancz, 1954, p. 60.

79. Numerous petitions for the recovery of their property were made by the ex-squatters while on transit to Central Province, detention camps or prisons. These were never heeded. Interview, Gachago Kagere, 28 October 1976, Nakuru.

80. Tamarkin, 'Mau Mau in Nakuru', p. 237.

81. AAD, RVP Annual Report, 1952, p. 65.

82. Spencer, 'KAU and Mau Mau', p. 215. See also Rosberg and Nottingham, *Myth of Mau Mau*, p. 268.

83. Tamarkin, 'Mau Mau in Nakuru', p. 236.

84. Interview, Wanjiru Nyamarutu, 18 December 1976.

85. KNA, DC NVA 6/1, Naivasha Annual Report, 1953, p. 1.

86. Interview, Mbaria Kaniu, November 1984, Granada Television Copyright.

87. See the extensive correspondence between Reginald E.V. Denning and colonial administrators as he sought to exonerate himself of pro-Mau Mau activities, in RH, MSS Afr. S. 1676, 'Mau Mau Miscellaneous reports, Emergency Controls, etc., 1953–1962', pp. 34–52.

88. RH, MSS Afr. S. 1580 (i), Lieut. Col. Mackay to Major Gen. W. Hinde, 27 September 1954, p. 4.

89. RH, MSS Afr. S. 424, O. H. Knight to the Editor, Trans Nzoia Post, Kitale, 25 February 1952.

90. ibid.

91. RH, MSS Afr. S. 1506, Njoro Settlers Association (NSA) Special meeting, 1 December 1952.

92. RH, MSS Afr. S. 1506, President, NSA to Hon. Michael Blundell, MCL, 28 November 1952.

93. ibid., meeting, 8 December 1952.

94. RH, MSS Afr. S. 1506, NSA, meeting, 8 December 1952.

95. RH, MSS Afr. S. 1506, Box 15/1, Samuel Mochu to Sec. NSA, Re: 'Control of Returning Kikuyu', 19 March 1957.
96. RH, MSS Afr. S. 1506, Box 15/1, Minutes of Turi-Elburgon Ward meeting, 4 March 1954.
97. RH, MSS Afr. S. 1506, NSA, Pip Beverley to Chairman NSA, 23 December 1954.
98. See RH MSS Afr. S. 1506, NSA, Box 15/1, Minutes, 8 December 1952, where the need was emphasised for settlers to reduce their Kikuyu labour to 25–30 per cent of their total labour. See also ibid., Townsend to Chairman, NSA, 5 December 1952.
99. Interview, Kirugumi Kagunda, November 1984, Nyeri, Granada Television Copyright.
100. Interview, Wanjugu Mbutu, November 1984, Nyeri, Granada Television Copyright; Kirugumi Kagunda, November 1984, Nyeri, Granada Television Copyright.
101. Interview, Wanjugu Mbutu, November 1984, Nyeri, Granada Television Copyright.
102. See RH, MSS Afr. S. 1676, 'Mau Mau Miscellaneous Reports, Emergency Controls, etc., 1953–1963', p. 32.
103. ibid. See also RH, MSS Afr. S. 1506, NSA, Box 15/1 Njoro, 1952–1967, R.G. Night to Provincial Emergency Committee, 'Denial of Food to Mau Mau Gangs', 8 August 1953.
104. RH, MSS Afr. S. 1676, 'Mau Mau Miscellaneous Reports'.
105. ibid.
106. Interview, Wanjiru Nyamarutu, 16 January 1984, Nakuru.
107. Interview, Ruth Gathoni Gitahi, 21 January 1984, Nakuru. See also interviews, Kuria Kamaru, 2 October 1976, Rongai and Mary Wacuka Cege, 23 January 1984, Rongai.
108. Interview, Flora Nyokabi, 16 January 1984, Rongai.
109. Interview, Ruth Gathoni Gitahi, 29 January 1984, Nakuru.
110. Interviews, Suleiman Gichure, 16 January 1984, Nakuru, and Wanjiru Nyamarutu, 16 January 1984, Nakuru.
111. This was rule number 28 in 'Rules for Mau Mau District and Locational Committees' found on 10 April 1953 and translated from Kikuyu. See RH, MSS Afr. S. 1676, 'Mau Mau Miscellaneous Reports'.
112. Interview, Ruth Gathoni Gitahi, 29 January 1984, Nakuru.
113. Interviews, Suleiman Gichure, 16 January 1984, Nakuru and Gakenia Wachira, 21 January 1984, Nakuru.
114. Interviews, Gakonyo Ndungi, 27 January 1984, Nakuru, and Ruth Gathoni Gitahi, 29 January 1984, Nakuru.
115. Interview, Ruth Gathoni Gitahi, 29 January 1984, Nakuru.
116. ibid.
117. ibid. and Gakonyo Ndungi, 27 January 1984, Nakuru.
118. Interview, Gakonyo Ndungi, 27 January 1984, Nakuru.
119. ibid.
120. RH, MSS Afr. S. 1676, 'Mau Mau Miscellaneous Reports, Rules for Mau Mau District and Locational Committees' found on 10 April 1953.
121. Interview, Ruth Gathoni Gitahi, 21 January 1984, Nakuru.

122. KNA, DC NVA 6/1, June 1955.
123. RH, MSS Afr. S. 1506, NSA, 1952–1957, Secretary NSA to R. V. H. Parker, Divisional Forest Officer, Londiani, 25 January 1955. The settlers passed a resolution requesting a ban on maize growing and the keeping of livestock by forest squatters who, it was said, were maintaining gangs in the East Mau area as late as 1955.
124. See KNA, DC KER 1/19, Kericho District Annual Report 1946, p. 3. See also Brett, E. A., *Colonialism and Underdevelopment in East Africa: The Politics of Economic Change, 1919–1939*, London, Heinemann, 1973, pp. 177–8, for the alienation of Kipsigis land for white settlement. *Kenya Land Commission Evidence*, Vol. III, p. 2440, stresses the Kipsigis claim to alienated land.
125. Pavlis, A.P., 'The Maasai and the Mau Mau Movement: Avenues for Future Research', *Kenya Historical Review*, Vol. 5, No. 2, 1977, pp. 253–73.
126. Corfield, *Origins and Growth of Mau Mau*, pp. 202–218.
127. Barnett, D. C., 'Mau Mau: The Structural Integration and Disintegration of Aberdare Guerrilla Forces', unpublished Ph.D. thesis, University of California, 1971, p. 38.
128. Maina wa Kinyatti, *Thunder from Mountains*, p. 28.
129. ibid., pp. 39–40.
130. Interview, Gachago Kagere, 28 October 1976, Nakuru.
131. This could be said to have evolved sufficiently by 1953 by which date the ideology was lucidly articulated in Mau Mau songs. See Maina wa Kinyatti, *Thunder from Mountains*, pp. 28–9 and 39–40.
132. Interview, Gacheru Manja, 4 October 1976, Elburgon.
133. Barnett, 'Mau Mau', p. 219.
134. Interview, James Mumbu Muya (alias Kinuthia Muya), 23 October 1976, Elburgon.
135. See KNA, DC NVA 1, Labour Office, Thompson's Falls, April-June 1953. The settlers had to come to regard the 'lake tribes' as 'lazy and thoroughly unreliable' where labour was concerned. See KNA, Naivasha District Annual Report, 1956, p. 5.
136. KNA, DC NVA 1, Month ending 31 January 1956. See also RH, MSS Afr. S. 1506, Box 15/1, Sec. NSA to DC NKU, 22 March 1956 informing him of area's decision to accept return of Kikuyu labour.
137. KNA, DC NVA 1, Month ending 29 February 1956. Subsequent labourers were offered lower salaries ranging between 14 and 20 shillings per month. This necessarily reduced the number of Kikuyu offering themselves for employment on farms. See ibid Month ending 31 March 1956.
138. KNA, DC NVA 1, Month ending 29 February 1956.
139. KNA, DC NVA 1, Month ending 31 March 1956.
140. Clayton and Savage, *Government and Labour*, p. 363. The figures included squatters from other ethnic groups.
141. See KNA, DC NVA 6/1, Month ending 31 March 1955.
142. KNA, DC NKU Deposit 2, Serial No. 402, Local Government, District Councils, Nakuru County Councils, 1937–1957: Resident Labourers (Nakuru District Council) Rules, 1953.
143. ibid.
144. KNA, DC NKU Deposit 2, Serial No. 402, Local Government, District

Councils, Nakuru County Councils, 1937–1957, Mr W. D. C. L. Purves to DC Nakuru: 'Reduction of Squatter Stock in Njoro Ward', 16 December 1952.
145. KNA, DC NKU Deposit 2, Serial No. 402, Local Government, District Councils, Nakuru County Councils, 1937–1957, Resident Labourers (Nakuru District Council) Rules, 1953.
146. KNA, Deposit 2/401, Local Government District Councils, 1948–60, Minutes of the Meeting in the Ministry of Local Government, Health and Housing, 6 November 1955, between Representatives of the Government and of the Nakuru County Councils.
147. ibid.

Six

The Post-Mau Mau Period:
The Independence Bargain and the
Plight of the Squatters, 1955–63

Among the many intriguing aspects of Mau Mau is the length of time
that the freedom fighters survived in the thick forest environment of
Mount Kenya and the Nyandarua range. Without prior preparations
or established arrangements for the supply of provisions, ammunition
and firearms, thousands of discontented Kikuyu, Embu and Meru
peasants trekked to the forests to strengthen the swelling numbers of
Mau Mau freedom fighters. Faced with the sophisticated weapons of
the British and loyalist troops, the freedom fighters' only advantage
was the forest environment within which the war was fought.
Camouflage was easy and the thick vegetation made further penet-
ration by the official troops difficult.

Amidst the struggle to improvise shelter and to obtain food and
weaponry, the freedom fighters persevered in adverse conditions
throughout the period of active armed confrontation between 1952 and
1956. Several hundred peasants had entered the forest before 1953 and
some of these were still in the forest long after the achievement of
formal independence in 1963. Mau Mau was a traumatic experience for
both the British and the Africans. Among the peasants it precipitated
many hardships, including thousands of deaths, loss of property and
indeterminate stretches of detention and imprisonment. The lives of the
majority of Kikuyu, Embu and Meru were seriously dislocated, both in
the urban centres and in the rural areas.

While it lasted, the Mau Mau struggle proved far more difficult to
quell than the colonial government had anticipated. What had initially
appeared as a localised uprising became a fully-fledged war that lasted
over three years and necessitated the importation of British troops,

advanced artillery and an extensive expenditure from the British treasury. The war rocked the very foundations of the colonial regime in Kenya and forced British colonial officials and Whitehall into rethinking the whole colonial policy. Whereas before there had never been a policy on the socio-economic and political progress of Africans, colonial administrators were now having to restructure the whole administrative machinery in such a manner as to ensure that an experience such as Mau Mau never happened again. In other words, Britain was awakened to the urgency of bringing Africans into the mainstream of the country's economic and political developments.

It was in the context of these events that the long drawn-outout process of decolonisation, which lasted from 1954 to 1962, was initiated. This was a process punctuated by periods of tense stalemate, tenacious demands, cordial 'compromises' and mutual suspicions between the European settler community, African national leaders and the British-backed colonial regime,[1] culminating in 1963 with the Africans becoming Kenya's legitimate political leaders. The decolonis-ation process involved all but those who had dared to participate in the Mau Mau struggle for independence. Mau Mau represented a major landmark and its sobering effects had forced Britain to abandon, albeit gradually, her racially-structured economic and socio-political policy in Kenya, which she had so carefully nurtured for over five decades.[2]

Decolonisation demanded that at least sections of the White Highlands be made available to the Africans, but the only way in which this could be achieved was to uproot the settlers. In the wrangle that ensued, the scrambling parties included settlers, colonial administra-tors, Whitehall officials and an emergent African elite who, ironically, were referred to as militant nationalists, despite their moderate and constitutional stance during both Mau Mau and the Lancaster House talks. Most evident was the way in which the British government was able to influence the outcomes of major decisions so that in the end the settlers were adequately compensated and Britain still retained a considerable influence over the independent state. This has been referred to as the 'Europeanisation' of the transfer of land and political control in Kenya.[3]

Attaining political independence became the national leaders' major goal and one they pursued at the expense of land, which had been the freedom fighters' single most important objective.[4] In the Rift Valley, especially among squatters and the urban militants of Nakuru, the land issue was very important. Land was all that the landless, impoverished and disgruntled squatters, whose plight had become worse during and after the Mau Mau struggle, really asked of independence, for it was through acquiring land that they gained their security and economic freedom. By accepting loan-financed schemes for buying land in the

White Highlands, the leaders had automatically pre-empted wide-spread distribution of free land to the landless, including ex-freedom fighters and squatters. As a result, in the post-1963 period, former squatters joined other landless Kikuyu to create self-help co-operative societies and limited companies, through which they could purchase land in the White Highlands. But, in the wake of the nationalist fervour that swept over Kenya in the late 1950s and early 1960s, the squatter's cause became submerged by other national interests.[5]

It is beyond the scope of this book to delve into the intricacies of decolonisation in Kenya, but it necessary to say that decolonisation occurred in such a way as to ensure that the settlers were fully compensated and that British metropolitan interests in Kenya were safeguarded. In other words, what was termed decolonisation was in effect Kenya's transition from a colonial to a neo-colonial state.[6]

The Kenya Land Freedom Army

Between 1956, when Mau Mau came to an end, and 1960, when it became clear that it was only a matter of time before Kenya emerged as an independent state under African rule, the nationalist struggle continued to simmer at grass-roots level, especially in the Rift Valley and Central Province. The Mau Mau crisis in Central Province had sharpened the colonial government's awareness of the need to introduce reform measures to avoid a similar calamity.

The Swynnerton Plan was designed by the colonial government's agricultural specialists to consolidate scattered landholdings in Central Province so that land ownership could be concentrated in the hands of a few peasants. These peasants would then become transformed into 'an African middle class' that engaged in economic production, while at the same time offering employment to the bulk of those rendered landless by the plan. It was anticipated that the remaining landless peasants would become small-scale rural craftsmen. The newly landed Kikuyu would act as a collaborator-buffer class between the masses of impoverished militant and landless peasants and the colonial government.[7]

But, contrary to colonial expectations, the Swynnerton Plan resulted in neither large scale land alienation nor extensive land ownership for a few Kikuyu. Many of the peasants emerged as owners of uneconomic holdings of on average 0.25 to 3 acres, so that they could neither engage in economic production, nor provide employment for the landless peasants. The majority of these peasant landowners were unable to subsist on their landholdings and had to resort to wage labour to supplement the produce from their land. The plan failed to generate the expected economic transformation in Central Province, in fact it made the situation worse.[8] Even after massive and intensive government involvement in the Swynnerton Plan, economic development in Central Province was not immediately visible. Here, as in the Rift Valley, disgruntled and pent-up feelings soon found expression in a new political organisation, the Kenya Land Freedom Army (KLFA).

Former freedom fighters were highly suspicious of the provisions made by the government for establishing political parties at the end of Mau Mau, for they were well aware of the limitations inherent in constitutional parties. At the national level, however, 'the tone of speeches and statements emanating from African nominated members of the Legislative Council was more conciliatory toward the government's policies'.[9] But the Lyttelton Constitution of 1954, which broadly pointed towards a conciliatory approach to the government, left much to be desired. Separately determined representation in the legislative and executive bodies on a racial basis ensured a European majority, for European representation was on a par with that of all non-Europeans. For example, of the six unofficial ministers, three were elected Europeans, two were elected Asians, with the one African representative being nominated rather than elected. And, being handpicked by the Governor, the African representative was bound to be an 'agreeable' candidate and thus unlikely to plead diligently for the African cause. In fact he was not even a representative in the democratic sense of the word, for the people he supposedly represented had not elected him.[10] The Lyttelton Constitution also maintained its monopoly of legislation on the more fundamental issue of land rights. Therefore, despite these early doses of multi-racialism, which in the context of previous racial animosity comprised a shift in outlook, the immediate position of the Europeans remained secure, which even further exasperated the African peasants.

In the period between 1955 and 1960, before the constitutional whirlwind of the Lancaster House talks, newly released Mau Mau detainees maintained a recalcitrant spirit of struggle through the recently formed KLFA movement.[11] The humiliation and intimidation accompanying the defeat of Mau Mau had failed to kill the spirit of protest among the Kikuyu peasants. Rather, they served to widen their political scope so that in the period before independence, defeated freedom fighters sought once again to revitalise protest. Like Mau Mau, the KLFA campaigned for the recovery of the White Highlands and the attainment of national independence. An almost exclusively Kikuyu organisation, the KLFA was better organised, commanded stronger allegiance and had greater clarity of purpose than Mau Mau. Composed of hard-core ex-Mau Mau leaders and followers, it clearly anticipated using physical violence if events went contrary to their expectations.[12]

In analysing the KLFA, Tamarkin hesitates to make the obvious connection between it and Mau Mau.[13] But in Central Province, as in the Rift Valley, veteran hard-core Mau Mau leaders refused to give up the struggle after their military defeat in the forest and, on their release, reorganised themselves into the KLFA. Kimunya Kamana, a former freedom fighter and KLFA member, insisted that 'KLFA was only Mau Mau under a new name. It was composed of soldiers who would watch the land to ensure that it was not taken over'.[14] KLFA members often referred to themselves as *thigari cia bururi* (soldiers, or guards, of the land)[15] as they sought to ensure that the land did not get into the wrong hands,[16] such as those of loyalist Kikuyu, other groups like the Kalenjin or Maasai who might claim land in the Rift Valley, or even settlers who might want to stay. The KLFA's members tended to be former Mau Mau leaders who had either fought in the forests, been central figures in Mau Mau's civil wing, or been detained for their Mau Mau activities. In essence, KLFA was motivated by exactly the same driving force that had been behind Mau Mau. And again, like Mau Mau, it had its grass-roots and local origins in the Rift Valley.[17] Former detainees in the Rift Valley had felt the need to reorganise themselves politically as early as 1958. An added advantage had been that many of the ex-freedom fighters were still armed and could therefore engage in war should the situation make this necessary.

By the beginning of 1960, it was apparent that it was only a matter of time before Kenya emerged as an independent state with African majority rule, but in the meanwhile ethnic fears and suspicions over land and power were causing serious divisions in the country. These in turn became translated into two political parties, the Kenya African National Union (KANU) and the Kenya African Democratic Union (KADU).[18] The KLFA then began to feel that its own interests were in jeopardy, especially after 1960 when KANU and KADU were starting to compete with, and indeed eventually displaced, the KLFA, particularly in its campaign for land.

KADU was basically the product of the minority pastoral and agricultural tribes' fear of being dominated after independence by the larger agricultural tribes, especially the Kikuyu and Luo. To counteract the intense land hunger of the Kikuyu, these small groups, which included the Kalenjin, various coastal tribes and the Abaluyia, advocated regionalism as the only possible political option if their land rights were to be safeguarded. In this respect, KADU's interests were close to those of the European community, which in itself, quite apart from their anti-Kikuyu posture, was enough to arouse KLFA hostility. For example, KADU advocated multi-racial government, as opposed to KANU's demand for African majority rule, and showed no wish to promote African ownership of land in the White Highlands. On the contrary, the party even seemed keen to preserve European holdings there[19] to prevent Kikuyu expansion into the area. Equally offensive, perhaps, was KADU's passive attitude towards the release of Kenyatta. It was this conciliatory stand, as against KANU's demand for African majority rule, that so appealed to the colonial government and made it look as if KADU might be given the reins of power on independence.[20] This was something that the KLFA wanted to prevent at all costs, but as it turned out, even KANU, which included the Kikuyu, failed to live up to the KLFA's expectations.

Although the freedom fighters recognised that Mau Mau had not achieved any tangible results, they were none the less impressed by its performance and exhilarated by the strong defence that their movement had mounted against the British before their final defeat. The KLFA intended to ensure that subsequent political developments in the country would not distort or destroy Mau Mau's, and therefore the freedom fighters', objectives of ousting the European settlers, acquiring the White Highlands and gaining political independence. Of these objectives, they considered the emancipation of land the most significant and anticipated that if KANU failed to obtain land and independence in the White Highlands, the hard-core Mau Mau would continue to operate underground. But the KLFA would certainly 'continue to fight if KADU won' in the independence bargain.[21]

The KLFA was most active between 1960 and 1962 when, despite definite political advancement toward African majority rule, the manoeuvres involved in the political bargaining and the divisions evident among the Africans themselves threatened to undermine the KLFA's basic interest, land. As we shall see later, the KLFA's fears were not without basis. The independence package left a lot to be desired. As a peasant grass-roots movement at the most crucial moment the KLFA found itself on the political periphery. Even at its most articulate, in the wake of constitutional talks between the British government and Kenya nationalist leaders, the KLFA, which was a militant and exclusive movement, could only hope to influence rather than direct the trend of political developments. And yet the KLFA was the last visible hope for thousands of landless squatters.

Although the KLFA had the same objectives as its parent body, it was not a mass movement for, unlike Mau Mau, it had an exclusive and select membership. [22] As it had been started by hard-core ex-Mau Mau leaders, membership of the KLFA depended on an intimate knowledge of prospective recruits who had to have an outstanding record of participation in Mau Mau engagements during the previous struggle.[23] Without open membership or the use of intimidation as a recruitment device, KLFA membership was consequently rather small, but, in the immediate aftermath of Mau Mau's defeat, KLFA members were wary of mass recruitment, which had proved so disastrous for Mau Mau. But, even then, with its militant stand and oath-taking activities, it was not long before someone betrayed the KLFA to the authorities.

Unlike other political parties, which adopted prescribed strategies for achieving their defined objectives, the KLFA, which armed all its members, was really a 'vigilante committee' designed to keep watch and to mobilise ex-Mau Mau forces in the event of other political movements failing to achieve the desired results.

In the Rift Valley, the KLFA was organised along the same structural lines as Mau Mau, i.e. with provincial, district, locational and sub-locational hierarchies of authority. Although it is unclear exactly to what extent communications were maintained at levels higher than the district, the freedom fighters' commitment to Kenyatta as the spiritual figurehead in their political struggle was as dominant in the KLFA as it had been in Mau Mau.[24] Like Mau Mau, the KLFA drew upon Kenyatta's apparent sanction of violence in the liberation struggle which he was supposed to have uttered at Gatharaini (Kasarani) on the northern outskirts of Nairobi immediately before he was arrested. But his challenge '*Ndanyita rwa thatha nimukurumia mateke?*' – If I hold on to the lion's jaw will you withstand the kicks? – in fact became the Achilles' heel of the struggle. The new style of conference-table politics ('holding on to the lion's jaw'), which characterised the post-Mau Mau period, effectively pre-empted the KLFA's strategy.

The KLFA stayed true to Kikuyu politics in another area as well. At a time when multi-ethnic political parties were being formed, it remained almost exclusively Kikuyu. This was seen as the pillar of its strength and the emergence of KANU and KADU brought its ethnic loyalty into even sharper focus. The KLFA was seen by its leaders as the 'strong man' that would come to KANU's aid should the latter fail to emerge victorious from the political struggle: the KLFA's ethnic purity and thus strength would be directed against the non-Kikuyu coalition, KADU. As one informant stated, 'KANU included all ethnic groups, but KLFA was all Kikuyu, ready to fight if KADU won.'[25]

KADU's regionalist proposal appealed to the settler community, largely because it meant that they would be allowed to stay in the White Highlands, but a KADU-settler alliance would obviously undercut the KLFA's hopes of acquiring the White Highlands for the Kikuyu. The KLFA interpreted KADU's policy as active support for settler occupation of the White Highlands and the entrenchment of settler hegemony in Kenya. On the other hand, the KLFA's determination to put up an armed struggle if KADU won the political battle not only spelled the upsurge of ethnic antagonisms over the White Highlands but also showed ethnocentric overtones in that the

Kikuyu accorded themselves a prior claim to political leadership in the country. The dual custodial and colonist roles adopted by the freedom fighters were expressed in the KLFA's expansionist intentions with regard to land in the White Highlands. The KLFA was obviously determined that the Kikuyu should get the lion's share of what had been defended on behalf of the other tribes.

Despite the apparent political conflicts being waged on economic and ethnic grounds, an inter-ethnic alliance eventually emerged between the Kikuyu and Luo, particularly in Nakuru Town where Wesonga Sijeyo[26] was elected on a KLFA ticket during KANU's Nakuru District elections in 1960. And at the national level Tom Mboya was commanding trans-ethnic allegiances in Nairobi. Politics had begun to take on a truly national flavour and, as a Kikuyu stronghold, the KLFA began to fight a losing battle. In any case, the immediate fate of the White Highlands and the nature of independence, when it did come, were determined as much by the needs of capital and by consultations between national and international bodies that functioned independently of KLFA considerations, as by the deliberations of national leaders.

Liberal European politics

While the KLFA was still clinging to its militant politics, a last-ditch attempt was made to safeguard European interests in Kenya[27] by a group of European moderates, led by Michael (later Sir Michael) Blundell (a member of the Legislative Council and later Minister for Agriculture) and including Wilfred Havelock and Bruce Mackenzie, who floated the idea of multi-racialism through the New Kenya Group Party. This group, which believed that settlers were indispensable to the Kenyan economy,[28] did not, however, oppose the need to remove race barriers to land ownership in the White Highlands, a policy which was adopted in 1960.[29] In giving their support to KADU, the European moderates had hoped to forestall the formation of an all KANU government which, they feared, would be extremist and would result in the elimination of the European community.[30]

Land and politics

How land was transferred from the European settlers to the Africans has been dealt with elsewhere,[31] but it is necessary to look at how the freedom fighters and other landless Kikuyu perceived these transactions which so drastically affected their economic predicament. How did party politics affect the transfer of land? What was the significance of the involvement of commercial and international bodies in the transaction? And did the nationalist leaders ignore the aspirations of the freedom fighters?

As Kenya approached independence, European settlers became anxious, even hysterical, about their future, especially with regard to their landholdings. At worst, they feared their lands would be seized without compensation or that they would be inadequately compensated. Some of the settlers found it impossible even to contemplate remaining in Kenya under an African majority government. A minority of settlers were, however, prepared to stay on. For both groups, it was considered necessary for the British government to give them guarantees for their property and its fair sale should a settler wish to sell.[32] The settlers' body, the Kenya National Farmers Union, undertook to lobby for these and other safeguards.[33] But the settlers were not the only ones who were agitated over the land issue. Landless Africans were also agitated and were threatening to seize settler land.

To quell the rising wave of the Africans' clamour for land and to give settlers time to devise suitable land transfer measures, token settlement programmes, such as the 'million acre scheme', were introduced. This approach was designed 'to help the European community prepare for independence rather than to realise the historic objective of Kenya African nationalism for the recovery of the White Highlands'.[34] The scheme involved the settlement of about 35,000 landless families on some 1.2 million acres of land excised from the White Highlands. The project was a massive undertaking requiring delicate political and economic negotiations.[35]

After extensive discussions between settler representatives, Whitehall officials and African politicians, a working programme on the transfer of land to Africans was established. An international pool of finance was set up, with contributions from the British government, the World Bank with its International Bank for Reconstruction and Development, and the Colonial Development Corporation. This was to be overseen by a non-political organisation and the money used for buying land from willing settlers to sell to willing African buyers. By internationalising the loan scheme to Kenya for buying land in the White Highlands, Britain hoped to ward off the possibility of financial default.

Kenyatta explained to puzzled freedom fighters that the land transactions did not amount to the purchase of African land, but were only compensation to the settlers for developing the land.[36] African political leaders had proceeded with the transaction despite the fact that the 'land transfer deal' effectively committed the Kenyan government to heavy financial debts.[37] The African nationalist leaders had hoped to postpone discussing the land issue until after independence when they might possibly bargain from a position of strength.[38]

Besides Whitehall being impatient to implement the 'willing settler, willing buyer' policy, KANU and KADU went along with the compromise through mutual mistrust. While KADU settled for the above deal and a regional government to pre-empt possible domination by KANU, KANU accepted the arrangement for fear that any further opposition on its part might lead to a KADU enthronement. In this manner, political expediency overrode the economic repercussions of the land transfer process. Such rationalisations did not, however, go down well with the landless, who had been hoping for free land grants.

The freedom fighters did not expect KANU to subscribe to this 'land purchasing' programme, so when it did they began to feel alienated from the party. Although, as a representative body, KANU saw no need to articulate the particular interests of either the freedom fighters or the former squatters, there were, even within the party's ranks, people like Bildad Kaggia and Oginga Odinga who remained strongly opposed to the land compromise, both before and after independence.[39] The Mau Mau struggle for land was kept alive in the Central and Rift Valley Provinces by the KLFA[40] which, militant to the end, soon lost favour with KANU, which joined hands with the colonial government to denounce the KLFA. Then, in the person of Kenyatta, KANU also declared that there would be no free grants of land.

Kenyatta's statement about land came as a great shock to the many landless Kikuyu. The peasants had come to equate Kenyatta's release and person with the inception of a millenium that would be epitomised by the recapturing and redistribution of the stolen lands. Kenyatta sounded strong warnings against any Africans who anticipated, then or after independence, free grants of land from the government. There would be limited settlement schemes for some landless people. But this did not mean that all land procured from settlers would be freely redistributed. He reiterated:

> I did not say that Africans should sit idle and wait until *Uhuru* to get land for nothing. All that I said was that the present government should get down to work and face realities and help the landless, unemployed Africans, that if there was any land going it ought to be given to somebody who needed it and not the man with 500 [acres] or however much he may have.[41]

Bildad Kaggia, who was a strong supporter of the freedom fighters, openly stated the absurdity of Africans having to pay for land that was rightly theirs.[42]

For those freedom fighters who had given everything they had fighting in the forest, or wasting away in detention camps and prisons, Kenyatta's stand was construed as a great betrayal. They had emerged from the forests an impoverished, disinherited and maimed people.

They expected official recognition of their sacrifice, which they thought would be rewarded by land grants. Understandably, the majority of landless people were unable to raise even the basic sum needed as a downpayment for the purchase of land.[43] Among the squatters, the issue was straightforward. They had nourished the White Highlands with their sweat; it was only logical that they should occupy the region when the settlers left.[44]

No immediate political achievements accompanied Kenyatta's release, and this frustrated the KLFA even more. Independence seemed further away than ever, especially after Kenyatta's address, at his Gatundu home after his release, to Rift Valley KLFA and KANU officials. His open confession that, although he had been released, he was in no position to prevent the detention of KLFA people who continued to take the oath, strengthened the KLFA's refusal to disarm. On his part, Kenyatta urged the people to stop engaging in underground activities, to join KANU and to await the elections.[45] KANU officials who were also KLFA members saw the dangers of the party's alliance with the KLFA, for they realised that the British government might use this alliance as a pretext for handing over the reigns of power to KADU. Consequently, KANU leaders joined other groups in a strategic move to ward off government suspicion, but the colonial government was not fooled. It kept a close watch on any KANU leaders who were also KLFA members.[46]

Even when it became clear that KANU would form the government in independent Kenya, the KLFA remained disgruntled about KANU's policy on the future of the White Highlands, especially in relation to the purchase of land and the continued presence of settlers in the region. As Tamarkin observed, 'in this respect, their views [KLFA's and KANU's policies on land] were diametrically opposed'.[47] Subsequent anger and feelings of betrayal among the dispossessed and impoverished people thus emanated from the disappointment of their earlier expectations. The local press stated that some of the disgruntled KLFA members took an oath with the avowed intent of killing Kenyatta.[48]

Avoiding the central issue of the free redistribution of land to ex-freedom fighters and other landless people, Kenyatta joined in the attack against the KLFA. He reprimanded them for engaging in oath-taking ceremonies and stated that 'after this meeting, I do not want to hear that Kikuyu are taking oaths. In the past Kikuyu took an oath to release Kenyatta from restriction, now he is free'.[49]

The Rift Valley witnessed another upsurge of militant politics, which was hardly surprising considering the great concentration of discontented squatters, some of whom had drifted to the province's urban centres to create a lumpenproletariat. Here, and especially in Nakuru

District, the KLFA played a special role in the political arena. In Nakuru District, the KLFA's leadership hoped to control the course of politics by penetrating the rank and file of KANU's leadership. Although the alliance was short-lived and in the end took a bitter turn, while it lasted, the KLFA injected militancy into the district's politics. During 1961–2, KANU's leadership in Nakuru reflected such a high level of militancy that it threatened to bring about an armed conflict against ethnic groups that had agreed to join KADU should KANU's discussions on the fate of the White Highlands fail to bear fruit.

In Nakuru, a joint Kikuyu, Luo and Kamba armed resistance seemed imminent against the Kalenjin, who were trying to enforce a prior claim to land in the White Highlands.[50] What had hitherto been portrayed as a national battle for lost lands, now assumed ethnic dimensions with the Kalenjin, Kikuyu, Luyia and Luo as the major protagonists. When the Abaluyia Union proposed that, under the federal arrangement, Kitale should be their capital, the Kalenjin (and more specifically the Sabaot, West Pokot and Marakwet sub-tribes) saw this as a plot to disinherit them. In the meanwhile, on behalf of the wider Kalenjin group, Kikuyu forest residents in the Rift Valley were given a month to vacate the area or expect a Kalenjin invasion. The Luo, who had no immediate claim to the White Highlands, then formed the Luo Union Movement as a safeguard against the possibility of Kikuyu domination at independence. The Akamba, who had remained in KANU until November 1962, now also pulled out of the party and formed the Akamba Peoples' Party.[51]

By 1962, therefore, the nationalist struggle was characterised by ethnic parochialism with each individual group seeking to strengthen its position against Kikuyu domination. The knowledge of impending independence had created mutual suspicions among the major ethnic groups, each of which reorganised itself in preparation for its rightful share of the independence cake. In terms of land, each ethnic group 'demanded the fulfilment of their wildest expansionist dreams'.[52]

While most of the ethnic groups could and did base their claims to land in the White Highlands on historical rights, the Kikuyu Union in Nakuru made its claim on the basis that Kikuyu 'sweat and blood had helped to develop' the area.[53] In the face of impending opposition, the Kikuyu Union argued that the long history of Kikuyu labour in the White Highlands provided legitimate grounds for Kikuyu claims to land in the region. As a result, by 1962, the White Highlands had become the centre of racial and ethnic controversy. The fate of the area, however, was decided, not by African peasants, but by the recommendations of the European settler community, whose influence was felt long after the attainment of political independence. Theirs was an economic hold that swayed major political decisions both under the colonial regime and in independent Kenya. It was left to the Kenyan government to appease the peasants as best it could within the provisions laid down during the decolonisation process.

At the same time as the colonial regime was carrying out its vindictive drive against the KLFA, KANU was also starting to adopt a hostile attitude towards this organisation, which it thought might become a possible threat and political rival after independence. Labelled as subversive,[54] the KLFA, which was the last formally constituted protest body to voice the grievances of the landless peasants, squatters and ex-freedom fighters before independence, was subjected to intensive vetting by both the colonial and the independent Kenya regimes before it eventually disappeared in about 1965. After 1962 the government stepped up its campaign even further and arrested, tortured and detained many of the movement's followers. But, in the same way as the KCA leaders had joined KAU (which they considered too moderate) to continue their underground activities, so also did the KLFA leaders, especially in Nakuru, now join KANU (which they too considered over moderate and constitution oriented)[55] to maintain their underground existence while canvassing under the banner of a formally constituted organisation.[56]

The peasantisation of the White Highlands

At independence, it had become clear to the large numbers of landless people that there were to be no massive free grants of land. Their high expectations had evaporated overnight. As a former freedom fighter and member of the KLFA put it:

> If *shambas* were not to be given for free, were we paid when we were in jail so that we could use the money to buy *shambas*? I stayed in jail for seven years, others stayed in the forest for over ten years. Did they have money from the forest to buy land? Detainees got 'token' money but what would such money buy, would it buy land? Since he told us to persevere during the freedom struggle, we thought he would give us land.[57]

Kenyatta's apparent betrayal of the freedom fighters has been partly attributed to his prolonged removal from the political scene between 1952 and 1961, when he was supposedly unaware of the extent of the people's suffering and sacrifice during his absence. As Kenyatta had been idolised during the freedom struggle, despite his absence over the crucial years, it is hardly surprising that he was the one who should receive the blame for the eventual outcome of the whole decolonisation and independence bargain, especially the unpopular land policy. For the freedom fighters, the intricacies of the Lancaster House talks were overlooked and emphasis was laid on the fact that the talks did not provide for a massive free distribution of land.

The squatters did not hesitate to approach their national leaders for help in buying land in the White Highlands. It was only logical that they should seek the co-operation of their government's leaders, especially Kenyatta, who became the country's President in 1964 and who came to play a major role in trying to help former freedom fighters in their quest to acquire land. Because of their financial difficulties, most of them could only hope to own land by joining co-operative societies or limited companies that purchased large farms, which were later subdivided and shared out among the various members. Despite the government's concern and advice that these large farms should be farmed co-operatively to ensure economic production, the peasants usually insisted on subdividing the land into individual plots averaging between two and three acres. Numerous co-operative societies and limited companies, most of which were exclusively Kikuyu, sprang up all over the Rift Valley, especially in Nakuru District, and were instrumental in acquiring land for several thousand formerly landless Kikuyu.

After independence, the government introduced alternative and cheaper schemes for settling landless people. In 1965, the Squatter Settlement Scheme was initiated, for which land was obtained through government excisions, donated lands and mismanaged farms. The scheme was intended to supply land to about 46,000 registered squatters from the Rift Valley and elsewhere, of which 12,000 were residing in urban areas.

By 1971, about 31,000 of these squatters had been settled. However the joint problems of landlessness and inadequate land holdings linger on.

Notes

1. The process of decolonisation underwent several changes as multi-racialism was rejected, and an acceptable politico-economic set-up and a collaborative African national leadership evolved. See Gordon, D. F., 'Mau Mau and Decolonization: Kenya and the Defeat of Multi-racialism in East and Central Africa', Kipkorir, B. E., 'Mau Mau and the Politics of the Transfer of Power in Kenya, 1957–1960', in Ochieng, W. R. and Janmohamed, K. K. (eds.), 'Some Perspectives of the Mau Mau Movement', *Kenya Historical Review*, Vol. 5, No. 2, 1977, pp. 327–48 and pp. 318–23. *Kenya Historical Review, op. cit.*, pp. 318–328. See also Harbeson, J. K., *Nation Building in Kenya: The Role of Land Reform*, Evanston, Northwestern University Press, 1978, and Wasserman, G., *Politics of*

Decolonisation: Kenya Europeans and the Land Use, 1960–65, Cambridge, Cambridge University Press, 1976.

2. Kipkorir, 'The Mau Mau and Politics', p. 326.

3. Harberson, *Nation Building*, pp. 81–134.

4. See Leys, C., *Underdevelopment in Kenya: A Political Economy of Neo-Colonialism, 1964–1971*, London, Heinemann, 1975, p. 60.

5. To a large extent, the grass-roots freedom fighters, the land hungry people and the peasantry failed to appreciate the intricacies and complexities of the interplay between the ethnic, racial, national and international interest groups that formed the decolonisation drama.

6. See Wanjohi, N. G., 'Socio-Economic Inequalities in Kenya: The Case of the Rift Valley Province', M.A. thesis, University of Nairobi, 1976, p. 289.

7. Sorrenson, M. P. K., *Land Reform in Kikuyu Country*, Nairobi, OUP, 1967, Chapter 7.

8. ibid.,, pp. 97–121.

9. Rosberg, C. and Nottingham, J., *The Myth of Mau Mau: Nationalism in Kenya*, Nairobi, EAPH, 1966, p. 310.

10. Kanogo, T. M. J., 'Politics of Collaboration or Domination? Case Study of the Capricorn African Society', *Kenya Historical Review*, Vol. 2, No. 2, 1974, p. 128.

11. Also identified as the Kenya Land Freedom Party, Kenya Parliament, Rift Valley Government and the Rift Valley Parliament, KLFA was operative in the Rift Valley and Central Province between 1957 and 1965. It included Kikuyu squatters, ex-squatters, landless and land-hungry Kikuyu.

12. Interviews, Wanjiru Nyamarutu, 3 January 1979, Nakuru, Gathogo Mwitumi, 4 January 1980, Nakuru, and Kiarie Waihobo, 4 January 1980, Nakuru. Part of the oath committed KLFA members to start tracing and accumulating weapons, especially rifles, in preparation for war. The *Kigaanda* blacksmith groups were entrusted with the task of repairing and keeping the rifles in working order. See Barnett, D. (ed.), *The Urban Guerrilla*, Richmond, LSM Information Centre, 1974, pp. 89–94, for earlier Land Freedom Army activities and Land Freedom Army oaths.

13. Tamarkin, M., 'Social and Political Change in a Twentieth Century African Community in Kenya', unpublished Ph.D. thesis, London University, 1973, p. 374.

14. Interview, Kimunya Kamana, 5 January 1980, Nakuru. See also Kiarie Waihobo, 4 January 1980, Nakuru.

15. Interview, Kiarie Waihobo, 4 January 1980, Nakuru.

16. Interview, Gathogo Mwitumi, 4 January 1980, Nakuru.

17. There was a great distrust of educated people among the KLFA leaders and education was not a prerequisite for leadership, although some literate members, such as Mark Mwithaga, were brought into the organisation. All the organisation required was loyalty and 'intelligence of the head' (interview, Kiarie Waihobo, 4 January 1980, Nakuru). The Mau Mau movement was itself at times referred to as the Land Freedom Army during its early stages (see Barnett, *Urban Guerrilla*, pp. 89–94).

18. Rosberg and Nottingham, *Myth of Mau Mau*, p. 317.

19. See Wasserman, *Politics of Decolonization*, pp. 62–4. See also Carey Jones,

N. S., *Anatomy of Uhuru*, Manchester University Press, Manchester, 1966, pp. 139–41.
20. Rosberg and Nottingham, *Myth of Mau Mau*, p. 319.
21. Personal communication.
22. For a long time KLFA members were prosecuted as members of Mau Mau. See Tamarkin, 'Social and Political Change', p. 396.
23. Interview, Kiarie Waihobo, 4 January 1980, Nakuru.
24. Interview, Wanjiru Nyamarutu, 3 January 1979.
25. Personal communication.
26. Wesonga Sijeyo was a militant and prominent Luo politician who was one of the few non-Kikuyu members of the KLFA in Nakuru. See Tamarkin, 'Social and Political Change', p. 384.
27. Harberson, *Nation Building*, pp. 88–9 and 92–3. See also Rawcliffe, D. H., *The Struggle for Kenya*, London, Gollancz, 1954, p. 151.
28. See KNA, Legislative Council Debates, Vol. LXXXXVI, 1960, pp. 31ff.
29. Harberson, *Nation Building*, p. 92.
30. Wasserman, *Politics of Decolonization*, p. 98.
31. Leo, C. P., *Land and Class in Kenya*, Toronto, Toronto University Press, 1984; see also Wasserman, G., *Politics of Decolonization*.
32. Wasserman, G., *Politics of Decolonization*, p. 48.
33. ibid., pp. 47–53 ff.
34. Harberson, *Nation Building*, p. 85.
35. See Wasserman, *Politics of Decolonization*, pp. 109–15 and 144–50.
36. Interviews, Gathogo Mwitumi, 4 January 1980, Nakuru, Kimunya Kamana, 5 January 1980, Nakuru, and Wanjiru Nyamarutu, 3 January 1979, Nakuru.
37. Wanjohi, 'Socio-Economic Inequalities', p. 293.
38. *Sunday Post*, 4 February 1962, p. 4.
39. Oginga O., *Not Yet Uhuru*, London, Heinemann, 1968, pp. 258–9 and 263.
40. As Kiarie Waihobo put it, 'Now that Mau Mau was over we would ensure that people did not forget what they had been fighting for. It would keep the struggle for land going on'. Interview, Kiarie Waihobo, 4 January 1980, Nakuru.
41. *EAS*, 26 January 1962.
42. *EAS*, 27 January 1962.
43. Leys, *Underdevelopment in Kenya*, p. 91.
44. Interviews, Gathogo Murtumi, 4 January 1980, Nakuru, Kimunya Kamana, 5 January 1980, Nakuru, and Wanjiru Nyamarutu, 3 January 1979, Nakuru.
45. Interview, Gathogo Mwitumi, 4 January 1980, Nakuru.
46. Tamarkin, 'Social and Political Change', p. 405.
47. ibid., p. 404.
48. *EAS*, 7 December 1961.
49. KNA, DC NKU Depart. 2/175/740/60, Special Branch, Nakuru Information Report, 21 May 1962, p. 15.
50. Tamarkin, 'Social and Political Change', p. 418
51. ibid., p. 403.
52. ibid., p. 421.

53. ibid.
54. *EAS*, 14 July 1964.
55. Personal communication.
56. At the time, KLFA members viewed KANU as a helpless organsiation that could not resist colonial machinations.
57. Personal communication.

Conclusion

The conflicts inherent in the squatter-settler relationship can be seen in their true perspective only within the context of the essentially brutal and exploitative relationship of colonialism. In Kenya, this was expressed by a dominant settler community which was heavily backed by the state. Uprooted from their areas of origin, the squatters felt the loss of their dignity and economic independence particularly keenly because they lived and worked in such close proximity to the settlers.

As this study has shown, squatter resistance to repressive regulations merely elicited even more stringent measures, so that by the outbreak of the Mau Mau revolt, squatters were disinherited and desperately insecure.

The initial Kikuyu movement to the Rift Valley was partially prompted by the entrepreneurial drive of a people intent on acquiring a more lucrative and independent lifestyle. This was achieved through exploiting the pioneer stage of European settler agriculture, during which the settlers allowed the squatters extensive use of alienated lands in exchange for a minimal amount of labour. In this early period, there was a large measure of mutually beneficial co-existence between the Kikuyu squatters and the European settlers, especially those engaged in kaffir farming.

An important feature of the squatter system was that it propped up pioneer European farming by enabling the settlers to acquire labour at well below the market price. They were able to do this through allowing squatters to use part of their land for grazing and cultivation, thereby meeting the wage deficit in kind. Under the kaffir farming system, Kikuyu squatters enjoyed considerable independence and operated within a framework of *laissez-faire*.

Pre-1918 European agriculture provided the basis for a frontier squatter community that visualised unlimited room for expansion, little or no official restrictions and, in that the squatters were allowed to keep an unlimited amount of livestock and to cultivate extensively, ample economic opportunities. It was hardly surprising that they sought to have, to hold and to guard jealously the fruits of this 'golden age' with all that it entailed, for this was the period when the squatters enjoyed their greatest autonomy before being crushed by demanding labour obligations and other restrictions. It has been important to study this early period because, not only does it reveal how squatter labour evolved, but also, and more importantly, it provides an insight into the basic values, aspirations and self-perceptions of the squatters within the settler economy.

While the squatter peasant option had thrived in the period before 1918, the inter-war period brought extensive contradictions and conflicts of purpose to the White Highlands, where it became glaringly apparent that independent squatter production and settler agriculture were no longer mutually compatible. The squatters bitterly resented the reversal of the circumstances under which they had enjoyed such intense economic satisfaction and being struck down by the settlers just as they were on the point of consolidating their gains. To argue that the White Highlands had been alienated expressly for European use was of little consolation to the squatters who had been promised unlimited land for cultivation and grazing by pioneer settlers on labour-recruitment drives, for the squatters too had been building up their dreams for the White Highlands. It is little wonder that from then on the conflict in the Settled Areas took an antagonistic turn as each community sought to consolidate its position at the expense of the other.

We have seen how the settlers strengthened their hold, especially in the immediate aftermath of the First World War, as they sought to establish their dominant position by exercising firmer control over squatter labour. Government legislation helped them to attain this end, with a publicly supervised labour system being initiated through the introduction of the 1918 Resident Native Labourers Ordinance. We have seen also how the settlers set about changing the squatters from independent producer-cum-labourers into closely supervised and restricted servants, penalised for the slightest infringement.

Totally arbitrary measures were adopted both to limit the squatter's own economic production and to increase his labour obligation to the farmer. Although *kifagio* was the most obvious of these, the government also introduced other legislation for purposes of subordinating squatter labour. The 1937 Resident Native Labourers Ordinance, for example, which drastically reduced land under squatter cultivation and the number of livestock a squatter was allowed to keep, drove a deep wedge into the socio-economic fabric of the squatter community. The subsequent increase in the squatter's labour obligation and the overall reduction of squatters *per se* precipitated a crisis with unprecedented consequences. It is thus no exaggeration to say that the colonial government was at its most brutal in the White Highlands and actively participated in creating an oppressive labour policy.

Although the squatters were subjected to all manner of restrictions by the colonial situation in the White Highlands, they by no means succumbed readily. On the contrary, as we have shown, they evolved subtle and sometimes very successful methods of countering the colonial assault. Even before the Olenguruone crisis and the Mau Mau revolt, which were obviously the two most organised examples of squatter resistance, Kikuyu squatters had expressed their discontent by flagrantly disregarding labour regulations, squatting illegally, deserting, maiming settler stock, and using more settler land than they were allowed.

In attempting to establish a foothold in the White Highlands, the squatters had begun to replicate their former lifestyle in Central Province, with all its incumbent cultural norms and practices. But to some extent the economic sub-system thereby created posed a threat to the settler economy. The settlers showed little concern for the welfare of Africans in colonial Kenya. They saw Kikuyu squatters and their families in the Settled Areas merely as a source of cheap labour, and squatter attempts to provide even rudimentary education for their children were harshly thwarted. This conflict between squatter initiative and settler oppression was largely responsible for the outbreak of the Mau Mau revolt in which squatters readily participated in the hope that they would receive economic and political rewards, i.e land in the White Highlands which would ensure their economic independence. None the less, as this study has shown, by no means all the squatters espoused the Mau Mau cause.

The fate of the White Highlands was ultimately decided by Britain with the consent of an elite African leadership that was becoming increasingly alienated from its grass-roots. Britain sought to safeguard her economic and political interests in Kenya by incorporating international credit-finance bodies into the decolonisation process. In the bargain that ensued, British and settler interests were safeguarded, while those of the squatters were sacrificed and their aspirations overlooked. The squatters were left to develop their own co-operative societies through which they could buy land in the White Highlands.

The history of the Kikuyu squatters in the Rift Valley has thus been one of an ardent determination to survive – there were even some moments of prosperity – amidst an oppressive colonial situation. But, in the White Highlands, the interaction between squatter strategies for survival and settler repression constituted only one aspect of the colonial conflict. It was enough to destroy white supremacy, but not enough to realise the peasant dream.

List of Informants

1. Joseph Matahe, 30/9/76, Bahati.
2. Njoroge Kahonoki, 1/10/76, Rongai.
3. Njau Kanyungu, 2/10/76, Rongai.
4. Wanjiku wa Kigo, 2/10/76, Rongai.
5. Nganga Githiomi, 2/10/76, Rongai.
6. Kuria Kamaru, 2/10/76, Rongai.
7. Wangari Thuku, 3/10/76, Njoro.
8. Ndegwa Wambugu, 3/10/76, Njoro.
9. Njoroge Mambo, 4/10/76, Elburgon.
10. Gacheru Manja, 4/10/76, Elburgon.
11. Icogeri Nyaga, 6/10/76, Njoro.
12. Muya Ngari, 23/10/76, Njoro.
13. Kimondo Muchemi, 8/10/76, Subukia.
14. Bethuel Kamau, 8/10/76, Subukia.
15. Munge Mbuthia, 8/10/76, Subukia.
16. Martim Chirchir Maina, 12/10/76, Bahati.
17. Githu Ikua, 12/10/76, Nakuru.
18. Mureithi Gathiga, 12/10/76, Nakuru.
19. Ernest Kiberethi Kanyanja, 13/10/76, Elburgon.
20. Wanjiru Nyamarutu, 18/12/76, 3/1/79, 15/1/84, 16/1/84, Nakuru.
21. Daudi wa Chief Murugu, 23/12/76, Nakuru.
22. Gatutu wa Kamathengani, 29/12/76, Nakuru.
23. Joyce Nyambura Kimani, 29/12/76, Nakuru.
24. Ngoci Ndegwa, 29/12/76, Nakuru.
25. Riiyu Ngare, 30/12/76, Nakuru.
26. Muthoni Ngugi, 30/2/76, Nakuru.
27. X, 2/12/76, Nakuru.
28. Kiarie Waihobo, 4/1/80, Nakuru.
29. Gathogo Mwitumi, 4/1/80, Nakuru.
30. Kimunya Kamana, 5/1/80, Nakuru.
31. Wilson Mwangi Njau, 13/10/76, Elburgon.
32. James Mumbu Muya, alias Kinuthia Muya, 14/10/76, Elburgon.
33. Maria Wanjiku, 18/10/76, Nakuru.
34. Kago, 18/12/76, Nakuru.
35. Gikunju Gakuo, 18/12/76, Nakuru.
36. Njuguna Kiorogo, 12/10/76, Nakuru.
37. Karanja Kamau, 21/10/76, Nakuru.
38. Shuranga Wegunyi, 25/10/76, Nakuru.
39. Kihiko Wa Mwega, 28/10/76, Nakuru.

40. Gachago Kagere, 28/10/76, Nakuru.
41. Muta Njuhiga, 1/11/76, Bahati.
42. Mary Teresa Wanjiku, 10/9/76, Turi.
43. Hannah Njoki, 10/9/76, Turi.
44. Ngugi Kuri Kamore, 10/9/76, Turi.
45. Lucia Ngugi, 10/9/76, Turi.
46. Jane Kanyina, 10/9/76, Turi.
47. Jane Wangeci, 10/9/76, Turi.
48. Wanyoko Kamau, 13/9/76, Londiani.
49. Mrs Kamau Wanyoko, 13/9/76, Londiani.
50. 'Major' Mithanga Kanyumba, 14/9/76, Molo.
51. Njuguna Muharu, 14/9/76, Molo.
52. John Kamau, 16/9/76, Njoro.
53. Mary Wangui Macharia, 16/9/76, Njoro.
54. Waitherero Gichuki, 16/9/76, Njoro.
55. Maria Njeri Kimani, 16/9/76, Njoro.
56. Kimani Kungu, 16/10/76, Njoro.
57. Nganga Karanja Koinange, 16/9/76, Njoro.
58. Solomon Muchangi, 16/9/76, Njoro.
59. Nganga Kimani, 16/9/76, Njoro.
60. Gitau Gathukia, 16/9/76, Njoro.
61. Njuguna Gakara, 10/9/76, Njoro.
62. Ngushu Kamara, 17/9/76, Njoro.
63. Waithaka Githongo, 17/9/76, Njoro.
64. Ben Karume, 17/9/76, Njoro.
65. Bedan Mwaura, 17/9/76, Njoro.
66. Kiiru Arphaxad Kuria, 21/9/76, Elburgon.
67. Peter Kariuki Wangengi, 23/9/76, Elburgon.
68. Kariuki Konji Mwangi, 24/9/76, Elburgon.
69. Kariuki Kimutui Gachaiya, 24/9/76, Elburgon.
70. Arphaxad Mwaura, 27/9/76, Elburgon.
71. Jackton Oyoo, 14/10/77, Kericho.
72. Ochama Omolo, 17/10/77, Kericho.
73. Patrice Okare, 18/10/77, Kericho.
74. Joseph Madanyi, 14/10/77, Kericho.
75. Jasper Odongo, 14/10/77, Kericho.
76. Daniel Ogire Orwa, 14/10/77, Kericho.
77. Midamba, 24/10/77, Kericho.
78. Suleiman Gichure, 16/1/84, Nakuru.
79. Ruth Gathoni Gitahi, 21/1/84 and 29/1/84, Nakuru.
80. Wanjugu Mbutu, (Granada Copyright), November 1984, Nyeri.
81. Gathoni Ndungu, 21/1/84.
82. Gakenia Wachira, 21/1/84, Nakuru.
83. Kanyoi Muita (Granada Copyright), November 1984, Nyeri.
84. Njoroge Gakuha, 18/9/76, Njoro.
85. Gakonyo Ndungi, 27/1/84, Nakuru.
86. Kirugumi Kagunda (Granada Copyright), November 1984, Nyeri.
87. Rev. James Gakunju Gathiga (Granada Copyright), November 1984, Nyeri.
88. Mbaria Kaniu (Granada Copyright), November 1984, Nyeri.
89. Mary Wacuka Cege, 23/1/84, Rongai.
90. Flora Nyokabi, 16/1/84, Rongai.

Biographical Notes
on Key Informants

1. Wanjiru wa Nyamarutu

Interviewed at Nakuru on 18 December 1976, 3 January 1979 and 15 and 16 January 1984. An ex-squatter's daughter. She belongs to the Mambo-Leo, Karara or Muthirigu age group of 1930. She was a member and leader of KAU in Nakuru. Was an oath administrator in Nessuit Forest in Njoro from where she ran to Nakuru on being pursued by security forces. In Nakuru, Wanjiru was responsible, together with others, for the storage of firearms and ammunition, the administration of the Mau Mau oath at Jack's farm in Lanet, the welfare of freedom fighters (by providing food, medicine and clothing) and the dispatch of freedom fighters to the various Mau Mau forest centres. She was a judge in Nakuru's Mau Mau Court number 4, which dealt with traitors. Her involvement with the freedom fighters earned her the title of *nyina wa anake* (young men's mother) and led to her detention in Lamu for 22 months. As an insider, Wanjiru provided a wealth of information on various aspects of the Mau Mau struggle.

2. Wanyoko Kamau

Interviewed at Londiani on 13 September 1976. Arrived at Molo before the outbreak of the First World War. Was a *nyapara*. Wanyoko was very informative about the pioneer period of Kikuyu movement to the Rift Valley. He clearly articulated the 'wealth' theory of pioneer migrants whose aspirations, achievements and declining fortunes he discusses lucidly. Was a Mau Mau supporter responsible for feeding the freedom fighters. Was a good example of squatters who accumulated wealth – i.e. he married nine wives, ran a butchery at Molo, bought plots at Londiani and ran a dairy and shop. Just before independence he established a KANU Office at his plot in Londiani which was visited by the late President, Jomo Kenyatta, after his release from Lodwar.

3. *Wanjiku wa Kigo*

Interviewed at Rongai on 2 October 1976. She belongs to the Kimiri age group (approximately between 1918 and 1920). She went to the Rift Valley from Karura (Kiambu) during the *Mbara ya Njeremani* (First World War). She was very knowledgeable about the lifestyles of the pioneer Kikuyu squatters, especially their cultural activities.

4. *Nganga Githiomi*

Interviewed at Rongai on 2 October 1976. Was born in 1914. Moved to the Rift Valley as a young boy in 1923 with his father. Was circumcised in 1931. He was a field squatter and was very important on information regarding squatter Mau Mau organisation and squatter attempts to establish education.

5. *Gacheru Manja*

Interviewed at Elburgon on 4 October 1976. He belongs to the Kimiri age group. Was an ox-cart driver, cream maker and later a field squatter. He showed great insight into and had a lot of information on the commercial transactions undertaken by squatters and the changing fortunes that the squatters encountered. Portrayed squatter grievances and rationale for their participation in Mau Mau analytically.

6. *Muya Ngari*

Interviewed at Njoro on 6 October 1976. Belongs to the Githingithia age-group (approximately 1926–1928). Went to the Rift Valley from Nyeri largely because the home *shamba* was inadequate. He was a field squatter. Was well informed about the Mau Mau oathing procedure among the squatters. He provided a lucid portrayal of the social status differentiations among the squatters in the order of cook, *nyapara* (foreman), farm clerks, tractor drivers, fencing hands, milk-men, *shamba* boys and field squatters respectively.

7. *Bethuel Kamau*

Interviewed at Subukia on 8 October 1976. He moved to the Rift Valley in 1933 from Nairobi and started off as a domestic servant. He was vital in the portrayal of socio-economic differentiation within the squatter community. Lucidly related the intricacies of the breaking-in of the *nyapara* during the Mau Mau oath taking ceremonies.

8. *Wilson Mwangi Njau*

Interviewed at Elburgon on 13 October 1976. Was born in 1916 at Kahuhia in Muranga. Went to the Rift Valley in 1936. He was a *nyapara* from 1938 to 1939. In 1939 he was employed as a farm clerk at Elburgon. He was semi-literate, having gone to school at Kahuhia. He provided vital information on the socio-economic status of the non-Kiyuyu labourers on settler farms in Nakuru District. Gave vivid accounts of conflicts relating to the squatter demand for education and how this impinged on settler juvenile labour demands.

9. *James Mumbu Muya or Kinuthia Muya*

Interviewed at Elburgon on 14 October 1976. Went to the Rift Valley from Muthangari (now Msongari) area of Nairobi. Muya expounded on the 'wealth' theory of squatter movement to the Rift Valley. He clearly articulated the squatters' sense of betrayal and the extent of their grievances. He also portrayed the socio-economic basis of Mau Mau among squatters in Nakuru District.

10. *Ernest Kiberethi Kanyanja*

Interviewed at Elburgon on 13 October 1976. Went to the Rift Valley with his father in 1917. Came from Githunguri. Informant started work as an ox-cart driver in 1923 at Turi. Recollected with great clarity cultural activities among Kikuyu squatters in Nakuru District and squatter endeavours to establish an educational network for their children. Was a Mau Mau activist. Arrested, together with 59 other squatters, at a settler farm in Keringet for refusing to sign a contract in 1949 and repatriated to Central Province. He was arrested in 1953 for administering the Mau Mau oath. Was detained at Lari and Manyani for four years to be released in 1957.

11. *Kimondo Muchemi*

Interviewed at Subukia on 8 October 1976. Belongs to the Githingithia age group. Moved to the Rift Valley in 1918 with his father to flee conscription for the Carrier Corps. Represents the category of squatters who began working for settlers as juveniles. Kiberethi gave an analytical account of the squatters' lives and grievances in the Settled Areas and their reasons for participating in the Mau Mau struggle. Portrayed the severity of the breaking-in of *nyaparas* in the Mau Mau oath taking procedure. Revealed a clear sense of former squatters' various political leanings.

12. *Kiiru Arphaxad Kuria*

Interviewed at Elburgon on 21 September 1976. Went to the Rift Valley in 1908 from Nyeri. Had received mission education in Central Province and, in the absence of schools in the Rift Valley, took responsibility for organising trips for girls to be educated in Kijabe. As a pioneer squatter, he was well informed about the squatters early aspirations, socio-economic activities and squatter or missionary endeavours in the field of education. As a squatter, he amassed wealth and purchased residential plots in Elburgon town.

13. *Kimunya Kamana*

Interviewed at Nakuru on 5 January 1980. An ex-freedom fighter from Nyeri. Served a seven year jail sentence for Mau Mau activities. On his release, he became one of the founder members of KLFA in Nakuru. Was also central in mobilising former freedom fighters from Nakuru into the Nakuru District Ex-Freedom Fighters Organization, an organisation that sought to buy land on a co-operative basis after independence, and was at one time its Managing Director. Gave useful information on the economic aspirations of freedom fighters and their attitudes towards decolonisation and 'Uhuru'.

14. *Kiarie Waihobo*

Interviewed at Nakuru on 4 January 1980. An ex-freedom fighter. Was among the founding members of the KLFA in Nakuru. Was very knowledgeable about the organisational structure of the Mau Mau movement both in Nakuru town and its hinterland in the White Highlands.

Select Bibliography

The following bibliography includes only a selective list of sources and is therefore not an exhaustive account of the existent literature and primary sources on colonial labour history.

PRIMARY SOURCES

Oral Sources

Extensive interviews were conducted with ex-squatters and some ex-guerrillas over a number of years between 1976 and 1984. It is intended to deposit the information in a public library. A list of informants is to be found on pp. 000–000

Unpublished Material

Official
Kenya National Archives (KNA)
Departmental Annual Reports
Provincial Annual Reports
District Annual Reports
Political Record Books
Intelligence Reports etc.

Rhodes House Library, Oxford (RH)
Rhodes House offers a wealth of official, personal and private documents, too many to list here. These included various deposits of private papers donated by ex-settlers and administrative officers at various levels of the civil service, personal letters and memoirs of visitors and wives of the above, and Fabian Colonial Bureau, Coryndon, Creech Jones and Settlers' Associations' papers. There is also a large collection of official papers and correspondence from various persons in the Civil and Military Service throughout the colonial period in Kenya.

Public Records Office

Of special interest were the Colonial Office Records, East Africa Protectorate, Kenya – original correspondence (CO 533).

Newspapers

East African Standard (EAS)
Kenya Weekly News
The Leader of British East Africa
The Nation
Sunday Post

Government Publications

Clayton, E. S., 'Some Factors Affecting European Agricultural Policy in Kenya', *East Africa Economic Review*, Nairobi, Government Printer, 1957.

Corfield, F. D., *The Origins and Growth of Mau Mau: an Historical Survey*, Nairobi, Government Printer, 1960.

Humphrey, N., 'The Relationship of Population to the Land in Southern Nyeri', in Lambert, H. E. and Wyn Harris, P. (eds), *Memorandum on Policy in the Native Lands*, Nairobi, Government Printer, 1945.

——, 'Thoughts on the Foundations of Prosperity in the Kikuyu Lands', in Lambert, H. E. and Wyn Harris, P. (eds), *Memorandum on Policy in the Native Lands*, Nairobi, Government Printer, 1945.

Knowles, O. S., 'The Development of Agricultural Marketing in Kenya', *East Africa Economic Review*, Nairobi, Government Printer, 1956.

Orde Browne, Major G. St. J., *Labour Conditions in East Africa*, Report by Major G. St. J. Orde Browne, Labour Advisor to the Secretary of State for the Colonies, London: HMSO, 1946.

Swynnerton, R. J. M., *A Plan to Intensify the Development of African Agriculture in Kenya*, Nairobi, Government Printer, 1955.

Watkins, O. F., *Kenya Colony and Protectorate: Labour Bureau Commission 1921 Report*, Nairobi, Government Printer 1921.

Seminar and Conference Papers

Atieno-Odhiambo, E. S., 'The Economic Basis of Kenya Settler Politics in the 1930's', University of East Africa Social Sciences Conference, Dar es Salaam, December 1970.

Bowles, B. D., 'The Underdevelopment of Agriculture in Kenya', Historical Association of Kenya (HAK) Conference, August 1975.

Cone, L. W., 'Politics in Agriculture in Kenya, 1920–1940: an Historical Perspective', East Africa Institute of Social Research (EAISR) Conference, Kampala, January 1966.

Furedi, F., 'The Genesis of African Communities in the Settled Areas of Kenya', Seminar paper, History Department, University of Nairobi, 1972.

——, 'The Kikuyu Squatter in the Rift Valley, 1918–1929', HAK Conference, 1972.

King, K., 'Education and Social Change: the Impact of Technical Education in Colonial Kenya', HAK Conference, 1974.

Lamb, G. R., 'Peasants, Capitalists and Agricultural Development in Kenya', East Africa Universities Social Science Conference, Nairobi, December 1972.

Lonsdale, J., 'The Growth and Transformation of the Colonial State in Kenya, 1929–1952', History Department, University of Nairobi, 1980.

Miracle, M. P., 'The Application of Backward Supply Curve to Kikuyu Labour Migration up to 1908', Institute of Development Studies, University of Nairobi, April 1974.

——, 'Economic Change among the Kikuyu 1895–1905', Working Paper No. 158, Institute of Development Studies, University of Nairobi, April 1974.

Sandbrook, R., 'Union Power and the Public Interest: a Study of Union-Government Relations in Kenya', 5th Annual Meeting of the African Studies Association, Philadelphia, 1972.

Sorrenson, M. P. K., 'Counter-Revolution to Mau Mau: Lands Consolidation in Kikuyuland, 1952–1960', EAISR Conference, Kampala, June 1963.

——, 'The Official Mind and Kikuyu Land Tenure, 1895–1939', EAISR Conference, Dar es Salaam, January 1963.

Stichter, S. B., 'Women and the Labour Force in Kenya, 1895–1964', Discussion Paper No. 258, Institute for Development Studies, University of Nairobi.

——, 'Workers, Trade Unions and the Nationalist Movement in Kenya', Annual Meeting of the African Studies Association, Philadelphia, 1972.

Van Zwanenberg, R. M. A., 'The Land Question in Kenya from the 19th Century to the Present Day', Third International Congress of Africanists, Addis Ababa, December 1973.

Dissertations

Atieno-Odhiambo, E. S., 'History of the Kenya Executive Council from 1907 to 1939', unpublished Ph.D. thesis, University of Nairobi, 1973.

Barnett, D. C., 'Mau Mau: The Structural Integration and Disintegration of Aberdare Guerilla Forces', unpublished Ph.D. thesis, University of California, 1971.

Blunt, E. M., 'Problems of Political Representation in Multi-Racial Societies with Special Reference to British East Africa', unpublished Ph.D. thesis, University of London, 1956.

Bunyasi, J. S. M., 'Labour in the Kenya Coffee Industry: An Economic Analysis', unpublished M.Sc. thesis, University of Nairobi, 1973.

Clayton, A. H., 'Labour in the East Africa Protectorate, 1895–1918', unpublished Ph.D. thesis, University of St. Andrews, 1971.

Graham, J., 'Changing Patterns of Wage Labour in Tanzania: a History of the Relations between African Labour and European Capitalism in Njombe District, 1931–1961', Ph.D. thesis, Northwestern University, 1968.

Gupta, D. B., 'Labour Supplies and Economic Development in Rhodesia', unpublished M.Sc. thesis, University of London, 1967.

Janmohamed, K. K., 'A History of Mombasa c.1895–1939: Some Aspects of the Economic and Social Life in an East African Port Town during Colonial Rule', unpublished Ph.D. thesis, Northwestern University, 1977.

Kanogo, T. M. J., 'Politics of Collaboration or Domination? Case Study, the Capricorn African Society', unpublished B.A. dissertation, University of Nairobi, 1973.

Kipkorir, B. E., 'Alliance High School and the Making of the Kenya Elite', unpublished Ph.D. thesis, Cambridge University, 1969.

Lonsdale, J. M., 'A Political History of Nyanza, 1883–1945', unpublished Ph.D. thesis, Trinity College, Cambridge, 1964.

Mukaru-Nganga, D., 'A Political History of Muranga District, 1900–1970: a Study of Society and Politics', unpublished M.A. thesis, University of Nairobi, 1978.

Muketha, J. K., 'Labour Absorption in Kenya Modern Sector Agriculture', unpublished M.A. thesis, University of Nairobi, 1976.

Njonjo, A. L., 'The Africanisation of the "White Highlands": a Study in Agrarian Class Struggles in Kenya, 1950–1974', unpublished Ph.D. thesis, Princeton University, 1977.

Okumu, J. J., 'Kenya: 1900–1930: a Study in Conflict: Asian Challenge to European Domination in Kenya', unpublished Ph.D. thesis, UCLA, 1966.

Redley, M. G., 'The Politics of a Predicament: The White Community in Kenya 1918–1932', unpublished Ph.D. thesis, Cambridge University, 1976.

Rempel, H., 'Labour Migration into Urban Centres and Urban Unemployment in Kenya', Ph.D. thesis, University of Wisconsin, 1970.

Sandbrook, K. R. J., 'Politics in Emergent Trade Unions: Kenya, 1952–1970', unpublished Ph.D. thesis, University of Sussex, 1970.

Sandgren, D. P., 'The Kikuyu, Christianity and the African Inland Mission', unpublished Ph.D. thesis, University of Wisconsin, Madison, 1976.

Segal, A., 'Political Independence and Economic Inter-Dependence in East Africa', unpublished Ph.D. thesis, University of California, Berkeley, September 1965.

Tamarkin, M., 'Social and Political Change in a Twentieth Century African Community in Kenya', unpublished Ph.D. thesis, London University, 1973.

Throup, D. W., 'The Governorship of Sir Phillip Mitchell in Kenya, 1944–1952', unpublished Ph.D. thesis, Sidney Sussex College, Cambridge, 1983.

Wanyohi, N. G., 'Socio-Economic Inequalities in Kenya: The Case of the Rift Valley Province', unpublished M.A. thesis, University of Nairobi, 1976.

SECONDARY SOURCES

Published Books

Aaronovitch, S. and K., *Crisis in Kenya*, London: Lawrence & Wishart, 1947.

Abuor, C., *White Highlands No More*, Nairobi: Pan African Researchers, 1970.

Amsden, A., *International Firms and Labour in Kenya, 1945–1970*, London: Frank Cass, 1971.

Anderson, J., *The Struggle for the School*, London: Longman, 1970.

Arnold, Guy, *Kenyatta and the Politics of Kenya*, London: Dent, 1974.

Arrighi, G., 'International Corporations, Labour Aristocracies and Economic Development in Tropical Africa', in Rhodes, R. I. (ed.), *Imperialism and Underdevelopment*, New York: Monthly Review Press, 1970.

Arrighi, G. and Saul, J. S., *Essays on the Political Economy of Africa*, Nairobi: EAPH, 1974.

Atieno-Odhiambo, E. S., 'Seek Ye First the Economic Kingdom: a History of the Luo Thrift and Trading Corporation (LUTATCO) 1945–1956', in Ogot, B. A. (ed.), *Hadith 6: Economic and Social Change in East Africa*, Nairobi: EALB, 1976, pp. 165–85.

Audrey, R. I. (ed.), *Economic Development and Tribal Change: a Study of Immigrant Labour in Buganda*, Cambridge: W. Heffer & Sons, 1954.

Barnett, D. (ed.), *The Urban Guerrilla*, Richmond, LSM Information Centre, 1974.

Baxter, E. J., *Mau Mau: The Terror that has Come to Kenya*, Nairobi: East Africa News Review, 1950.

Bennett, G., *Kenya, a Political History: the Colonial Period*, London: OUP, 1963.

Bennett, G. and Rosberg, C., *The Kenyatta Election: Kenya 1960–61*, London: OUP, 1961.

Bewes, T. F. C., *Kikuyu Conflict, Mau Mau and the Christian Witness*, London: Highway Press, 1953.

Bienen, H., *Kenya: The Politics of Participation and Control*, Princeton, N.J.: Princeton University Press, 1974.

Blundell, Sir Michael, *So Rough a Wind*, London: Wiedenfeld & Nicholson, 1964.

Brett, E. A., *Colonialism and Underdevelopment in East Africa: The Politics of Economic Change, 1919–1939*, London: Heinemann, 1973.

Buell, R. L, *The Native Problem in Africa*, London: Frank Cass, 1965, 1st edn. 1928.

Buijtenhuijs, R., *Mau Mau – Twenty Years After: The Myth and the Survivors*, The Hague: Mouton, 1973.

Carey Jones, N. S., *Anatomy of Uhuru*, Manchester, Manchester University Press, 1966.

Clayton, A., *Counter-Insurgency in Kenya, 1952–1960*, Nairobi: Transafrica Publishers, 1976.

Clayton, A. and Savage, D. C., *Government and Labour in Kenya, 1895–1963*, London: Frank Cass, 1974.

Clayton, E. S., *Agrarian Development in Peasant Economies*, Oxford: Pergamon, 1964.

Cone, W. and Lipscomb, J. F., *The History of Kenya Agriculture*, Nairobi: University Press of Africa, 1972.

Ehrlich, C., 'Economic and Social Developments before Independence', in Ogot, B. A. (ed.), *Zamani: a Survey of East Africa History*, Nairobi: EAPH, 1974.

Eliot, Sir Charles, *The East Africa Protectorate*, (Third Impression). London: Frank Cass, 1966. (Originally published in 1905.)

Farson, N., *Last Chance in Africa*, London: Gollancz, 1949.

Fearn, H., *An African Economy: a Study of the Nyanza Province, 1903–1953*, London: OUP, 1961.

Furedi, F., 'The Kikuyu Squatters in the Rift Valley: 1918–1929', in Ogot, B. A. (ed.), *Hadith 5: Economic and Social Change in East Africa*, Nairobi: EALB, 1975, pp. 177–94.

Furley, O. W., 'The Historiography of Mau Mau', in Ogot, B. A. (ed.), *Hadith 4: Politics and Nationalism in Colonial Kenya*, Nairobi: EAPH, 1972.

Gertzel, C., *The Politics of Independent Kenya, 1963–1968*, Nairobi: EAPH, 1970.

Ghai, D. P. and Ghai, Y. P. (eds), *A Portrait of a Minority: Asians in East Africa*, Nairobi: OUP, 1970. (Second edition.)

Goldsmith, F. H., *John Ainsworth: Pioneer Kenya Administrator, 1864–1946*, London: Macmillan, 1955.

Harbeson, J. W., *Nation Building in Kenya: The Role of Land Reform*, Evanston: Northwestern University Press, 1973.

Harlow, V., Chilver, E. and Smith, A. (eds), *History of East Africa*, Vol. II, Oxford: Clarendon Press, 1965.

Hill, M. F., *The Dual Policy in Kenya*, Nakuru: Kenya Weekly News, 1944.

——, *The Permanent Way*, Nairobi: EAPH, 1957. (Second edition.)

——, *Planters Progress: The Story of Coffee in Kenya*, Nairobi: Coffee Board of Kenya, 1956.

Hobley, C. W., *Kenya: From Chartered Company to Crown Colony: Thirty Years of Exploration and Administration in British East Africa*, London: Frank Cass, 1970. (First published in 1929.)

Hodges, G. W. T., 'African Responses to European Rule in Kenya to 1914', in Ogot, B. A. (ed.), *Hadith 3*, Nairobi: EAPH, 1971, pp. 82–102.

Huxley, E., *White Man's Country, 1870–1914*, Vols. 1–2, New York: Praeger, 1967. (First published in 1935.)

——, *The Red Strangers*, London: Chatto & Windus, 1944.

——, *Settlers of Kenya*, Nairobi: Highway Press, 1948

——, *Sorcerer's Apprentice*, London: Chatto & Windus, 1948.

——, *The Flame Trees of Thika*, Harmondsworth: Penguin Books, 1962.

——, *The Challenge of Africa*, London: Aldus, 1971.

Huxley, E. and Perham, M., *Race and Politics in Kenya*, London: Faber & Faber, 1956. (Originally published in 1944.)

Iliffe, John, 'The Creation of Group Consciousness: a History of Dockworkers of Dar es Salaam', in Sandbrook, R. and Cohen, R. (eds), *The Development of an African Working Class*, London: Longman, 1975.

Itote, W., *Mau Mau General*, Nairobi: EAPH, 1967.

Kaggia, B., *The Roots of Freedom, 1921–1963*, Nairobi: EAPH, 1975.

Kanogo, T. M. J., 'Politics of Collaboration or Domination? Case Study of the Capricorn African Society', *Kenya Historical Review*, Vol. 2, No. 2, 1974.

Kariuki, J. M., *Mau Mau Detainee*, London: OUP, 1963.

Kenyatta, J., *Facing Mount Kenya*, Nairobi: Heinemann Educational Books, 1971. (First published in 1938.)

---, *Suffering Without Bitterness*, Nairobi: EAPH, 1969.

King, K., 'Education and Social Change: The Impact of Technical Training in Colonial Kenya', in Ogot, B. A. (ed.), *Hadith 6: Economic and Social Change in East Africa*, Nairobi: EALB, 1976, pp. 145–64.

Kipkorir, B. E., 'The Educated Elite and Local Society', in *Hadith 4: Politics and Nationalism in Colonial Kenya*, Nairobi: EAPH, 1972, pp. 252–69.

Kitching, G., *Class and Economic Change in Kenya: The Making of an African Petite Bourgeoisie*, London: Yale University Press, 1980.

Kuczynski, R. R., *Demographic Survey of the British Colonial Empire*, London: OUP, 1948.

Lamb, G., *Peasant Politics*, Lewes: Friedman, 1974.

Lambert, H. E., *Kikuyu Social and Political Institutions*, London: OUP, 1956.

Leakey, L. S. B., *Mau Mau and the Kikuyu*, London: Methuen, 1952.

——, *Defeating Mau Mau*, London: Methuen, 1954.

——, *The Southern Kikuyu before 1903*, London: Academic Press, 1977.

Leo, C., *Land and Class in Kenya*, Toronto: Toronto University Press, 1984.

Leys, C., *Underdevelopment in Kenya: The Political Economy of Neo-Colonialism, 1964–1971*, London: Heinemann, 1975.

Leys, N., *Kenya*, London: Frank Cass, 1973. (Fourth edition. First published in 1924.)

——, *A Last Chance in Kenya*, London: Hogarth Press, 1931.

Lipscomb, J. F., *We Built a Country*, London: Faber & Faber, 1956.

Lonsdale, J. M., 'State and Peasantry in Colonial Africa', in Samuel, R. (ed.), *People's History and Socialist Theory*, London: Routledge & Kegan Paul, 1981, pp. 106–18.

Low, D. A. and Smith, A., *History of East Africa*, Vol. III, Oxford: Clarendon Press, 1976.

Maina wa Kinyatti (ed.), *Thunder from the Mountains: Mau Mau Patriotic Songs*, London: Zed Press, 1980.

Mboya, T. J., *The Kenya Question: an African Answer*, London: Fabian Colonial Bureau, 1956.

——, *Freedom and After*, London: Deutsch, 1963.

McGregor Ross, W., *Kenya from Within: a Short Political History*, London: Frank Cass, 1968. (New impression. First published in 1927.)

Middleton, J., 'Kenya: Administration and Changes in African Life, 1912–1945', in V. Harlow and E. Chilver (eds), *History of East Africa*, Vol. II, Oxford: Clarendon Press, 1965, pp. 333–92.

Mitchell, P., *African Afterthoughts*, London: Hutchinson, 1954.

Mungeam, G. H., *British Rule in Kenya, 1895–1912*, Oxford: Clarendon Press, 1966.

Muriuki, G., *A History of the Kikuyu, 1500–1900*, Nairobi: OUP, 1974.

Ngugi wa Thiong'o and Mugo, G. M., *The Trial of Dedan Kimathi*, Nairobi: Heinemann, 1976.

Njama, K. and Barnett, D. C., *Mau Mau from Within*, New York: Monthly Review Press, 1966.

Odinga, O., *Not Yet Uhuru*, London: Heinemann, 1968.

Odinga, R. S., *The Kenya Highlands: Land Use and Agricultural Development*, Nairobi: EAPH, 1971.

Ogot, B. A. (ed.), *Hadith 4: Politics and Nationalism in Colonial Kenya*, Nairobi: EAPH, 1972.

——, *Hadith 6: Economic and Social Change in East Africa*, Nairobi: EALB, 1976.

Ominde, S. H., *Land and Population Movements in Kenya*, London: Heinemann, 1968.

Padmore, G., *Pan-Africanism or Communism*, London: Frank Cass, 1953.

Rawcliffe, D. H., *The Struggle for Kenya*, London: Gollancz, 1954.

Rosberg, C. and Nottingham, J., *The Myth of Mau Mau: Nationalism in Kenya*, Nairobi: EAPH, 1966.

Salim, A. I., *The Swahili Speaking Peoples of Kenya's Coast, 1895–1963*, Nairobi: EAPH, 1973.

Sandbrook, R., *Proletarians and African Capitalism: The Kenya Case, 1962–1970*, Cambridge: Cambridge University Press, 1975.

Sandbrook, R. and Cohen, R. (eds), *The Development of an African Working Class*, London: Longman, 1975.

Shanin, T., *Peasants and Peasant Societies*, Harmondsworth: Penguin, 1971.

Sifuna, D. N., *Vocational Education in Schools: A Historical Survey of Kenya and Tanzania*, Nairobi: EALB, 1976.

Singh, M., *History of Kenya's Trade Union Movement to 1952*, Nairobi: EAPH, 1969.

Sorrenson, M. P. K., *Land Reform in Kikuyu Country*, Nairobi: OUP, 1967.

———, *The Origins of European Settlement in Kenya*, London: OUP, 1968.

Stichter, S., 'The Formation of a Working Class in Kenya', in Sandbrook, R. and Cohen, R. (eds), *The Development of an African Working Class*, London: Longman, 1975.

Stoneham, C. T., *Mau Mau*, London: Museum Press, 1953.

Thomas, J. J., *Froudacity: West Indian Fables Explained*, London: New Beacon Books, 1969. (First published by T. Fisher Unwin in 1889, London.)

Thompson, E. P., *The Making of the English Working Class*, Harmondsworth: Penguin, 1967.

Tignor, R. L, *The Colonial Transformation of Kenya: The Kamba, Kikuyu and Maasai from 1900 to 1939*, Princeton, N.J.: Princeton University Press, 1976.

Van Zwanenberg, R. M. A., *Agricultural History of Kenya*, Nairobi: EAPH, 1972.

———, *Colonial Capitalism and Labour in Kenya, 1919–1939*, Nairobi: EALB, 1975.

Van Zwanenberg, R. M. A. and King, A., *An Economic History of Kenya and Uganda, 1870–1970*, Nairobi: EALB, 1975.

Wambaa, R. M. and King, K., 'The Political Economy of the Rift Valley: a Squatter Perspective', in Ogot, B. A. (ed.), *Hadith 5: Economic and Social Change in East Africa*, Nairobi: EALB, 1975, pp. 195–218.

Wasserman, G., *Politics of Decolonization: Kenya Europeans and the Land Use, 1960–65*, Cambridge: Cambridge University Press, 1976.

Wolff, R. D., *Britain and Kenya, 1870–1930: The Economics of Colonialism*, Nairobi: Transafrica Publishers, 1974.

Wray, J. A., *Kenya: Our Newest Colony, Reminiscences, 1882–1912*, London: Marshall Brothers, 1928.

Wrigley, C. C., 'Kenya: Patterns of Economic Life, 1902–1945', in Harlow, V., Chilver, E. and Smith, A., (eds), *History of East Africa*, Vol. II, Oxford: Clarendon Press, 1967, pp. 209–64.

Published Articles

Aaron, S., 'The Politics of Land in East Africa', *Economic Development and Cultural Change*, Vol. 16, No. 2, January 1968, pp. 275–96.

Anderson, D. M., 'Depression, Dustbowl and Drought: The Colonial State and Soil Conservation in East Africa during the 1930s', *African Affairs*, Vol. 83, No. 332, July 1984.

Atieno-Odhiambo, E. S., 'The Song of the Vultures: A Case Study of Misconceptions about Nationalism in Kenya', *The Journal of Eastern Africa Research and Development*, Vol. 1, No. 2, 1971.

——, 'The Colonial Governments, The Settlers, The Trust Principle in Kenya to 1939', *Transafrican Journal of History*, Vol. 2, No. 2, 1972.

——, 'The Rise and Decline of the Kenya Peasant 1882–1922', *East Africa Journal*, May 1972, pp. 11–15.

Belshaw, D. G. R., 'Agricultural Settlement Schemes in Kenya Highlands', *East Africa Geographical Review*, No. 2, 1964, pp. 30–7.

Farrell, C., 'Mau Mau: a Revolt or a Revolution?', in Ochieng, W. R. and Janmohamed, K. K. (eds), 'Some Perspectives on the Mau Mau Movement', *Kenya Historical Review*, Vol. 5, No. 2, 1977, pp. 187–99.

Furedi, F., 'The Social Composition of the Mau Mau Movement in the White Highlands', *Journal of Peasant Studies*, Vol. 1, No. 4, July 1974, pp. 486–505.

Gordon, F. G., 'Mau Mau and Decolonization: Kenya and the Defeat of Multi-racialism in East and Central Africa', in Ochieng, W. R. and Janmohamed, K. K. (eds), 'Some Perspectives on the Mau Mau Movement', *Kenya Historical Review*, Vol. 5, No. 2, 1977, pp. 329–48.

Kanogo, T. M. J., 'Rift Valley Squatters and Mau Mau', in Ochieng, W. R. and Janmohamed, K. K. (eds), 'Some Perspectives on the Mau Mau Movement', *Kenya Historical Review*, Vol. 5, No. 2, 1977, pp. 243–53.

Kauffman, D., 'Mau Mau: Peasant War or Revolution?', in Ochieng, W. R. and Janmohamed, K. K. (eds), 'Some Perspectives on the Mau Mau Movement', *Kenya Historical Review*, Vol. 5, No. 2, 1977, pp. 173–86.

Kipkorir, B. E., 'Mau Mau and the Politics of the Transfer of Power in Kenya, 1957–1960', in Ochieng, W. R. and Janmohamed, K. K. (eds), 'Some Perspectives on the Mau Mau Movement', *Kenya Historical Review*, Vol. 5, No. 2, 1977, pp. 313–28.

Lonsdale, J. M., 'Some Origins of Nationalism in East Africa', *Journal of African History*, Vol. 9, No. 1, 1968, pp. 119–46.

——, 'European Attitudes and African Pressures: Missions and Government in Kenya between the Wars', *Race*, No. 10, 1968/69, pp. 141–52.

——, 'Coping with the Contradictions: The Development of the Colonial State in Kenya, 1895–1914', *Journal of African History*, Vol. 20, No. 4, 1979.

Maina wa Kinyatti, 'Mau Mau: The Peak of African Nationalism in Kenya', in Ochieng, W. R. and Janmohamed, K. K. (eds), 'Some Perspectives on the Mau Mau Movement', *Kenya Historical Review*, Vol. 5, No. 2, 1977, pp. 287–311.

Mitchell, J. C., 'The Causes of Labour Migration', *Bulletin of Inter-African Labour Institute*, No. 6, 1959, pp. 12–47.

Monone Omusule, '*Kiama kia Muingi*: Kikuyu Reaction to Land Consolidation Policy in Kenya, 1955–1959', *Transafrica Journal of History*, Vol. 4, Nos. 1–2, 1974.

Mukaru Nganga, D., 'Mau Mau, Loyalists and Politics in Muranga,

1952–1970', in Ochieng, W. R. and Janmohamed, K. K. (eds), 'Some Perspectives on the Mau Mau Movement','*Kenya Historical Review*, Vol. 5, No. 2, 1977, pp. 365–84.

Odingo, R. S., 'Post-Independence Agricultural Changes in Kenya Highlands', *Geographia Polonica*, No. 19, 1970, pp. 207–26.

Ogot, B. A., 'Politics, Culture and Music in Central Kenya: a Study of Mau Mau Hymns, 1951–1956', in Ochieng, W. R. and Janmohamed, K. K. (eds), 'Some Perspectives on the Mau Mau Movement', *Kenya Historical Review*, Vol. 5, No. 2, 1977, pp. 275–86.

Pavlis, P. A., 'The Maasai and the Mau Mau Movement: Avenues for Future Research', in Ochieng, W. R. and Janmohamed, K. K. (eds), 'Some Perspectives on the Mau Mau Movement', *Kenya Historical Review*, Vol. 5, No. 2, 1977.

Spencer, J., 'KAU and Mau Mau: Some Connections', in Ochieng, W. R. and Janmohamed, K. K. (eds), 'Some Perspectives on the Mau Mau Movement', *Kenya Historical Review*, Vol. 5, No. 2, 1977, pp. 201–24.

Tamarkin, M., 'Mau Mau in Nakuru', in Ochieng, W. R. and Janmohamed, K. K. (eds), 'Some Perspectives on the Mau Mau Movement', *Kenya Historical Review*, Vol. 5, No. 2, 1977, pp. 225–41.

Throup, D. W., 'The Origins of Mau Mau', *African Affairs*, Vol. 84, No. 336, 1985, pp. 399–434.

Uzoigwe, G. N., 'The Mombasa-Victoria Railway, 1890–1902: Imperial Necessity, Humanitarian Venture or Economic Imperialism?', *Kenya Historical Review*, Vol. 4, No. 1, pp. 11–34.

Van Zwanenberg, R. M. A., 'Background to White Racialism in Kenya', *Kenya Historical Review*, Vol. 2, no. 1, 1974, pp. 5–11.

Wasserman, G., 'European Settlers and Kenya Colony: Thoughts on a Conflicted Affair', *African Studies Review*, Vol. 17, No. 2, 1974.

Yankwich, R., 'Continuity in Kenya: Negative Unity and the Legitimacy of the Mau Mau Rebellion', in Ochieng, W. R. and Janmohamed, K. K. (eds), 'Some Perspectives on the Mau Mau Movement', *Kenya Historical Review*, Vol. 5, No. 2, 1977, pp. 349–63.

Index